PASIÓN

MIGUEL LOURENÇO PEREIRA

PASIÓN

A JOURNEY TO THE SOUL OF SPANISH FOOTBALL

First published by Pitch Publishing, 2025

Pitch Publishing
9 Donnington Park,
85 Birdham Road,
Chichester, West Sussex,
PO20 7AJ
www.pitchpublishing.co.uk
info@pitchpublishing.co.uk

© 2025, Miguel Lourenço Pereira

Every effort has been made to trace the copyright. Any oversight will be rectified in future editions at the earliest opportunity by the publisher.

All rights reserved. No part of this book may be reproduced, sold or utilised in any form or transmitted in any form or by any means, electronic or mechanical, including photocopying, recording or by any information storage and retrieval system, without prior permission in writing from the publisher.

A CIP catalogue record is available for this book from the British Library.

ISBN 978 1 80150 957 2

Typesetting and origination by Pitch Publishing

Printed and bound on FSC® certified paper in line with our continuing commitment to ethical business practices, sustainability and the environment.

Printed and bound in India by Thomson Press

CONTENTS

Identities 7

The Pursuit of Happiness 11

Power to the People. 29

Viva La Vida 46

Stop the Clocks. 62

Go Out and Enjoy Yourselves 85

The Gates of Time 113

On Air 134

Lady Madrid 152

The Dreamers 174

Rock You Like a Hurricane. 197

Band of Brothers 219

Even More When We Lose 241

Those Lonely Bulls 272

Kings of Europe 288

Acknowledgements 312

Bibliography 315

IDENTITIES

THERE'S NO country like Spain. Over the years people have come to believe in all the travel agents' brochures. A land of sun, beaches and the most relaxed way of life you could imagine. That is only partially true. A fragment of something more complex. After all, like in almost everything, Spain is much more than what meets the eye. No other European country is as diverse, in any sense. It starts with the basics. Spain has the most diverse geographic landscape in all of Europe. Deserts, tropical islands, rainy shores, paradise beaches, green valleys, endless plains, stunning mountains. It's all there. Wherever you decide to go will determine what Spain looks like for you. Enjoy a magic sunset at any Mediterranean beach or walk on a chilly rainy afternoon around its northern coastline. It will not be the same experience, but it will be profoundly Spanish either way. Geography shapes and defines cultures and because of that Spain has found the ability to be many in one. A country that is a feast to the senses, whether through its natural or urban landscapes or the heart-warming people living there. Each piece of land has its own story to tell, many told in different languages, another unique trait you hardly find anywhere else. And, of course, many of those stories take you to its football identity. Or better said, identities.

After all, Spain is nothing but a country of nations. One that lived under a profound centralised dictatorship for decades and has since embraced a more diverse approach, even if it is way beyond the federalist ideal that probably suits its diversity and common history best. Divisions are there and always have been. Truth be said, few things can unite all Spanish people behind one common goal. One might think of their love for the outdoor life or their artistic soul but, in the end, everything faces the harsh reality of the most typical Spanish thing of all: either you're with me or you are against me. Few people see the world as purely black or white as they do. Even when it is something they love. Take beer, for example. Despite a well-known wine culture that goes back to the days of the Roman Empire, if there's anything anyone in Spain enjoys it is sharing a beer with friends. After all, this is the country with the most bars worldwide. Yet, as with everything, even here there are trenches and barricades. Every region has its brand of beer, with its particular flavour, and nobody will ever claim any beer from somewhere else is better than theirs. You can have a taste of Mahou in Madrid, Estrella in Galicia, Victoria in Málaga, Damm in Barcelona, Ambar in Zaragoza, Cruzcampo in Seville or San Miguel in Asturias and it doesn't matter if you decide to argue in favour or against any of those. For locals, everyone will think they are in the right and theirs is better. That works with just about anything. Especially with the thing Spain loves even more than its beer: football.

Their passion for the game comes second to none and it's driven by the same hardcore mentality of us against them. *Fútbol*, more than enjoyed, is lived. It runs through people's veins and bowels, a country of brothers forever quarrelling to the bitter end, an image so well represented by Francisco Goya's iconic paintings. Football rivalries are as intense as ancient feuds as if stadiums have turned into modern battlegrounds over and over again. That intensity is well known worldwide through the *El Clásico* rivalry between Real Madrid and FC Barcelona, but it goes much deeper than that, right into the heart of the football pyramid. That's where the most beautiful, tense and inspiring stories are. The almost exclusive media attention on two of the greatest giants of the game, as well as the recent golden age of the national side, has hidden in a chest all those tales but, like with any treasure, they are there for the taking. What makes them even more fascinating is that they are rarely just about football. They tell us the stories of places, people, ideas and worlds that were, that are and that will be. Of unsung heroes and forgotten feats. Of football clubs that will win your heart and realities you didn't deem possible.

This book is a journey into a nation that has it all but was never fully able to tell it to the rest of the world. Perhaps it's their pride in the Spanish language – the most spoken European first language in the world – that prevents them from even trying to express themselves in any other. Or their character, so in awe of their world that they don't seem to be bothered by how others perceive them. Either way, it seems Spain has become, over the centuries, one of the most undervalued nations in the world. And it's not just about the football either. Whether it's painting, literature, cinema or music, their genius is everywhere but the world never seems to pay attention. Take the uncountable number of architectural prodigies everywhere you move or their sense of artistry that can be found in anything they do. Think of their iconic footballers who seem to be actors, dancers, musicians and writers all wrapped into one on the pitch. Andrés Iniesta would paint you a portrait worthy of El Prado. Rodri Hernández could have played the bass in any Britpop band. Fernando Torres probably can write the most beautiful love sonnet, and when you glimpse Lamine Yamal, you know it's time to dance.

That is why our journey goes far beyond just the football. It's a trip around the country's geography, but also through its gastronomic riches, landmark sites and the most incredible artists you could dream of. A book with a soundtrack, a gourmet menu and a travel guide, all in one. It takes you from Vigo to Seville, north to south. From Madrid to Valencia, inland to the coast. From Salamanca to Logroño, west to east. From Bilbao to Barcelona, nation to nation. It throws you back in time to remember unforgettable matches played and titles fought for and won. Of players and managers who have shaped the nation's DNA and with it the rest of the world; but, most of all, of the hardcore identity of its supporters, some who have lived through heaven and hell without ever turning their backs on their club colours. A pathway right into the nation's soul. Once you reach the end you will never be able to think of Spain the same way. I know that for sure because I've been you.

I arrived in Spain fresh out of college, full of certainties about what to expect. Almost two decades later, I was proved wrong in everything. More than that, I fell in love with a nation and its people. So much so that I have become one of them, forever an adopted son. Spain taught me everything about life, love, commitment, art, dreams and football. Above all else, about *pasión*, that undying spirit that has made them elevate themselves as one of the greatest nations in history. They are certainly the greatest football nation of our time and, for that reason, it is also worthwhile to understand how it all came to pass to get us where we are today. They play and live the game as if the world is about to end. It doesn't matter if it's the dying minutes of *El Clásico* or a match of your local side in the lower leagues. No country senses things so feverously as they do, whether it's having a night out with your friends to see a match at the local bar, or simply watching the sunset at the top of a deserted mountain, away from everything. The feeling is always the same. That is how things are lived around there. A vibe that explains why this is a journey that will forever surprise and change you after you see how the world reverberates through their eyes.

THE PURSUIT OF HAPPINESS

GALICIA IS Spain's hidden paradise. It is also an enigma, even to the locals. They are quite similar to their southern neighbours from Portugal. Some even claim they should have become one nation. They are, however, also profoundly Catholic, lovers of outdoor life and talking loud like any Castilian would be. And yet Galicia is also one of the few remaining places, much like Ireland, where the Celtic tradition is still alive. Despite the extensive forests and the ever-present sense of rain and fog in many parts of the interior, they also have the most extended coastline of all Spanish regions. Between stony cliffs that cut defiantly into the Atlantic and paradise-like beaches in their Rías, Galicia is a land of blueish water as much as it is of greenish mountains. Everything, all at once. It is not too dissimilar to its football, capable of creating magical tales like the old Gaelic traditional songs and stories of whispering ghosts lost in the fog of the early hours of dawn.

* * *

There's a sense of perennial optimism whenever the sun seems to nutmeg the ever-present clouds and shines through the mild drops of rain falling from the sky. It's early Sunday morning and the weather couldn't be more typical of Vigo. One minute it is pouring, the other it is sunny. Doomed to live in this permanent indecision, Galicians were moulded by the climate like few people in Spain. They are perceived as indecisive, never saying affirmatively yes or no to anything.

Well, that is not exactly true, especially when it comes to football. If there is something that sparks a smile it's their love for the game, in any shape. Take for instance *Futbolín* – the most popular form of table football, still seen in every bar around Spain – patented in Barcelona but created by the Galician-born poet and inventor Alejandro Finisterre, as a distraction for handicapped children, victims of the Spanish Civil War.

By the late 1930s, football had become as popular as any sport in the region, especially around Vigo, where the company that first brought the telegraph to Spain settled in. The Exiles Cable Club de Vigo played exhibition matches against sailors from commercial vessels harboured in the beautiful city of the Rías Baixas. There is still dispute about whether they were the first-ever football club in the history of Spanish football. They are now long gone but the city – the biggest in Galicia, with around 300,000 inhabitants – remains passionate about the game and the local sky-blue colours of Celta de Vigo.

Blue is everywhere you look. In the different tones of the waves or the skyline. In the ever-present traditional flag of Galicia and, of course, in the shirt of Celta de Vigo. Walking in the direction of the Balaídos stadium it's impossible not to see it. In painted murals, in flags proudly placed on balconies. In scarves around people's necks. Every street leads to the place where past and present meet. Balaídos feels like time-travelling. The stadium belongs to the city hall and not to the club – which is an issue for its financial sustainability – and it has been renovated recently. It now boasts three futuristic stands that contrast immensely with the sole survivor of the days of old concrete stands, a recollection of the 1982 World

Cup when it hosted the first three matches of future world champions Italy.

Vigo is also a city with one foot in the past and another in the future. On one hand, it remains a place that encapsulates the spirit of the old fishing and canning industry that shaped the region for so long. The harbour might have been revamped, but Teis and Bouzas's old streets still smell distinctively humble, far from the new aspirational neighbourhoods of Navia or Coia. But Vigo is also vibrant and modern, full of life and with an eye on becoming the north-western capital of tourism in the country. It has much to be thankful for: the astounding beauty of the Cies Islands and its beaches, but also its people. They suffered greatly over the years and the city landscape changes have also reflected that. During the 1980s Vigo was assaulted by an epidemic of drug abuse that almost wiped out a generation. At the same time, the central government in Madrid, inspired by Thatcherite policies, started to dismantle a great part of the local shipyards, raising unemployment to an all-time high. The town suffered but it didn't stay silent. People marched on the streets in protest and reinforced their sense of belonging.

And to belong to Vigo was to belong to Celta. Today, the football club remains the long-standing Galician side in the Spanish first division. They have never won any silverware, losing three cup finals and qualifying only once for the Champions League. But, in Vigo, people have been used to losing so much it didn't matter. They were there for each other. That feeling is still present every time you bump into supporters around Balaídos. You can sense it inside the stadium, a love that crosses generations. But it's not only in the city. Support for Celta stretches from the southern tip of Galicia in A Guarda to the northern limits of the Pontevedra province, on the wild island of Arousa. Their sky-blue kit, inspired by the flag of Galicia that the side took on to the field one afternoon in 1977, defying the authorities of a country still clinging to old fascist ideals, is also a testimony of that connection. That devotion is reflected powerfully in the anthem created by the popular rap artist C. Tangana for the club's centennial back in 2023. 'Oliveira dos Cen Anos' became an immediate hit track when it was released, mixing the urban sounds of today with the folkloric musical tradition of old. Before each home match, more than 25,000 supporters sing the lyrics written in local Galician by Tangana, himself a Celta supporter despite having been born in Madrid: 'Sempre Celta'. Forever Celta.

Of course, music and Vigo have walked side by side for a long time. In Spain, many remember the *Movida* cultural movement in Madrid in the early 1980s as a symbol of the social period known as *Transición* after decades of fascism. What few know is that, around the same time, Vigo was living its own cultural revolution. The *Movida Viguesa* was a movement that brought the city to life. It all started with a car crash that inspired a group of teenagers to form a band. They called it Siniestro Total – meaning 'total write-off' – and their raunchy, provocative lyrics accompanied by punkish new wave guitar sounds became an instant hit and were quickly followed by other acts like Golpes Bajos and Aerolineas Federales, who introduced ska, reggae, funk and techno to Spanish audiences.

They also loved football. Regulars at the Balaídos, when the club was permanently moving between the top two tiers of Spanish football, Siniestro Total debuted a night after seeing Celta thrash Real Mallorca. Plus, they usually played Celta's club anthem in their concerts. The movement stretched the cultural and social horizons of the city. It ended abruptly when the mayors of Madrid and Vigo decided to stage an event with some of the most representative artists of both cities. The first trip brought popular Madrid acts to Vigo but ended in a riot. The seed was planted though, and empowered the city through dark times, with many local bands usually performing in benefit concerts for the striking workers of shipyards and factories that years later started to shut down one by one.

Celta was the first team from Galicia to play in the league, back in 1939. Their name of course comes from the Celtic origins of the region, after a merger of three other clubs in 1923. They were always an up-and-down side, capable of playing the cup final on three occasions but never reaching as high as fourth in the league. However, in the 1990s, everything changed. While the city tried to find its place in a new world, Celta became their guiding light. Around the same time local songwriter Ivan Ferreiro was leading his band, Los Piratas, into indie rock royalty, the arrival of Victor Fernàndez in 1998 was like hitting number one in the charts. Quickly Balaídos became used to a flashy, entertaining attacking side that played like no other team when the Spanish league was known as 'La Liga de las Estrellas'. And there were stars to behold in Vigo as well. From the Russian local icon Aleksander Mostovoi to Brazilian World Champion Mazinho, alongside players like Claude Makélélé, Haim Revivo, Luboslav Penev and Valeri Karpin.

Those were the glory days of Galician football, with Deportivo la Coruña, Celta's greatest rivals, also boasting one of the best sides in Europe. The rivalry left us with some of the most memorable matches in the league's history, but Celta were always more spectacular than effective. It was in Europe that they lived their most memorable nights. The club had been the first from the region to play in continental cups, back in 1971, beaten in the first round of the UEFA Cup by Aberdeen.

In 1998/99, however, they surprised everyone by beating favourites Aston Villa and Liverpool only to lose a tight quarter-final duel against Marseille. Proving it was no fluke, they went at it again the following season, hammering Benfica 7-0 at home before beating mighty Juventus 4-0, thanks to goals from Makélélé, Benni McCarthy and an Alessandro Birindelli own goal. That night remains the greatest in living memory for any Celta supporter. Unfortunately, once again a French rival, Lens, beat them in the last eight and it was Barcelona who frustrated the club's continental ambitions the following season.

The 'EuroCelta' tag, however, would not be forgotten. The team led by Fernàndez was 90 minutes away from touching the sky in that summer of 2001. On 30 June, in the asphyxiating heat of Seville, Celta met Zaragoza in the cup final. Mostovoi opened the score early in the match but three goals from Fernàndez's former club meant, once again, the prospect of glory faded away. The defeat was painful, not only because it meant the end of a golden era but because Deportivo had celebrated their first league title the year before and would win the cup the following season. They were as ruthless as Celta were enthralling.

But it's not by chance that the club motto is *Afouteza*, the Galician word for courage. Celta rose once again and have since become one of the most noted *Canteras* – the Spanish name for youth academies, literally referencing stone quarries – in the country. Without money to invest, they had to rely on local talent. And they had plenty to call upon: players such as Borja Oubiña, Dennis Suárez, Brais Mendez, Hugo Mallo, Rodrigo Moreno and, above all, Iago Aspas. Because if Celta are still around in the elite, they owe much to the forward born in Moaña, known as the 'Prince of the Bateas', the name of the characteristic platforms positioned alongside the Ría de Vigo. Aspas debuted with the first team in June 2008 when Celta were battling to avoid stepping out of professional football. He scored both goals as a substitute against Alavés, saving the club from bankruptcy.

It would not be the last time. Top scorer for the side a couple of seasons on, Aspas took Celta back to La Liga and scored the decisive goals that kept the club from being relegated once there. He proved to be one of the hottest prospects around and eventually signed for Liverpool in 2013. However, he struggled to adapt to a Brendan Rogers side that would finish second in the Premier League. He was briefly loaned to Sevilla but in 2015 opted to return to Vigo. A few weeks later he scored a brace in a 4-1 home win against Barcelona. Balaídos had its prodigal son back.

And there he remains, ten years on, guiding the club to a Europa League semi-final – lost against Mourinho's Manchester United – and proving to be an ever-decisive factor that has allowed Celta to stay as the sole representative of Galician football in La Liga. He also entered the goalscorers' hall of fame, having become one of the 20 top scorers in La Liga's history. Aspas is part of the club's crest and identity. An example for future graduates of the *Cantera* to follow. A local homegrown player who embodies the spirit of a club and city. Of a region. Leaving Balaídos under a surprisingly sunny sky, after another fantastic display of the club's number ten, the final verses of 'Oliveira dos Cen Anos' resonate powerfully once again: '*Sempre Celta*'.

***

Despite Galicia being one of the regions where football was played first, only four of its clubs have featured in La Liga. In 1969/70 Pontevedra Club de Fútbol joined Deportivo and Celta and, for the first time, there were three teams from the region in the elite. It was to be their fifth but also last season at the top. The club hails from a beautiful medieval town sitting over the banks of their own Ría and the river Lérez. Although much smaller than Vigo, which sits 20 miles to the south, Pontevedra is the provincial capital. The local ground,

Pasarón, remains an iconic setting in the mind of Galician supporters, an echo of a time long gone when football was played on muddy pitches and character was as important as talent.

SD Compostela had a shorter stay in La Liga, playing four consecutive seasons there between 1994 and 1998. They are most remembered for conceding an iconic solo goal by Ronaldo Nazário and the ensuing expression of disbelief on the face of Sir Bobby Robson when Barcelona came to town. The club rose only thanks to the patronage of chairman José Maria Caneda and went bankrupt shortly after their relegation but, as Galician writer and historian Sergio Vilariño explains, they are also a symbol of Galicia's football golden age. 'Compostela lived a beautiful story, with faithful supporters still behind the newly reborn club, despite competing in lower leagues nowadays. But back then they could only aspire to be in La Liga thanks to the local canning industry's support, Caneda's vision and money from the television deal. Without TV money, no football club in Galicia would ever be able to compete at the highest level.' Caneda had an eye for managers, first trusting in Fernando Castro Santos and, later on, Fernando Vazquez, who delivered results with a mix of local players and exciting signings like Bulgarian striker Luboslav Penev. That period was also decisive in reviving the spirit of the Road to Santiago.

Compostela is the historical capital of Galicia and became popular in the 10th century when a cathedral was built on the site where some claimed the bones of St James had been found, after being brought by boat from the Holy Land. It ended up as one of the most important pilgrimage sites in Europe, alongside Rome and Jerusalem, but its relevance faded with time. In the 80s, Galicia's regional government sought to revive the route and, in 1985, the city achieved UNESCO World Cultural Heritage status. Still, only a few hundred were known to take the road, so a huge publicity campaign began during the 90s to revive the tradition, with great success. Football was part of the revival of the *Camino de Santiago* pilgrimage route and Compostela's success in La Liga was seen as essential to spreading the city's name around Europe. Thirty years on, almost half a million pilgrims a year take, on foot, the different routes to arrive at the gates of the Doorway of Glory, the main entrance of the mighty cathedral, and admire its breathtaking beauty when the bells toll.

The *Camino* revival was one of the positive sides of the economic and social changes in 1990s Galicia. But there was a downside as well. Unemployment had been rising since the previous decade mostly because of the closure of many local industries. The award-winning movie *Lunes al Sol*, which includes footage of a real friendly match between Pontevedra and Celta Vigo and stars Oscar-winning actor Javier Bardem, tells the harsh story of how a group of jobless middle-aged workers contemplate the meaninglessness of their lives and serves as the perfect reflection of what was the spirit of the day.

But whenever unemployment rises so usually does organised crime. And Galicia, a poor region, had always been fertile territory for smugglers. So much so that many baptised the early 60s Celta as 'Marlboro Celta' because of the supposed connections between the club chairman Celso Lorenzo and the tobacco smuggling business. Some suggested the team bus was used to smuggle cigars all over Spain. The inclusion of many shady businessmen on the board didn't help either. But if tobacco was socially accepted, narcotics weren't. Unemployment and desperation made Galicia the perfect entrance point for South American drug cartels. Heroin and cocaine had already begun to arrive in Europe in the late 1970s but Galicia's complex coastline, with its coves and inlets, the craftsmanship of their small speedboat pilots and the closeness to the Americas paved the way for a large-scale drug invasion that took place the following decade. Some of the old-school smugglers stayed out but others embraced the new business. None became as famous as Sito Miñanco.

Born José Ramon Prado, he was a talented speedboat pilot who knew the trade from an early age. He was known to be one of the best pilots in the Ría de Arousa and quickly understood the potential offered by the South American narcos, setting himself aside from other smugglers from the region. He was also a football fanatic, a staunch Real Madrid supporter and an amateur player for his hometown side Juventud Cambados. The club currently plays in the Galician Segunda Autonómica – the seventh tier – and is part of the Celta Academy project. Cambados has changed as well. From a small greyish town in the 1980s, which depended exclusively on its fishing community, it's now a beautiful tourist site, known for its fabulous Albariño wines, the supreme quality of its beaches and popular local dishes like octopus, mussels and shellfish.

While walking along its old streets it's hard to believe this was once a place of suffering. The local ground is full of kids on a Saturday morning, wearing the club's yellow-and-blue colours. Parents watch proudly from the stands. Many probably were kids themselves when Miñanco, by then the most popular smuggler in Galicia, decided to take control of the club. He was named chairman in 1986 and immediately signed the best players available in the region, delegating to Rafa Lino, as sporting director, the responsibility of creating a winning project. Cambados were by then in the sixth tier. His ambition was to take them to La Liga, just like Pablo Escobar had done with Nacional Medellin. He invested heavily and the club started to climb divisions. He reached as high as the third tier – Segunda B – and to celebrate Miñanco took the players to Panama on tour. Many suspected that the team bus was used on occasions to smuggle drugs past police controls, although that was never proved. When they were on the brink of promotion to the Segunda, Miñanco was forced to leave as a result of the police hunt against Galician drug traffickers, called Operation Nécora. He never saw his team play against Real Madrid but, in the end, he did manage to see Cambados visit both Real and Atlético Madrid B sides. During those troubling years, while teenagers were dropping dead in the streets from overdoses by the dozens, Juventud Cambados' success was seen by locals as a way of Miñanco paying back the community. He did it for social recognition, but the goal celebrations were never loud enough to silence the cries of the mothers of destroyed families who took to the streets to protest against the drug culture fostered by the likes of him.

Many would believe drugs might have been used in a similar way to finance other clubs from Galicia. Nothing was ever proven but, as Sergio Vilariño says, the *fariña* – Galician slang for cocaine – was everywhere. 'We saw people with money that came out of nowhere. People who weren't supposed to have any. So, everyone assumed that money got its way into private companies, political parties, and football clubs as well, but besides Cambados there was never any proven connection.' What is a fact is that drugs killed hundreds, especially teenagers and young adults, and that affected Galician football deeply. 'Even if I am from a younger generation, I still saw how some team-mates of mine, 15- and 16-year-olds, died of an overdose,' Vilariño states. 'It became clear drugs were wiping out an entire generation and among those were certainly kids who were meant to be professional footballers. Probably some would have become very good but never got the chance.'

One of those kids was Luis Gallego, a Celta youth prospect who turned to crime. One day he got the help of two petty criminals to rob the club's headquarters. But things went wrong. At the premises, preparing for an away match to San Sebastián, was Joaquín Fernàndez, known as Quinocho, a former club legend who was part of that historical 'Marlboro Celta' side, and was the club's senior director. One of the most beloved figures in Spanish football, Quinocho tried to stop the robbers and was stabbed to death. Vigo mourned his passing, but he was just one of the hundreds who suffered the consequences of the arrival of the narcos culture in Galicia.

In the end, when Miñanco was finally arrested, Juventud Cambados inevitably descended back to where they had been. They have never left the lower leagues since and remain a sad footnote in the history of Galicia's football, even if locals still take pride in what the team achieved, albeit for a short time and in strange circumstances. Football always serves as the perfect excuse to search for better self-reflection in the mirror. Cambados may now be a very much changed city and Miñanco is still paying the price of a life of crime, after spending the last decades in and out of jail, but that darker side of Galicia's recent history contrasts immensely with the ravishing beauty of its shores and the warm-hearted essence of its people.

* * *

Denise Oliveira wasn't happy. And she had every reason not to be. A few weeks before, two men had knocked on the door of her house in the posh neighbourhood of Tijuca, in Rio de Janeiro. They knew her husband was set to sign for Borussia Dortmund and bluntly told her he was making a terrible mistake. The weather in Germany was horrible. In turn, if he accepted their offer to move to Coruña he would be able to enjoy beaches like the ones he had in Rio de Janeiro. To prove it they offered her a book full of colourful postcard images of the beach of Riazor, right next to where the club stadium was.

Denise was convinced. She picked up the phone, called her husband's agent and told him straight away he was not going to Dortmund. He was moving to a club called Deportivo. The two men at her doorstep were Augusto César Lendoiro, the club's chairman, and his right-hand man, Luis Sanchez. That conversation changed the club's history. It was July 1992, they had just miraculously avoided relegation from La Liga, and had now signed one of the best players in the world. When they arrived at A Coruña, Denise understood that Riazor was no Copacabana. The chilly wind of the North Atlantic and the ever-present clouds painted a very different picture from what she imagined. But, thankfully for the local supporters, there was no turning back. In a few weeks, they were already in love with their new star, a classy forward who went by the nickname of Bebeto.

Bebeto was the beginning of everything at A Coruña but, during that trip to Brazil, Lendoiro also managed to snatch a promising midfielder named Mauro Silva. In two years, both would be key players in Brazil's fourth World Cup title. It was another masterstroke by Lendoiro, a man who came to symbolise the most glorious moments of football in Galicia and, especially, in A Coruña. He wasn't even a football man to begin with. Years before he took control of the local roller-hockey club, Liceo, and transformed it into European royalty. By then he had been persuaded to lead Deportivo's revival after turbulent years in the lower divisions.

The club's debut in La Liga had come a year after their rivals Celta. For most of the previous decades, they had been fighting each other to be seen as the best team in the region. Now they were throwing punches in the first division. It was a good period for Galician football and Depor had, in Juan Acuña, one of the most decorated goalkeepers of his time, a decisive player in their ranks who enabled the club to finish runners-up to Atlético Madrid in 1950, using

Argentine Alejandro Scopelli's innovative version of the WM formation, with a team packed of talented South Americans. Around those parts, the Spanish are still known as 'Galicians' because of the mass emigration in the late 19th century, a consequence of the famines and lack of job opportunities that forced thousands to cross the Atlantic searching for a better life. Ironically football paved the way for many descendants of those immigrants to return home and, since then, Galicia has become a preferred entrance point for players from South America to Europe. Even some who triumphed in Argentina or Uruguay, like Independiente stars Manuel Seoane or José Vilariño, were proud of their family origins. Lendoiro was following a long-standing tradition that was halted when Franco's regime closed the borders at a time when Deportivo were already on a low.

The club has also had an important youth set-up over the years. The proof is that they nurtured two of the greatest footballers Spain ever produced, Luis Suárez and Amancio Amaro. Suárez was a cultured midfielder who led the team from a tender age and was finally signed by Helenio Herrera when the manager took control of Barcelona. He became the star figure of a side that included Ladislao Kubala, Sandro Kocsis and Zoltan Czibor, winning two league titles against mighty Real Madrid before moving along with Herrera to Milan. Wearing Inter's colours, he dominated 1960s Serie A like no other, guiding the *Nerazzurri* to their first two European Cups and winning the coveted Balón d'Or. Suárez was also the main figure of the Spanish national side that won the Euros in 1964. Alongside him was Amaro, by then already a Real Madrid player after showing all his goalscoring skills in his teens at Riazor. Amaro was one of the most elegant forwards ever to wear the white shirt. The leader of the so-called Ye-Ye's generation, he won the 1966 European Cup for *Los Blancos* alongside a total of nine league titles.

But Suárez and Amaro's exploits came at a time when Deportivo started to lose relevance. It took them almost two decades to become a contender again, all thanks to Lendoiro's hard work. He signed local manager Arsenio Iglesias and showed patience as the team tried year after year to clinch promotion, to no avail. But something was brewing in the shadows of the mighty Tower of Hercules, one of the wonders of the ancient world and the oldest remaining Roman lighthouse in use. A place where the Romans believed the world ended. In 1990/91 Deportivo finally got themselves back to La Liga, only for the celebrations to be cut short because one of the stands at the Riazor caught fire and a tragedy was on the brink of happening. The following season was a mess, the club forced to a play-off against Betis to avoid relegation. It was a turning point, followed by the arrival of Bebeto and Mauro Silva. The two Brazilians fitted perfectly in Iglesias's system and, against all odds, Deportivo began the following season leading the pack. It was not only the new signings. Paco Liaño in goal, López Rekarte, Aldana, Donato and especially a youth prospect by the name of Fran González all delivered and the club ended the season third, with Bebeto winning the Pichichi award for top scorer. The *SuperDepor* legend was born.

The following season Deportivo played like they never had done before. They were not spectacular, far from it. Iglesias had forged a rocky defensive system that exploited well Fran's speed on the wing and Bebeto's ability to score. They fought week in, and week out against Cruyff's Barcelona team and arrived at the last day of the season only needing to win at home against Valencia to clinch their first-ever league title. A Coruña were having the time of their lives. It was a fairy tale, coming from the dark days of the lower divisions in a city, like Vigo, who suffered deeply the closing of shipyards and saw their youth destroyed by drugs. Only it wasn't to be. With one minute to go and the scores level, Deportivo were awarded a penalty. Donato, the usual taker, had been taken off and Bebeto didn't step up, so it came to centre-back Miroslav Djukic to take the shot. It never crossed the line. While Barcelona celebrated their fourth consecutive league title, people cried in Riazor.

The following season they finished second again and won the Copa del Rey, their first-ever title, also in dramatic fashion as the match, played in Madrid, had to be suspended due to heavy rain when Depor and Valencia, once again, were level. Three days later a header from Alfredo proved to be decisive. Lendoiro and Iglesias at least had a trophy to show for their efforts but the romantic image of the *SuperDepor* was always linked to that missed opportunity. It was almost the end for the club as well. To compete against the elite, the debt had been increasing fast, and when Iglesias called it a day, Depor were once again at a low. But as Sergio Vilariño explains, the 1997 television rights deal saved the club.

'When Via Digital and Canal Plus started to push for the TV rights of the so-called 'Liga de las Estrellas', Lendoiro got an excellent deal for Depor,' he said, 'and with that inflow of cash, he started to sign top international players that allowed him to create another great team, much superior in quality to the *SuperDepor* days. Without that TV money deal, Depor would have probably gone back to oblivion.' Class players did come to A Coruña, international stars from the Brazilian Djalminha to Dutch striker Roy Makaay, to local Spanish prospects Juan Carlos Valeron and Diego Tristan. In also came a new manager, Javier Irureta, a former international who had a more attacking mindset than Iglesias. 'Arsenio's side was more romantic, Irureta's played much better football,' recalls Vilariño.

In 1999/2000 Deportivo finally won the league. They ended up six points clear of Barcelona, clinching the title on the last day with a 2-0 win against Espanyol. Donato, alongside Fran and Mauro Silva, one of the sole survivors of the *SuperDepor*, opened the scoring to make amends with the past. That season, however, is still remembered well in Galicia because of a match in December, when the *Blanquiazules* beat Celta at Riazor. It was the first time the two teams from Galicia were top of the league. The win rocked Depor to their destiny, sealed in May. The city partied all night long and, for once, Riazor beach did look like Copacabana after all.

Irureta's side proved to be much more than that everlasting memory. Over the following four seasons, they never finished as low as third and won the Copa del Rey in 2002 at the Bernabéu. That day became known as *Centenariazo* as Real Madrid expected to win to celebrate their centenary anniversary and, in turn, it was Deportivo supporters who ended up singing 'Happy Birthday'. They also enjoyed memorable European nights along the way. During those years Depor won at iconic grounds like Old Trafford, Highbury, San Siro, Delle Alpi and the Olympiastadion. The dream ended when they faced Mourinho's Porto in the 2003/04 Champions League semi-final. They had just beaten AC Milan in a historic 4-0 comeback, and many considered them favourites to win the trophy. They didn't, and the rising debt finished the club off. Deportivo went bankrupt, ended up in the hands of Abanca, Galicia's most important financial institution, and fell to the third tier.

But that became a much-needed catharsis. People felt the need to reconnect with the club, away from all the noise of the glory days. Little by little Riazor came back to life, with a packed stadium filled with younger supporters who had never witnessed the club's golden years. As local singer and club supporter, Xoel López, would write in one of his hits, 'Glaciar', they answered the call "Would you love me the same if you saw me down in the ring" with heart. If the previous generations had been Depor fans because they won, they now are behind it because they feel it. Even local hero and former Arsenal striker Lucas Pérez decided to leave first-division football, paying his release clause from his own pocket to help out his childhood club.

Of course, it had to be him who scored the decisive goal that clinched promotion back to professional football during the 2023/24 season. A son of a local fisherman, Pérez grew up playing in Arteixo, the same place where Arsenio Iglesias came from, a small town next to A Coruña. His childhood was rough, and football was his salvation. Depor was what drove him to become a first-class footballer. In the end, he rescued the club the same way the club had rescued him. Because of love. He put his name up alongside club legends like Lendoiro, Iglesias, Irureta, Bebeto or Djalminha.

By now fans know the good times are not likely to return but they don't care. It was no coincidence there were more people in Riazor when they were promoted in 2024 than when they won the league. Belonging is all that matters. And wherever you are in Galicia, even if you're not from around there, you always get the strange feeling that, somehow, it has already become part of you. Some say it has to do with the *Meigas*, the entities who survive in that magical and mystical world. To others, it's just the undisputed beauty of one of Europe's hidden paradises. Whatever it is, it will never let go.

POWER TO THE PEOPLE

30 JUNE 1992. Two years after it was first announced by the authorities, the deadline for football clubs to be converted into limited companies finally arrived. It was also the day Spanish football lost its soul. Only four sides – Real Madrid, Barcelona, Athletic Bilbao and Osasuna – were spared. Although most clubs were practically bankrupt, the new law turned out to be a complete failure with the accumulated debt increasing by more than five hundred million euros over the next decades. Football clubs, until then, belonged to their members – the *sócios* – who paid a monthly fee to have a voice in how their side was run. By forcing them into Sociedades Anónimas – limited companies – the government paved the way for dubious businessmen, from within and outside Spain, to take control with devastating effects for many. That last night of June, when the football world was still in awe of the Denmark fairy tale in Euro 92, Spanish supporters were cast out of the game. But not all of them remained silent.

* * *

Logroño is a four-hour drive from Madrid. Crossing large stretches of deserted land into dashing mountain roads, surrounded by small rivers and beautiful vineyards, one can understand better its heart-warming people's nature. They are northerners but not quite. The city serves as the capital of La Rioja, one of the smallest Comunidades – the name given to the different administrative regions – and breathes a mix of tradition and modernity. Some of the best wine produced in Spain comes from the lands above the banks of the local Ebro river. The always-crowded Laurel Street is known as one of the best places to eat in Spain, especially if you are a fan of tapas, their traditional small portions. It is always packed with both locals and tourists. At the end of the street, there's a small wine and cheese store called La Casa de los Quesos. It belongs to Agustin Abadía, a local legend. Known as 'Tato', he remains one of the most iconic centre-backs of Spanish football during the late 1980s, a hard-tackling man with a heavy moustache who led the charge for the local side CD Logroñés. When the club got promoted to the first division for the first time, in 1987, few could believe it. Many thought it wouldn't last. They stayed for almost a decade.

During that time Las Gaunas, the local ground, became a symbol of resilience. The expression 'Goal in Las Gaunas', echoed over radio broadcasts to the collective memory of an entire generation. To play there was like doing it on a rainy Wednesday night in Stoke. It was not for the faint of heart. When the club was forced, like all others, to convert into a limited company, things started to turn sour. Debt increased and after being relegated it wasn't long before they were forced to declare bankruptcy. It wasn't just CD Logroñés. All around Spain, more than a dozen historic professional sides disappeared, their supporters left shattered. Angel Iturriaga, a local author and football historian, lived through those days of wine and roses as a teenager. He recalls the excitement of playing against the best sides in Spain. 'It was huge for La Rioja, being able to sign players like Oscar Ruggeri, Manu Sarabia and Quique Setién and play against Barcelona or Madrid. As a region, we became known because of the local club. Even wine exports benefited from that. But it couldn't last, we were too small to sustain a project like that.'

In 2009, after tumultuous years, Club Deportivo Logroñés was no more. But football stayed alive in Logroño. A few weeks later a local businessman tried to take advantage of the situation and bought a competitive license from a smaller side in the third division and founded Unión Deportiva Logroñés, a club supposed to continue the legacy of the historical team of the city. Many were against it, especially hardcore supporters who had been gathering in the stadium, at Puerta Cero, searching for a way out. It was they who, on 4 June of that same year, founded Sociedad Deportiva Logroñés. But they didn't have any financial backing and neither did they buy a competitive licence. For them it was start from square one, playing in the lowest league in the region. A club managed exclusively by supporters who decided it was time to take control. Who's the manager they hire? 'Tato' Abadía, of course.

José Luis Ouro is on the club's board and has been there since day one. 'The end of CD Logroñés was a hard blow. I had lived the glorious days and the bitter end. At first, you don't realise how the club has changed once it converts into a limited company but then you see how the connection with the fans disappears. I was fed up with all of that. The city, the local businessmen let the club die and it was painful but, at the same time, gave us strength to create the sort of club that we would have liked CD Logroñés to have been.' SD Logroñés was one of the first clubs to break the wheel and return to the roots.

In Spain, those clubs are called *Clubes de Accionariado Popular* – clubs that are run exclusively by their associates. The echoes of AFC Wimbledon or FC United of Manchester were there but their story differs. They decided to take back what was theirs to begin with. Sixteen years on, the club remains a powerful symbol of resistance. SD Logroñés went as high as the third division, a semi-professional league – huge for a side with no financial backer – and now rents the renewed Las Gaunas while managing to break even each season. Day-to-day life is not easy. Raúl Rota, also from the boardroom, explains: 'It's all volunteer work. On matchdays we have volunteers coming to the stadium to sell merchandising, and tickets, or control the entrance gates. Only the football team is fully professionalised; for everything else, we use whatever free time we can spare from our families and regular jobs for the love of the club.'

It's matchday and the sun shines on Las Gaunas. Locals walk to the stadium calmly, aware it will not be a sold-out match. It never is. Logroño now has two clubs instead of one but neither managed to gain full support. That's a setback but the people who run SD Logroñés are not worried. For them, it's more about the values the club sets, especially with the younger generations. 'We have a hardcore group of supporters that understands the difficulties of running a club like this,' says Ouro. 'For the rest of the supporters who just want to see some football, we are perceived as any other normal club and like always they expect results or else they walk away. Yet, we are very proud of what we achieved. Out of nowhere, we ended up playing historic sides like Deportivo. They won a league; we are a team run by *sócios*. It's a different ball game but for us, to be here, despite all the ambition we carry in our hearts, is already worthy to be celebrated.'

SD Logroñés wear the same red and white stripes as the former club and have the same fighting spirit. Even down to ten men, they hold on and get a well-deserved draw against Real Irún, a club owned by Unai Emery's family. But is the project sustainable in the long run? 'It's a question of identity,' explains Rota. 'People in Spain always expect some businessman will invest millions to make them competitive. Especially in La Rioja. It's hard for them to understand we are happy writing our destiny.' He adds: 'We believe this sort of club will become more relevant in time. Of course, if you expect to be competing in European football, you can forget about it, but if you want something different, this is the way to go.' Ouro agrees: 'For me, success is not about Champions League football. It's about having no debt, and people who feel the club colours.' There's life around Las Gaunas. The game ends and people cheer the memory of the club that was and the survival of the club that is. SD Logroñés may still be a needle in a haystack, but they are not alone.

***

In 2007 the Atlético Club de Sócios was born. It was the first *Accionariado Popular club* in Spain, set up by a group of Atlético Madrid supporters tired of fighting against the men who took control of the club when it was converted into a limited company. The project set an example followed by others. Some only wanted to be part of a project close to the local community like UC Ceares. Others were supporters of clubs that suffered the same fate as Logroñés or who were bankrupted at the hands of unscrupulous owners. That was the case of Xerez Deportivo Fútbol Club in Jerez La Frontera, a town well known for its legendary temple of speed, a track where some of Spain's most decorated drivers such as Angel Nieto, Jorge Lorenzo or Marc Marquez won several motorcycle world championships.

The same could be said of CF Tarraco, created in 2013 by a group of former Gimnastic of Tarragona supporters tired of how the club was being run, taking no consideration of the local identity of one of the most beautiful cities on the Mediterranean shores, one that sits close by to Salou, a favoured travel destination for young British students partly because of the popular theme park Port Aventura. There was even the extreme case of Club Accionariado Popular Ciudad de Murcia, whose fans saw how the owner decided to relocate to Granada, a town more than 170 miles away, and took matters into their own hands by setting a new club away from all the noise.

Every single *Accionariado Popular* club has a different story to tell but there is unity in the same principle. They believe football has turned its back on fans. In a country where Barcelona and Real Madrid attract the lion's share of support, media time and money, the rest are forced to fight for crumbs. Without the backing of their local community, they won't survive. Historic teams like Racing Santander, Deportivo Alavés, Málaga, and even Valencia have paid a high price and set an example for others not to follow. But they belong to well-to-do cities and were able to dodge a bullet. Not everyone was so lucky, especially in the poorest regions. Football almost disappeared in the western region of Extremadura – Mérida, CF Extremadura and Badajoz all shut down between 2000 and 2012 – and the same happened miles north in Salamanca, a city where history and culture run so deep that the end was also the beginning of something new.

Salamanca sits in the western part of Spain; 70 miles west lies the border with Portugal; 130 miles south-east and you reach Madrid. The city is a key part of Spanish identity. It's home to Spain's oldest university, one of the most important in Europe. A place where knowledge and study have always been valued. The city's mighty cathedral that commands the landscape can be seen from miles away and immediately captures your heart. The old medieval streets are full of secrets and the presence of thousands of students makes it a place boiling with youth. The vast area around might be scarcely populated but walking its Plaza Mayor you can't tell. Once it was the favoured place for philosopher Miguel de Unamuno to take his morning coffee. He was one of the leading members of the Generation of 98, a group of philosophers and writers who helped define Spanish modern identity at the turn of the 20th century. Great men such as Antonio Machado, Pio Baroja or Ramón de Valle-Inclan. Unamuno became the headmaster of the university and was banned by the dictatorship of Primo de Rivera when famously, upon his return six years later, he started his first lecture: 'As we were saying yesterday.' Despite being born in Bilbao, he had a certain stubbornness shared by locals that you can also find in their football supporters. After all, they were the ones who didn't let their colours die.

If there is a club that represents the spirit of the *Accionariado Popular* in Spain, it is Unionistas Salamanca. They are closely connected with SD Logroñés and sponsor the Supporters Club Day, a festivity that takes place whenever they play each other. Unionistas now sit in the third tier, one step from professional football but, much like Logroñés, they are still run exclusively by their members. 'We do a lot of overtime,' says Nacho Sanchez, a board member. 'Our chairman dedicates more hours to the club than to his own professional life, but we are lucky to be surrounded by very able people who have helped make this club a success story. Every single one of us is here for love, even if that means staying away from home more than we should,' he laughs. Unionistas was born when the old Union Deportiva Salamanca disappeared. It was a historic club, one that had played in the first division in two different periods with good results, finishing as high as seventh in the 1970s. Twenty years later they got promoted partly to the genius of a young manager, Juan Manuel Lillo, credited with implementing in Spanish football a new tactical shape, the 4-2-3-1. But like so many others at the time, relegation was just the first step before bankruptcy.

As in Logroño two teams were set up as a result, one sponsored by local businessmen who sought to buy the legacy of the former club – Salamanca Club de Fútbol – and a club founded by the supporters of the UD, who called themselves Unionistas de Salamanca CF. Relations between the clubs were tense. Salamanca, much like Logroño, is a city not big enough to host two sides but the way things were done by Unionistas made them the true beloved entity in town. They even gained the backing of local celebrity Vicente del Bosque. The man who guided Spain to their World Cup title in 2010 was born there and spent his youth playing for the local side before signing for Real Madrid. Diplomatically, Del Bosque says that, despite being a *sócio* of Unionistas, he also has a membership card for Salamanca CF and takes no sides because, for him, the city is what matters.

'All of us who enjoyed the good years of UD in the elite feel a little bit nostalgic, of course,' he explains. 'It's clear football is losing part of its romanticism, but we have to accept times change.' But Del Bosque is also uplifted by the evolution of the club's project. 'For me, the third tier, despite being officially semi-amateur, is pretty much a professional competition and Unionistas are doing an excellent job, with young people who love the city, the club and the game, and we can see that the city feels itself again part of something special,' states a man who, despite having become a marquee name after winning the World Cup, still talks and behaves like he always was, a man of the people. His legacy is part of what Unionistas represent.

'We loved the UD, enjoyed those years in La Liga so much and wanted to honour that memory,' explains Sanchez. 'That was our guiding force throughout the years. We felt like orphans when the club disappeared and only wanted to give back to Salamanca what the UD gave to us.' And they did. The club climbed the football pyramid and has become the perfect example of how a supporters' club can be a success story. They have a fully packed stadium each week and suspended the number of new members to guarantee nobody is left out of a seat. Their marketing beats many first-division sides, and they have their club members voting each season on social media for the designs of their new kits. When the Spanish Federation made the use of grass turf mandatory in competitive games, it was thanks to the economic backing of admirers from all over the world, especially from the United Kingdom, that they were able to pay for it.

That club culture can be seen reflected on the pitch as well. When they hosted Real Madrid and Barcelona in the Copa del Rey, players always put up a good fight despite the huge differences between both sides. Since 2022 Unionistas are no longer forced to play only as high as the third tier because new legislation revoked the need for clubs to convert into limited companies to play professional football. Many now believe Unionistas are on a path to becoming the first *Accionariado Popular* club to make the jump to the professional leagues. Their stubbornness might well be rewarded in the end. Unamuno would be proud.

* * *

Unionistas and Logroñés are both representatives of a region. Some clubs survive in a different environment. When Club Esportiu Europa was founded, in 1907, Gràcia had just been annexed by the city of Barcelona. Once a proud village north of the mighty capital of Catalonia, with time Gràcia became a singular element in a cosmopolitan urban city. Today, the barrio has a life of its own, known for the love of arts, fashion, and pub life but the club, one of the founders of La Liga, has not had an easy life. In their early days, Europa became one of the first local rivals of mighty FC Barcelona. When they surprisingly won the Catalonia Championship in 1923 it allowed them to take part in the Copa del Rey. Against all odds CE Europa reached the final, only to lose against favourites Athletic Bilbao by a single goal.

Six years later, when the football league started, they were amongst the ten teams invited and played brilliantly for three consecutive seasons, until eventually being relegated. Darker days followed. The club suffered the consequences of the Civil War and wasn't able to climb back from the pit. They remained, however, deeply rooted within the neighbourhood and, come the 2010s, a rivalry with Sant Andreu, another local side from a working-class neighbourhood, arose. It came to be known as the 'other' Barcelona derby. In the words of Alex López, a board member, it is a new-found rivalry but full of meaning. 'It began with a dispute between the ultra groups of both clubs during a match but, in the end, helped both institutions to grow in popularity and to bring attention to lower league football. The derbies are very intense, with both grounds packed, which is good, but as clubs we have more things in common than people might expect.' And those values are what have made Europa such a special club.

Run by their fans, the Escapulats were the first football club to include in its statutes an anti-fascist, anti-bullying and anti-homophobe core of values. 'We are a club proud of our ideals,' López says. 'We are historically a Catalanist side and some of our supporters are indeed pro-independence of Catalonia but as a club, we are, above all else, a club that wants to do good. We work closely with the community in social projects, and literary journeys, and get together with people from the neighbourhood. We want to be much more than just a football club.' And they are. CE Europa is an example of how a club run by its members can do so much for a local community, especially in a place like Gràcia. The way many have become fed up with the increasing commercialisation of Barcelona also increased support for Europa. They have come to be seen as the representatives of a purer form of football, where supporters not only matter but also get to dictate how the club takes a stand on what they feel is right. Although they all know Europa will hardly ever again play against the likes of Barcelona or Madrid, they strongly believe that if they have to slowly climb the football pyramid, they might as well do it the right way. 'Glòries tornarèm', says in Catalan a sign displayed by the ultra group L'Escapulats at the beautiful Nou Sardenya, a ground surrounded by housing that is a refreshing sigh for those fed up with stadiums turned shopping centres. Glory days will return. They just might.

* * *

Football is always more than just a game. But life sometimes hits hard when one least expects and makes everything look smaller in comparison. On the morning of 11 March 2004, Cristina Pereira's alarm clock never went off, so she couldn't catch the 7.10 am train that was supposed to take her from the university city of Alcalá de Henares to a student protest in downtown Madrid. A train that never got there. Twenty-eight minutes later two bombs exploded in one of the carriages while the train stopped at the station of El Pozo. At the same time, bombs in three other trains, one in the station of Santa Eugenia and two in Madrid's Atocha station, also went off. It was the largest terrorist attack ever to take place on Spanish soil; 193 people died, 2,057 were injured. The 11M became a memory of pain and suffering. A wound that never truly healed. Two trains exploded in the Vallecas district, the biggest neighbourhood south of Madrid. A place forged by people who suffered the hardships of life like no other in the capital. That tragic event reinforced their strength of will. Locals bravely immediately took to the streets to help the injured as they always did.

Vallecas started as a shanty town, a small village south of Madrid where the poor from the southern regions of Castilla, Extremadura and Andalusia arrived, believing they would find a better life. Many were forced to stay there, living in shanties built with their own hands. But they were never alone. When authorities forbade anyone who arrived to settle, they met resistance from the locals who found a loophole in the law that allowed anyone who could claim a house of their own before dawn to be considered a permanent resident. During the dark hours of the night, everyone got together to aid newcomers in building their homes in record time to avoid eviction the next morning. That communal spirit lives on and is represented perfectly in the identity of its football club: Rayo Vallecano.

'Rayo is Vallecas and Vallecas is Rayo,' says writer Ignacio Pato, author of a seminal book on the club's history. 'It's a club full of grateful people. Vallecas always opens her heart to whoever comes by. It's a neighbourhood of suffering people, they know what it's like to have nothing, they are normal people with real problems and when it comes to football, they live it like that, with authenticity. It's not as much as if Rayo wins or loses. It's the sense of belonging, the possibility of celebrating a goal around your neighbours that lightens up a week of hardship.' The club with the iconic diagonal red stripe is said to be inspired by River Plate – although the real historical reason was that Atlético de Madrid helped them financially and in return asked them to add some red to their usual white shirt to separate them from their rivals Real Madrid – was founded in 1924 in Prudencia Priego's house. She was the template of what you would expect from a woman from Vallecas. Widow of the first club chairman, she had her house serve as club headquarters for years, where all the football and kits, which she washed herself, were stored. Those were hard years in Vallecas and the club was an important element in bonding relations inside the neighbourhood. Since the beginning, it became a working-class institution, profoundly left wing and very down to earth. They also paid a price for that. When Franco's army finally conquered Madrid, Rayo's ground was used as a prison camp. Many who were detained and shot there were also Rayo supporters. It wasn't until the 1970s that the club finally got its chance to play at the highest level. It was 1977 and they became known as giantkillers, playing heroically and often beating the likes of Athletic Bilbao, Real Madrid or Barcelona at home. It wouldn't last long, but in the late 1980s they went up again and established themselves professionally at the top for the following decade. During those years Vallecas had expanded geographically and demographically as well. The first waves of immigrants from South America were forced to settle in the area, much like the poor people from Andalusia or Extremadura had done. The same happened with African immigrants, and soon Vallecas became the most multicultural place in Madrid. A poor, working-class neighbourhood but also full of life and communal spirit, something that caused an impact on its culture, fuelling the work of its local artists, whether they were *rumberos* of gypsy background such as Los Chichos or Los Chunguitos, hard-rock legends like Obus or hip-hop artists such as Ska-P. The latter even included in their 1994 debut album a theme dedicated to the club, 'Como un Rayo'. The supporters adopted it as their unofficial anthem. The band even witnessed first-hand how local legend – and later Girona's manager – Michel celebrated a goal by taking his shirt off, only to show another with the Ska-P logo. Cinema during those years was also attracted by the complex social reality of its working-class streets and the remaining slums where gypsies, drug addicts and poor emigrants tried to survive. The *Quinqui* exploitation film genre, extremely popular in Spain during those years, served as a testimony of that period. *Deprisa, deprisa*, directed by Carlos Saura and shot entirely in Vallecas with many locals as extras, won the Golden Bear at the 1981 Berlin Film Festival and marked the artistic pinnacle of the genre.

During the early 1990s much changed within the club. On one side, the forced conversion to a limited company paved the way for the arrival of José Maria Ruiz-Mateos, a dodgy businessman who ended up appointing his wife, Teresa Rivero, as club chairman. She became the first woman to preside over a football club in Spain, although she had little to no interest in the game. Still, she was welcomed by the supporters for her down-to-earth style and became a symbol of a decade where Vallecas became also renowned for their political stance. Because if you talk about football and politics in Spain, you have to talk about the Bukaneros.

Over the previous decade, right-wing ultras began to control the stands at Vallecas, much as they were doing in almost every ground in Spain. But the neighbourhood was never a place for far-right extremists. Today they remain the only district in Madrid that has never given any electoral victory to the right-wing Partido Popular, which usually runs both the city and regional government. The way Bukaneros, a militant left-wing group, was able to take back control of the stadium made them a worldwide symbol of resistance within the ultra movement. They had Rayo become the first football club to take a stand against racism after their Nigerian goalkeeper Wilfried Agbonavbare was racially abused by Real Madrid supporters at an away match. Since then, Vallecas has become a pillar in the anti-racism fight in Spanish football, an ever-present reality that still affects today's world-class players like Vinicius Jr. as it did in the past with other black-skinned footballers such as Samuel Eto'o. They have also fought against homophobic policies, the eviction of hundreds of people out of their homes when the banks started to cancel mortgages during the 2012 economic crisis and the increasing persecution of immigrants by right-wing movements. 'La Vida Pirata' – a pirate's life – has become their most celebrated anthem, and they sing it along with the players at the end of each game. When ultra groups from rival clubs mocked them by calling them gypsies and junkies, they simply created an anthem that dwelt on how proud they were of their background. Their popularity has allowed them to rank alongside other iconic left-wing clubs such as Sankt Pauli.

Despite being known as a club where supporters have a huge role, the truth is that Rayo Vallecano is owned by someone who is the opposite of its fanbase. After Ruiz-Mateos was forced to sell, it ended up in the hands of entrepreneur Martin Presa. Since then, he has been in open war against the Bukaneros and most supporters, often promoting decisions that go against everything the club stands for, from trying to sign a Ukrainian striker with far-right beliefs to inviting the leader of the extremist party Vox to the directors' box. He also has vowed to sell the stadium, an iconic ground that sits right in the centre of Vallecas, to move the team to the outskirts, closer to one of the train stations where the 11M bombs exploded. That would enable him to convert the land into blocks of apartments in the hands of a powerful real-estate company. Many believe that what he aspires to, alongside the regional government who always saw the club as a thorn in their side, is to take the communal spirit of Vallecas out of Rayo. Ignacio Pato explains that a decision like that might well be the end of the club as we know it. 'Vallecas is a working-class club and to be so in a time like today is hard,' he says. 'It has survived mostly thanks to where it's located, in Avenida de la Albufera, the main centre of the neighbourhood. Even aesthetically, the stadium, with those typical redbricked tower blocks surrounding it, is an exception in a world where all grounds look the same and fans seem more interested in taking selfies than supporting.'

Walk around the streets of Vallecas and you can easily share that feeling. From the Cerro do Tio Pio one can easily see the beautiful 15,000-seater ground and how it mingles perfectly with the urbanity around it. That might be all gone if the club moves. Over the past decades, Rayo suffered relegations that took them very close to bankruptcy and have only been able to fight back and stay in La Liga because of that strong local connection. Those chaotic streets, those old-school bars where the players usually go out for a *caña*, a small pint, sharing tables with supporters. That is the spirit that best defines Vallecas.

However, Presa's way of running the club had already taken a toll on Rayo and many supporters, fed up with how things were going, decided to take a stand. That's how Independiente de Vallecas was born. The club belongs to the ever-growing *Accionariado Popular* community. Diego Muñoz, the club secretary, explains how it all began. 'Independiente resulted from the necessity to offer the community a type of football institution that brought people together. As such we are not only a football club, but we also serve as a space for the neighbourhood of Vallecas to feel alive, supporting any struggle against vicious elements of society like betting companies, real-estate speculation and racism. We are a working-class club made by and for working-class people. We bring our core values to our football identity.'

The club was founded by former Rayo supporters who believed in its social ethos but not in what their owner was trying to do. The inspiration drawn from AFC Wimbledon is clear. For Carlos Castellanos, who serves as vice-president and is also the manager, 'we follow the example of other *Accionariado Popular* clubs, where all the decisions are voted on in assemblies and that reflects how we believe football should be. We are not interested in the commercialisation of the game, ever dependent on television networks.' While Rayo supporters gather around the Stadium of Vallecas to usually see spectacular attacking football, a local trademark going back to the days of Paco Jemez's moving on to Michel or Andoni Iraola, Independiente supporters are forced to travel around Madrid each season to find a ground to play in. In compensation, they don't have to pay for a ticket and can enjoy a beer or two even if the football is not very good, as it wasn't expected when you are in the eighth tier. But that's not why they are there. For them, the game is much more than a perfect cross from the wing that ends up with a powering header towards the goal.

Some clubs run by their *sócios* have inherited a long-standing tradition of now-gone historic sides. They might aim to play, once again, in the professional leagues if everything goes their way. Others are just trying to work alongside the community, forging important values for younger generations to follow, whether they are in Barcelona or Madrid. And there are those whose supporters know they live on the permanent edge between the reality of playing in the elite, with all its consequences, and the necessity of maintaining their social values. Wherever they sit, one thing unites them all. They believe in people. They believe in the indispensable role of the football supporter. They believe in the power football has to change lives and shape local communities. In a world of expanding zeros in wages and transfer fees, of football grounds turned theme parks, they are the sole representatives of another ball game. They are not only against modern football. They are raising their voices and shaping their future in the process.

VIVA LA VIDA

ON 12 June 2008, Coldplay launched one of the century's greatest hits. 'Viva La Vida', the second single from the album of the same name, immediately impacted the cultural world and quickly crossed borders to the sporting arena. It recurrently played over the following weeks as the Euros 2008 unfolded in Austria and Switzerland. That was the tournament that showed to the world what the all-powerful figure of the Spanish holding midfielder could do as *La Roja* put an end to more than 40 years of hurt. One year later, inspired by Guardiola's love for the band, 'Viva la Vida' became the main theme song at Barcelona, often playing before and after matches during an extraordinarily successful year. It was even used as the soundtrack for one of his emotional motivational videos, just before the Champions League Final. That was the year the world became familiar with the name of Sergio Busquets. And like players such as himself, Xabi Alonso or Marcos Senna, who were all over the pitch, the song could be heard anywhere you went, transforming an already renowned indie rock act into the greatest band in the world. It seemed almost mystical that lead singer Chris Martin had chosen a Spanish name for a smash hit that would appear right when Spain started to dominate world football. It was a song that celebrated life, the same way the holding midfielder celebrated a new aesthetic approach to playing the game – a time when they ruled the world.

***

After Spain lost against Switzerland in the opening match of the 2010 World Cup the Spanish press was furious with the national manager Vicente del Bosque. No one understood why he insisted on playing a holding midfielder in the shape of Sergio Busquets against a side that rarely attacked, while having so many talented options he could call upon to play upfront. Del Bosque, one of the most cultured midfielders Spanish football had ever seen, shrugged his shoulders and claimed that, if he could become a professional footballer again, he would love to be like Busquets. The Barcelona midfielder played the following six matches as Spain went on to win their first-ever World Cup. Two years prior, Busquets was playing third-division football with the Barcelona B team. He proved to be an exceptional player throughout his career but, looking back, it is easy to see that his success was also a consequence of something that had started two decades earlier. Today it's impossible not to look at Spanish football and think about the holding midfielder as the first tactical position that springs to mind. Quality players, clever on the ball, able to read the game, and capable of helping in defence while commanding the attack, they became a symbol of Spain's golden era. Yet, it was a foreigner that precipitated a revolution.

Busquets is a family name deeply rooted in Barcelona's history. Sergio's father, Carles Busquets, had been the stand-in goalkeeper for Andoni Zubizarreta during Johan Cruyff's years in charge. It was during that period that the Spanish holding midfielder was born. Until the 1990s local sides usually followed the European tactical trend of the moment, unable to create a system that best suited their abilities. Players were forced to adapt to survive, instead of being nurtured to express their natural game. Cruyff saw it differently. For him, it was all about having players in a system that best benefited them.

Despite being groomed in the ideals of the Danubian school that evolved into Total Football, he was his own man. By 1988, even his mentor Rinus Michels was back to playing a traditional 4-4-2 but Johan insisted on moving to a 3-4-3 that defied conventions. It was supposed to be an all-out attacking formation but, for it to work, a huge deal of responsibility had to be put on the holding midfielder, which in Barcelona became known as the 'number four'. They needed to bring balance to the side and be the creative force behind all attacking movements while capable of closing down whenever the team lost possession. There was no historical precedent for a similar role. It was just the result of Cruyff's way of thinking, ever the improviser.

Football analyst Alejandro Arroyo explains that, before the Dutchman's arrival to the Spanish league, football was only played out, not thought about. 'Cruyff is the pioneer,' says the former *Ecos del Balón* author. 'He opens minds to the need to create a football identity. The latest greatest side before his arrival, Real Madrid's *Quinta del Buitre*, was a sum of talented individuals but his Dream Team is already a side that plays and thinks about the game collectively. Establishing that way of thought became key for a new type of player to emerge from the youth ranks, players with more tactical awareness who would later become managers themselves. That was the beginning of positional play.'

Positional play meant that players had to have a special awareness and none more than the holding midfielder. It demanded specific qualities that had been flying under the radar until then. Johan first tried Luis Milla, a talented midfielder who adapted well to the position. So well that, when his contract was up, Real Madrid decided to snatch him after seeing how important he was to the Barcelona way of playing. The transfer was meant to abort Cruyff's project but karma works in mysterious ways. Milla never had the career he might have had if he had stayed at the Camp Nou but by leaving he paved the way for Cruyff to search for an alternative in the youth set-up. There he found his soulmate.

Look at Pep Guardiola and you don't immediately understand why he was such a dominant holding midfielder. He was slim, not excessively tall and looked like he would faint if forced to run more than five kilometres. It was precisely because of all that that he was the perfect choice. The Dutchman didn't want a runner or a strong man to patrol the midfield. He was searching for other skills and Pep had plenty of those. He could read the game like no other and had exquisite technique, which made him able to deliver first-time passes with the precision of a surgeon. His job was to run the show. And he did. Born in Santpedor, a ball-boy for the club in his teens and the first renowned graduate of La Masia, Guardiola was a symbol of the Catalan identity of Barcelona. He was also their first modern all-round footballer. With him at the bottom of a diamond-shaped midfield, Cruyff's side controlled matches like few did in the past. He was often the assist man for quick forwards like Hristo Stoichkov or Romário but mainly served as the player who created the decisive penultimate pass.

Guardiola was skilful, witty and extremely disciplined. He was not the first Spanish player to display those traits so clearly, but he was the first being able to do so in a position on the pitch that best favoured his qualities. That became Cruyff's greatest tactical legacy. He developed the idea of a different kind of player for a specific role in a new ecosystem based on possession football and positional play. Of course, as with all of Cruyff's experiments there was no theoretical background. The Dutchman always worked on instinct and occasionally was left wanting. Never more so than when Barcelona travelled to Athens to meet AC Milan in the 1994 Champions League Final. The Catalan side was considered heavy favourites but ended up knocked down by a much superior Italian team in one of the most one-sided finals ever. The match was decided from the moment Fabio Capello's plan to take Guardiola out of the game by pressing him permanently worked. The constant shadowing of Marcel Desailly restrained Guardiola from playing to the full extent of his abilities and short-circuited the Dream Team's creative spirit. In doing so, Capello set out the recipe that would be followed for the next decade: hard-tackling and physical midfielders pressing the creative holding midfielders out of the game. Clubs went for the next Desailly rather than a new Guardiola. When Claude Makélélé, who had been playing in Spain, arrived at Chelsea his destroyer role was eventually christened the 'Makélelé' role essentially because he was the most accomplished pupil of his fellow international partner.

Michael Cox, one of the world's most renowned tactical analysts, wrote on the impact of the Spanish holding midfielder in his book *Zonal Marking*. For him, 'Ultimately Spanish holding midfielders were a very different type from the defensive midfielders who dominated in most other countries. In England and Italy, they were workers and tacklers, I don't think there was too much emphasis on passing quality as there was in Spain.' There they remained faithful to the concept of *mediocentro* – the name they gave the role – and many started to search for replicas of the talented player from Santpedor.

None was as successful as Argentinian international Fernando Redondo. Coming from a country where the tactical position of the holding midfielder had an immense cultural value, Redondo was fully apt to play the game the way Cruyff imagined it. Jorge Valdano, an admirer of the Dutchman, was the first to fully take advantage of his abilities, while at Tenerife. A relatively unknown club from the Canary Islands, Tenerife came to the spotlight when Valdano took over and led the side to European football, twice beating his former club Real Madrid in the process. Those victories gifted back-to-back league titles to Cruyff's Barcelona and were greatly a result of Redondo's genius, thus making the Dutchman twice lucky.

When Valdano, alongside his sporting partner Angel Cappa, moved to Real Madrid in 1994 he took Redondo with him and over six seasons he became one of the best players in the world from that creative holding midfield position. He was a cornerstone of the side that won the league in his first season at the Bernabéu, linking with Michael Laudrup the same way Guardiola had done with the Dane previously. When Real Madrid beat the *Blaugrana* 5-0 on a cold January night in 1995 – after losing themselves by the same result a year prior at the Camp Nou – the Argentine was lauded as the key figure of the side. They both played at the bottom of that midfield diamond, although Valdano preferred a classic back four.

Like Guardiola, however, Redondo suffered recurrent injuries, sometimes a consequence of how rivals used to target him hard, knowing the influence he commanded. He returned briefly to his best when Vicente del Bosque took the helm and led Real Madrid to their eighth Champions League trophy win in 2000, a season that went down in the history of the club as the one when Redondo silenced Old Trafford with a spectacular back-heeled pass to himself that made the Manchester United defence look amateurish. Guardiola and Redondo were very similar players, philosophically, although Redondo roamed more freely, as both spoke the same positional language. They also set an example for others to follow. Their success at the two biggest clubs in Spain had, by the end of the 1990s, several clubs already searching for the next big thing who could fill out the role of the *mediocentro*.

By the turn of the millennium, the tactical influence of Juanma Lillo had already started to spread around Spanish football in the same way Cruyff's had done a few years prior. The Dutchman's diamond midfield in a 3-4-3 that could convert into a more conservative 4-3-3 was one of the most-used tactical systems in the league. The other was the 4-2-3-1, first put into practice by Lillo's Salamanca side in the mid-90s. By playing two holding midfielders – José Luis Sukunza and António Díaz – Lillo's tactical plan allowed for a more creative display, as he could move between more physical or technical players, complementing themselves in different approaches to the same role. Some, following Arrigo Sacchi's revolution at Milan, had already advocated for two midfielders who could press constantly, managers like Albacete's Benito Floro, who later coached Real Madrid, and Hector Cúper and then Rafael Benítez at Valencia. Their midfield duo focused more on defensive roles. Lillo, on the other hand, was all in favour of combining a creative profile with a more physical one. Either way, the wide spread of both schools of thought paved the way for what became known in Spain as the *doble pivote*.

Successful sides of that time such as Irureta's Deportivo la Coruña, Ranieri's Valencia or Aragonés' Mallorca usually boasted two players as holding midfielders, mixing creativity with physicality. The positional number four in the Cruyff way was replicated by the likes of Victor Fernàndez during his stints at Zaragoza and Vigo but remained closely associated with the Catalan side. Cruyff's legacy survived through both his foe Louis van Gaal and protege Frank Rijkaard, who had different approaches to the game but remained followers of the holding midfielder. Van Gaal still enjoyed Guardiola's final years as a top-class footballer. When injuries started to affect him regularly, he tried out Albert Cclades, and then Xavi Hernández. Even Andrés Iniesta was initially tried in the number four position as it became synonymous with class players who graduated from La Masia. Famously Guardiola told Xavi, who was then already playing as a holding midfielder, that he would be chosen to succeed him in the side but that then Iniesta would own the role for the years to come. For much of the early 2000s, Spanish football's cultural debates were focused on the right type of *mediocentro* and how different footballing identities evolved from Cruyff's original idea. It reflected how Spanish society had evolved from the old days of *La Furia* into a new cultured approach that would plant the seed for successes to come.

* * *

For decades football in Spain was all about fury and balls. The trait most valued in footballers was grit – players who showed cojones were much preferred to those who displayed artistry. Not only was the national side known as the Spanish Fury – a nickname earned during their international debut at the 1920 Olympic Games – but Franco's fascist regime made sure those values of bravery remained the core of club football as well. Supporters learned to value tackles or limitless courage over those who preferred to embellish plays or dwelled too much on the ball. It was a social reflection of the Spain of the time, a country that still adored bullfighting above all else and remembered with fondness the days when the military corps of the Tercios was the most feared army in all of Europe. The brutal violence that had swept the regime to power and was behind the fascist ideal had been transported to the pitch. Technical players suffered. There were plenty but, eventually, many ended up deployed in wider positions if they had the pace, while others languished in the dugout.

That mentality was partially why the national side rarely fared well in international football. And why there were so few great historical individual players in Spanish football during large parts of the 20th century. Talent was usually a trait appreciated in foreigners – and the reputation of Spanish football guaranteed plenty of them came knocking – but locals had to be made of other stuff to get popular approval. That mentality endured until the late 1990s, with Javier Clemente, former manager of Athletic Bilbao, serving as national coach. Clemente had been a talented player himself but, as a coach, preferred a much more direct approach, famously starting seven defenders for the last-16 duel against Switzerland in the 1994 World Cup. Spain won 3-0. He represented a world where talented playmakers and midfielders had to put in extra effort to thrive, famously replacing all the leading members of the free-flowing attacking generation of Real Madrid stars with more down-to-earth footballers. By the time Clemente was forced to resign, Spain was already celebrating 20 years of its democratic constitution. The country had changed and so did mentalities.

The period immediately after Franco's death was complex. Unlike their Portuguese neighbours, the Spanish people never took to the streets against the fascist regime and the army remained pretty much right-wing. Adolfo Suárez, appointed as prime minister by the new head of state, King Juan Carlos I, was a civil servant during the late stages of the previous regime and a decisive figure during the transition towards democracy. In a country still divided between supporters of the late dictator and a generation who wanted to live in freedom, Suárez was forced to compromise. It was what he did best. While he appeased the military on one hand, he allowed for the return of political refugees and the legalisation of the Communist Party. With the king's support, he helped to draw a new political constitution that returned Spain to Western European democratic regimes. To achieve all that, he managed the unthinkable. A silent pact of 'forgive and forget' between Franco's heirs and the leaders of the Socialist, Communist and Nationalist parties.

The period became known as the *Transición*, and it was not such a bed of roses as people were made to believe. There were killings, revolts, terrorist groups from both factions and even a failed attempted fascist military coup but, in the end, democracy prevailed. The following decades allowed Spain to recover economically and socially as the country entered the European Union in 1986 and, organised the 1982 World Cup, the 1992 Olympic Games and the Expo in Seville the same year. It was a time of concord and permanent dialogue between different political factions and after the divisionism of the past, it seemed that the Spanish had finally learned to talk with one another. Everything changed accordingly, in arts, economics and sports. After decades of underachievement, national sports planted the seeds for a future glorious period, while celebrating the first heroes of a new era, such as golfer Severiano Ballesteros, cycling hero Miguel Indurain, female tennis star Arantxa Sanchez-Vicario or waterpolo superstar Manuel Estiarte. Football joined the trend, first with the popularity of the *Quinta del Buitre*, the first post-Franco generation of entertaining footballers, but mainly during the 1990s with the rise of the holding midfielders.

Here were, for the first time, creative, talented footballers lauded for their skills and ability to control games and entertain rather than for fighting for every ball as if the world was about to end. During the previous decades that sort of player would have been cast into oblivion and many, because of their physicality, probably would never have turned professional. When Cruyff first went to watch Guardiola play for the reserves he was shocked to find out that he was a regular sub because the team coach thought he didn't possess the physical ability to perform. Until then many players expected to be shorter than 1.7m ended up vetoed by youth academies. Yet, the Spanish were not known for being tall or strong, much on the contrary. Also, they rarely genetically mingled with other nations, a consequence of the previous regime's hatred for multiculturality. Immigration, especially from South America or Africa, only started to thrive in the early 1990s. Only now, 30 years on, can we begin to appreciate a trend of second-generation immigrants playing for the national side.

Back in those days, there was almost only one sort of footballer. Cadena Ser journalist Bruno Alemany explains: 'One of the things that the holding midfielder culture in Spanish football does is that it mirrors our lack of multiculturality. The type of player Spain produced was physically different from other European countries. Small, and thin, they had to make themselves valuable by controlling the ball better than anyone, to get a better peripherical vision of what was happening around them. It was a physical limitation turned in our favour.' The mental change that came with a new society – greatly thanks to Suárez's political efforts – was also key to bringing a new way to understand the on-pitch dynamics. The *doble pivote* reflected that permanent sense of concord, players often very different who were forced by circumstances to understand one another for the good of the team. It became a metaphor for a country that had embraced beauty, artistry, and dialogue after decades of heralding the glories of violence and grit. A country that found its voice.

* * *

'Busquets has a superlative intelligence when reading the game. He knows exactly when and how to pass, and where to position himself to help the team at any moment. These players are vital for team play to work, they are the brain of the side,' says Vicente del Bosque. He should know. Once one of Spain's most talented midfielders he was also the man that first called up Sergio Busquets for the national side in 2009. He went on to play a pivotal part in the greatest era of Spanish football until his international retirement in 2022.

If there ever was a player so linked to a particular role, that would surely be him. Born in Sabadell, and raised in Badía, Busquets played most of his formative years in local small clubs. He only entered La Masía at 17. Despite becoming the perfect representation of the Barcelona way of playing, the fact that he spent so many years in smaller sides gave him a different perspective on the game. He was street-smart, always had a few tricks up his sleeve and knew how to impose himself. He was also taller than the usual graduate, another trait that helped him greatly. Guardiola knew all about him, being close to his father Carles, but when he started to coach him in the Barcelona B team back in 2007 he realised he had found a player that was even better than he had been for that role.

Busquets had all of Pep's traits but could add a physicality that the Santpedor man never could. He was born to dominate matches. When Guardiola was promoted to the first team the following season, he took Busquets with him and made him a pillar of the side. Over the following seasons, while the world fell in love with Messi, Xavi and Iniesta, it was Busquets who made everything work. His huge personality and ability to read the game was second to none, so much that even Cruyff himself anointed him as the key figure of the side. All the coaches that followed Guardiola found in Busquets their main man.

As Michael Cox stresses, 'For me the key with Busquets was that he was never flashy. You had to see him play a handful of times before realising how good he was. Even his line-breaking passes were done in a nice, subtle, understated way.' As Xavi and Iniesta's careers faded, he kept being decisive, providing the much-needed balance for Luis Enrique's attacking trio of Lionel Messi, Neymar Jr and Luis Suárez. Even as he was getting older, Busquets never managed to lose the ability to control the game. So much so that in 2021 he was considered the best player in the Nations League finals – at 31 – more than a decade after Del Bosque had resisted the pressing claims that he should leave his place in the side that eventually won the World Cup.

During the South Africa World Cup Busquets had been paired by the national coach with Xabi Alonso. If the Badía boy represented the ethos of Cruyff's idea of a holding midfielder, Alonso was the perfect representative of the other version, which grew in relevance with the 4-2-3-1 of the previous decades. He was more physical, hard-tackling and ran more than the Barcelona man. He was also one of the best long-range passers of the ball ever to grace the pitch, a trait that first made him a vital player for his hometown club of Real Sociedad and later at Anfield, where he paired Steven Gerrard in the Rafa Benítez years. 'Alonso was much more spectacular,' says Michael Cox, 'but I think less positionally reliable. He often fired the first pass out to a winger who would then break at speed, and was at his best at Bayern under Pep when he learned how to play as the sole holding midfielder.' Used as a substitute in Euro 2008, after Senna left the stage, he, like Busquets, became a decisive figure under Del Bosque. The former Real Madrid manager usually played with two holding midfielders but allowed Busquets to move into his more preferred number four role. At the same time, Alonso had the freedom to roam and connect with the likes of Xavi, Iniesta, Silva, Fàbregas or Cazorla. It was the most dominant international side history has ever known, a team that won everything between 2008 and 2013, often accumulating more than 70per cent ball possession.

During those moments the role of both players was decisive in giving fluidity to their passing game. Del Bosque explains: 'Having those two was vital for everything we achieved. They control the distances between the lines, always make the best possible decisions and represent the true creative nature of the Spanish footballer.' They became a winning partnership as vital as Xavi and Iniesta's a few metres higher up the pitch and, because of that, many talented holding midfielders rarely had the chance to compete in the national side. Players like Mikel Arteta, Javi Martinez, Gabi, Asier Illaramendi, Bruno Soriano and Dani Parejo were dominant in their football clubs but never played regularly for the national side. Another of those skilled footballers was Mikel San José who, at Athletic Bilbao, moved from centre-back to play as a holding midfielder and started to enjoy the game more. 'You are closer to the action. To be able to press higher, mark your position, always offering yourself to team-mates and, at the same time, move around to find solutions for what is happening at each moment is highly enjoyable,' explains the man who Del Bosque called up as back-up for Busquets for the 2016 Euros once Alonso retired from international football.

As time went by Spain became obsessed with finding a new holding midfielder who would allow them to keep dominating games. None reached the same heights as Rodrigo Hernández. The Manchester City midfielder was born in 1996 in Madrid and arrived in Atlético de Madrid's youth set-up when he was 11. Spain was about to rule the world, so he grew up wanting to be like Busquets and Alonso. He became easily the most talented player of his generation but, surprisingly, was told that he lacked physical strength and ended up signing for Villarreal instead. In the Spanish Levante, Rodri proved his doubters wrong, converting himself into one of the most dominant figures in La Liga, so much so that Simeone insisted on signing him back and handing him the keys of his side's midfield. He was so good that it took only a season at the Metropolitano until Pep Guardiola recognised all the traits that reminded him of Busquets and signed him for Manchester City.

Since then, he has become one of the most decisive figures for the Citizens, regularly one of the best players in the Premier League by showing not only what the Spanish holding midfielder can do but also adding a physicality and goalscoring prowess that reminds of the old-school box-to-box. 'Rodri is a genuine blend of the two,' explains the author of *Zonal Marking*. 'He has physicality, mobility, and also goalscoring ability. It feels like he's as much an all-rounder as football has seen in that position for a long time. I can't see a weakness other than perhaps in terms of discipline.' The boy who grew up admiring the classic holding midfielder evolved with the game and became a reflection of how times have changed. As Marti Perarnau, who wrote a seminal work on Barcelona's youth academies as well as a trilogy of Pep Guardiola's career, says, 'The holding midfielder has become a symbol for the Spanish modern way of playing but it has already inspired players around the world. Think of Joshua Kimmich, Toni Kroos or Granit Xhaka. They too have benefited from the path set out by the likes of Guardiola, Busquets or Alonso.'

So much so that when *France Football* announced Rodri as the surprise winner of the 2024 Balón d'Or, the midfielder publicly acknowledged that the award was not just a recognition of his unforgettable season but also the role of the Spanish *mediocentro* over the years. Rodri became only the second Spanish player to receive the prized accolade, something that not even the likes of Andrés Iniesta, Xavi Hernández or Sergio Busquets could do. His win, after guiding Spain to victory at the Euros and a memorable season in the Manchester City shirt, served as a reminder of the impact that the Spanish holding midfielder had in the modern game, so much so that no other player who bossed the midfield had ever been recognised above talented wingers, playmakers or goalscorers. The likes of Frank Lampard, Steven Gerrard, Andrea Pirlo or Toni Kroos were never able to achieve such individual recognition as Rodrigo did, partly because, by honouring him, in fact, the *France Football* jury was celebrating the impact of a specific group of Spanish players who changed how the game was played.

Spain is now a very different country than it was three decades ago. It's a more multicultural, dynamic and creative nation. They have also become winners. When Guardiola began his footballing career, he did so with a side that had never won the European Cup in a country that rarely went beyond the last eight in big tournaments. Now, not only has Barcelona's 'number four' become synonymous with continental trophies but also the *doble pivote* led Spain to glory. They have left behind prejudices and a football culture excessively focused on aggression and grit. Players are now proud of their artistry and ability to interpret the game like few can. For decades the world didn't know what to think of the Spanish footballer. There was always something missing. Now all doubts have been left behind. They are regarded as creative, clear-minded, winners and are sought-after by the biggest clubs in the world. Despite being a Dutchman's idea, the holding midfielder fits in the way Spain lives the game. With *pasión*, yes, but also with knowledge and a special ability to read between the lines. In a nation deeply rooted in duality, they became the central hub of a lacking football identity. Football was not supposed to be something that just came out of bravery and *cojones*. It was to be thought of and celebrated. Like life. Or that Coldplay song that still echoes in eternity.

STOP THE CLOCKS

THE SPANISH have their slang word for slow life. They call it 'Mediterraneamente'. Indeed, life moves at a different pace as you walk along the ever-sunny shores of the Mediterranean Sea. For a moment it seems clocks can stop ticking when the radiant lights enter the open windows of any of their pearly white houses. It is a place for relaxation. Coffee on the table, shades of bright colours all around, days that last longer than anywhere else. Perhaps because no one is bothering with the pressure of time. But all that doesn't mean the Levante coastline lacks complexity or diversity. They too have quite a story to tell. From being the seminal point of the Roman Hispanic identity to becoming the doorstep for modernity during the sombre late years of Franco's regime, the region can surprise those who believe it's all only about sun, beaches, late-hour drinks and a round of good paella. A place that holds deep and dark secrets as well as fascinating tales of underdogs, sleeping giants and Moneyball adventurers.

* * *

Even a man like Oliver Kahn could not look away and do nothing. Amid wild celebrations, the giant German goalkeeper showed unexpected empathy and embraced his fellow rival. Santiago Cañizares sat on the ground, head in his hands, crying. It was a mixture of rage and sadness. Kahn knew all too well what it was like to lose a Champions League final abruptly, but he had no idea what was like to lose it twice in consecutive years. Knowing there would be no third time. Valencia had just lost in a penalty shoot-out against Bayern Munich and, in the stands of the San Siro as in the city streets, people somehow knew their time had come and gone. No Spanish club other than Real Madrid and Barcelona had won the Champions League before. None did afterwards. But to lose back-to-back finals was all too much. Valencia would eventually win the Spanish league the following season and again in 2004, a year when they also conquered the UEFA Cup and the European Supercup, to make an historic treble. Those were their golden years, as a club and as a region that had been through exciting and hard times, without imagining they were about to embark on a tragic journey that came to epitomise the end of the so-called Spanish economic miracle.

Valencia sits right in the middle of Spain's eastern shore, a region that came to be known as Levante. It stretches from the delta of the Ebro river, in the province of Castellón, out to the popular beach resorts around Alicante. Phoenicians, Greeks, Carthaginians and Romans all entered the Iberian Peninsula through those shiny shores, and since that moment, Valencia represented a sense of openness to the world that differed from other big Spanish cities. It was also one of the landmark symbols of the medieval days of the Reconquista, the period in which the Christian warlords of the northern Iberian kingdoms set out to reconquer the land previously occupied by the Muslim invasion of the 8th century. The city became ever attached to the mighty figure of Rodrigo Díaz de Vivar, a warrior from the northern area of Burgos, who decided to go rogue after confronting his newly crowned king, whom he deemed responsible for his elder brother's death. He single-handedly established a kingdom, making the city his capital from where he and his men resisted the Moors until his death. He became known as *El Cid*, and his figure, revered by both sides, not only represented the warrior spirit of the Spanish people during those troubled times but also a sense of ideal of what men should aspire to be. Loyal but independent, a warrior but compassionate.

That spirit lingered in the Spanish ethos, especially in Valencia, above all places. Eventually, supporters came to look upon those traits when football became the talk of the town during the 1920s but, most of all, 20 years later when Valencia CF lived its first golden age. The city had been punished severely by the Nazi Luftwaffe during the Civil War as it was there that the last Republican government reunited before moving to exile once it became clear Franco was going to prevail. Despite ending on the losing side, locals felt proud of their spirit of resistance, much as they had done during the Cid years. When the war was over, they transferred that passion to football. Luckily the team was about to perform to expectations. A series of decisive signings paved the way for what became known as *La Delantera Electrica*, a quintet of creative and deadly strikers put together by the iconic figure of Luis Casanova, the club's most decorated chairman. Epi, Guillermo Gorostiza, Mundo, Vicente Asensi and Amadeo Ibañez led the Valencia side to three league titles and two cup wins between 1941 and 1949, losing three other cup finals and ending as runners-up on other three occasions. In a time when the modern-day hierarchy of Spanish football was still to be consummated, Valencia represented an independence from the powers to be and provided a sense of belonging for those who packed the Mestalla stadium, the oldest still in activity today in La Liga. The following decade, with the arrival of Dutch winger Faas Wilkes, brought more flair than silverware but in the 1960s there was a short-lived revival that saw the club win back-to-back Inter-Cities Fairs Cups, the competition UEFA decided not to recognise as the predecessor of the UEFA Cup. They would win another league in the 1970s and a Cup-Winners' Cup Final in 1980, in a penalty shoot-out against Arsenal, on both occasions coached by the legendary Alfredo di Stéfano, with the 1980 side led by the goalscoring prowess of Argentine star Mario Kempes. However, by that time, football wasn't what mattered the most.

During the early 1960s, Franco's regime was forced by circumstances to endorse a more open policy to the world. The hunger years after the cruel Civil War were a thing of the past and the nation needed to boost its economy. The regime sought tourism as the easiest solution, taking advantage of its fantastic landscape and a growing will from more well-to-do northern Europeans to seek sun and relaxing times. The Propaganda Minister and later founder of the Partido Popular, Manuel Fraga, launched a campaign tagged 'Spain is Different' to attract investment and tourists. He had been involved in some of the darkest moments of the regime, such as a nuclear accident in Palomares, the execution of political prisoner Julián Grimau and the assassination of student activist Enrique Ruano, but later became one the most proactive reformist ministers in the cabinet.

When tourists first arrived at the beaches of Castellón, Valencia and Alicante, he was forced to battle against the mighty forces of the Catholic Church and the Opus Dei, two key pillars of the regime alongside the army. The debate about how visiting northern European women were wearing bikinis or even going topless, things forbidden to the Spanish women, raised many eyebrows. After the pioneering years of the Spanish Republic that granted women the right to vote and divorce, the Church fought hard to guarantee that they behaved as exemplary housewives. Franco's legislation treated women as the property of their fathers or husbands.

The arrival of foreigners caused a deep impact on locals. Censorship had acted unmercifully so few in Spain knew how the world had evolved. Censors of moral costumes were not only at the beaches and public spaces but especially in the arts. Many Hollywood historical couples in film were made brothers and sisters to abide by the conservative and catholic values of the regime. When northern tourists started to populate the sunny beaches of the Mediterranean it became impossible to hide what was in plain sight. Women now had something to aspire to and men rediscovered a lost sense of lust. That propelled a shift in movie censorship, with Fraga loosening the rope and allowing more freedom, including the first nudity to appear on screen.

In due course that drastic policy change would partly cost him his job as he was forced to accept the role of ambassador in the United Kingdom but it would also pave the way for the *Destape*, a popular local movie genre that became the king of the box office in the late days of the regime right until the end of the decade. It was a mix of comedy and eroticism, depicting young Scandinavian tourist women, often nude, accompanied by provincial Spanish men played by popular actors like Alfredo Landa, Andrés Pajares or Fernando Esteso in odd circumstances. Eventually, the movement expanded to include more artistic works and Spanish actresses, like well-known icons Rocío Durcal and Carmen Sevilla, and entertainers such as Barbara Rey and Norma Duval. It paved the way for the country's much-needed sexual revolution. Without it the work of iconic directors like Bigas Luna and the success of magazines such as *Interviú* probably wouldn't have been possible.

Despite many of those movies being set on the Mediterranean shore, by then, Valencia was already so accustomed to that reality that it didn't matter. They were moving on to establish their own cultural and social revolution. At first, it seemed solely an artistic movement, greatly inspired by the punk pub culture and electronic sounds that mixed well with traditional dances and visual spectacles. Around the breathtaking area of El Saler, a huge natural salty lake only inhabited until then by rice producers and fishermen where you can today eat the best paellas in Spain, locals flocked to enjoy the shows and music concerts in places like Barraca, Chocolate or Spook. Eventually, this movement evolved from an artistry identity to embrace the Hacienda and Madchester spirit of dance culture. It only made it even more popular. With it came a new leading figure, the DJ, and a new drug culture that replaced the common use of mescaline or cannabis with speed and ecstasy pills. The phenomenon became so huge that each weekend people arrived by the thousands, in cars and buses, just to attend parties where they could mix alongside cultural icons like The Cure's Robert Smith or Suede's Brett Anderson. They called it *Ruta del Bakalao*. DJs like Chimo Bayo and Paul Pills pushed boundaries and, alongside the popularity of nearby Ibiza disco clubs, made Valencia Europe's epicentre for clubbing at the turn of the 90s. All that partying ended in a disaster hangover. Teenagers were getting killed by the dozens in road accidents because of alcohol and drug consumption, and when the prices to access the ever-popular clubs rose, many just opted to party outside, in parking lots, drinking and taking drugs in clear sight of the police authorities. The *botellón* culture, still popular among teenagers, shocked a more conservative sector of society, so when the right-wing Partido Popular ousted the socialist government that had backed the movement from the early days, lights went off and loudspeakers fell silent.

At the same time, Valencia CF also experienced their first relegation and were living through turbulent times but in 1994, just months after the end of the Bakalao Route, Francisco Roig was appointed club chairman. Part of a business family in Valencia with a long-standing connection to sports, Roig was set to make the club a symbol of a new and prosperous idea of Spain. His early projects were not as successful as he hoped but in 1997, just before he abandoned the presidency, Roig finally hit the jackpot. Claudio Ranieri was signed as coach with the season already running and slowly started to rebuild a winning mentality at a club that had long had nothing to celebrate. The team already included several youngsters that grew in relevance with the Italian at the helm, such as Gaizka Mendieta, Miguel Angulo, David Albelda or Javier Farinós, and upcoming stars like Claudio 'Piojo' López, Ariel Ortega and Adrian Illie. Suddenly Mestalla became a fortress once again. In the following season, the club lifted its first Copa del Rey in two decades and finished third in the league, a result that would pave the way for a historic season in the Champions League with the Argentine Héctor Cúper in charge. The Spanish side topped the first group stage and came second behind Manchester United in the second group round, before offering their long-suffering supporters a night to remember when Lazio came to town. The Italians were much-favoured to win the trophy but were eventually hammered by the locals, who beat them 5-2, with Gérard López scoring a hat-trick. When everyone was convinced that an *El Classico* final was in order, once again Cúper's men proved them wrong by destroying Barcelona in the semi-finals. A 4-1 thrashing at Mestalla was enough to book an all-Spanish final against Real Madrid in Paris. Suddenly they were now everyone's favourites and the extra pressure took hold of the side, beaten by a much more experienced Real Madrid squad. Some might have thought Valencia had lost their only shot but they eventually reached the final again the following season. López, Gerard and Farinós were sold for record fees, replaced by Ruben Baraja, John Carew, Zlakto Zahovic, Vicente and Pablo Aimar. During the knockout stages, Valencia beat both Wenger's Arsenal and the much-fancied Leeds United of David O'Leary. In a tense, well-disputed final in San Siro, the Spanish team was the superior side, but Bayern Munich held on and in the endh they took the trophy after a penalty shoot-out. Cúper was by then out, as was Gaizka Mendieta, the symbol of that generation and later himself a DJ, following in the steps of Chimo Bayo, forever representing the mix of the local football identity with the celebrated dance culture of the 90s. In came a young unknown manager named Rafa Benítez. The *Ches* would never again go as high as the last 16 in the Champions League, but the refurbished team built by Benítez won two leagues in 2002 and 2004, and a UEFA Cup, before he too left, for Liverpool. It was the end of a golden era in Mestalla, yet few could have predicted it then. It was also the end of a way of doing business in Spain that used Valencia as its favoured playground.

Rafael Chirbes, perhaps Valencia's most brilliant author, wrote in his celebrated work *Crematorio* the story of a Machiavellian real-estate businessman who took whatever means necessary to expand his business, using corruption and force if needed. He was the blueprint for many nameless faces who had shaped Valencia's economy for the previous decades, from Franco's late regime to the new millennium. The success brought by the expansion of tourism paved the way for real-estate speculators and constructors who forever changed the region's urban landscape. Benidorm, a small fishing village transformed into the favoured Spanish summer destination, with its skyline resembling a North American city, full of hotels and skyscrapers, set the example. North and south of Valencia changes were profound. For each traditional place like Denia or Peñiscola, several new resorts built almost exclusively for outsiders came out of nowhere. German, British or Dutch pensioners chose those shores to live their retirement, and prices rose. The consecutive regional elections won by the right-wing Partido Popular paved the way for more dodgy connections between politicians and local entrepreneurs. Valencia itself became a very modern city, with the transformation of the old course of the river Turia into public gardens and the inauguration of the splendid City of Arts and Sciences near the old harbour, serving as symbols of modernity. But all that investment, which also flocked into football clubs thanks to local sponsorships, was for many directly connected with a corruption network that was eventually brought to public knowledge during the 2010s in the so-called Gürtel affair. It ended with several local Valencia businessmen and high-profile politicians from the Partido Popular condemned to serve jail time. Some names attached to the investigation also died in strange circumstances. The region became closely linked with urbanistic corruption over the years and football suffered. None more than Valencia CF itself.

In 2004, while supporters were still celebrating the success of the Benítez era, a real-estate developer named Juan Soler arrived in the presidency. He came with a megalomaniac project for a new stadium and promised a huge investment in the squad. He splashed 25 million euros on Joaquín Sanchez, then a club record, to make a point. He was just the first of many. Soon players like Patrick Kluivert and David Villa followed but all that spending only brought back a single Copa del Rey win in 2008. When the economic crisis reached Spain over the following months, it hit harder in Valencia than anywhere else, a consequence of the property bubble. The club almost declared bankruptcy and ended up being saved at the last hour thanks to a loan from the regional government. Inevitably, the construction works for a futuristic new ground stopped and the best players of a squad full of World Cup winners, including the likes of David Silva or David Villa, were sold at bargain prices to avoid closure. But that wasn't enough. When the possibility of outside intervention from the IMF started to loom, not even local authorities could keep the club safe any more and, eventually, Peter Lim, a businessman from Singapore who previously sought to buy Liverpool and had by then worked closely with sports agent Jorge Mendes, took control.

It was the moment supporters most feared and one that has shaped the last decade of the club's life. Local fans have always tried to take back some sense of control, taking to the streets on several occasions, but met only disdain from an owner who gradually started to show little to no interest in the club whatsoever. At the same time, despite an unexpected cup win in the centenary year, the team has struggled just to be competitive in La Liga, without any financial support to aspire to anything else. There's no sign that things might change in the short term, nor any interest from outside investors. *Marca* sports journalist Nahuel Miranda has lived the past two decades in the city and understands the current state of affairs better than most.

'Valencia is a very intense city and even when the club was winning or performing people were always demanding more,' he says. 'To live in this situation now throws back some nostalgia for a time that should have been enjoyed more than perhaps it was. In a sense, the club is the representative of the sins of an entire region for the past two decades.' Just as the hangover of the Bakalao Route took a toll on a culturally forward-thinking local society, so the years of real-estate speculation and political corruption ended up putting in danger the very survival of Spain's fifth most successful football club. A side that has been known to represent the identity of the Valencians in all their splendour. Deep down, supporters know that times will change and eventually Valencia will rise. The question is not if, but when. Like the bat, an iconic symbol of the city also present in the club's crest, Mestalla awaits a sign in the sky to know that it's time to fly once again.

***

When Francisco Roig left Valencia his brother Fernando decided to enter the football business a few miles north. The Roig family is key to understanding the entrepreneurial spirit of the people of Valencia. Francisco Roig Senior started Mercadona, one of the biggest and most successful supermarket chains in the Iberian peninsula, alongside his wife Trinidad Alfonso in 1977. His younger son, Juan Roig, ran the company during the 60s and took control of Pamesa Valencia, the local basketball club. Francisco, the eldest, was chairman of Valencia, and Fernando, the middle brother, got to control Pamesa, a successful ceramics company. In 1997 he bought Villarreal, a club from a very small town just south of Castellón, the provincial capital north of Valencia who, by that time, were playing for the first time in the second tier. They were practically unknown outside the region, and only in 1992 reached the professional game for the first time. Six years on, already with Roig in charge, the club was finally promoted to La Liga. They since have become a symbol of how Spanish football also has its fairy tale stories to tell.

Not many live in Villarreal. There are more seats at the Cerámica Stadium, a huge yellow building right in the middle of town, than registered inhabitants. Originally known for their trade in oranges, one of the local symbols, it was ceramics that helped finance the region. The town is what the Spanish call a pueblo, a small place with a strong identity. Walking alongside its streets feels like living in the past. And, of course, everyone around knows that if any stranger happens to pass by, it's probably because of the football club. There's just not much else to see. Fernando Roig showed the skills of a visionary. He applied the policy of managing the club as if it were a company in his portfolio but with a human touch. The club aspires never to get into debt, but at the same time constantly searches for new ways of doing business and expanding the brand, while providing exciting results. Alongside the fundamental figure of José Manuel Llaneza, who ran masterfully the day-to-day life of Villarreal, the owner set out a blueprint of a club different from any other in Spanish football. The team had to play attractive football and serve as a platform for developing players with high potential, while never taking a step too far. Most of all, amid all the usual chaos clubs were used to, they would show patience. When Villarreal got relegated in their first season at the top, nobody panicked. They went back up immediately.

In 2004 the club took a bold step by signing Chilean coach Manuel Pellegrini. South America had been, since the early days, a preferred place for signings, following the successful example of Valencia. In came internationals like Martin Palermo, Rodolfo Arrubarrena, Juan Roman Riquelme and Diego Forlán and out went the blue shorts, with the side playing in full yellow. Originally, they started by wearing Valencia's black-and-white combination but then opted for yellow instead to better represent their sunny shores. Without knowing it at the time, the legend of the 'Yellow Submarine', as they became known in Europe, was born. The season before the Chilean's arrival Villarreal played in the UEFA Cup for the first time but Pellegrini took them one step beyond. In his first full season in charge, not only did Villarreal win the Intertoto Cup before reaching the last eight of the UEFA Cup, but they also finished third in the league. The year before, Valencia had been league champions and now they were four places below Villarreal in the league table. Something was changing.

Pellegrini's attacking mindset fitted Roig's vision. Riquelme's passing skills, Forlán's goalscoring ability and

Marcos Senna's leadership made all the difference. Villarreal were only seventh in 2006 but their European campaign was nothing short of a miracle. They disposed of Everton in a play-off and topped a group stage against Benfica, Lille and Manchester United. They then beat Rangers and Inter to reach the semi-finals. Suddenly all of Europe started to pay attention. They faced an Arsenal side that was saying their goodbyes to Highbury, and it was there that a solo Kolo Touré goal sealed the Spanish side's fate. Well, not quite. On the return leg, in front of a packed stadium, Villarreal outplayed the likes of Thierry Henry, Dennis Bergkamp and Robert Pires but squandered chance after chance. Then, in the very last minute, after a foul on José Mari, Russian referee Valentin Ivanov pointed to the spot. Riquelme picked up the ball but could not hold his nerve. The Argentine playmaker shot low to his right and allowed Jens Lehman to dive and save. The dream was no more.

Other clubs would have entered a state of emotional breakdown after a night like that. Not Villarreal. The club had already started to invest in infrastructure to improve their youth system, quickly becoming a reference point in Spanish football, and they just kept on going. Two years on, they finished the league second, their highest league finish ever. Santi Cazorla now led the pack, alongside Nihat, Giuseppe Rossi, Robert Pires and Cani, playing in front of the midfield duo of Bruno and Senna, a key element in that summer's Spain Euro 2008 triumph. Pellegrini had already proven himself and moved on to coach Real Madrid, but the club soon found in Juan Carlos Garrido an apt successor, once again reaching the Champions League and then the semi-finals of the Europa League, with Borja Valero and Brazilian Nilmar joining the attacking force. Against all odds, however, the club was relegated the following season. Many suspected it was the end of the *Groguets*, but Roig and Llaneza again played things cool. The club had a sound financial backbone and good infrastructure, and they were promoted without fuss. Since then, with a single exception, they have never finished a season below seventh and have become regulars in continental cups. Players came and went but the structure stayed the same.

But something was missing. Twenty-five years after Roig's arrival, they were yet to win any kind of silverware. When they finally did, it couldn't have been more dramatic. During the 2020/21 season, with COVID-19 conditioning the competition calendar, Villarreal entered the Europa League with low expectations. They had just signed Unai Emery, after his spell as Arsenal coach, and took advantage of their southern rivals from Valencia's dreadful financial situation to sign Dani Parejo and Francis Coquelin. If in the league things were going according to expectations, with the team finishing seventh, it was in Europe that the season started to shine unexpectedly. After beating Red Bull Salzburg, Dinamo Kyiv, and Dinamo Zagreb, a showdown against Arsenal was in order. It was the semis all over again versus the Gunners, a traumatic affair for the local supporters. Yet things couldn't have gone better when Raúl Albiol scored the decisive goal in a 2-1 home victory. After a goalless draw in London, with Emery celebrating against his former team, Villarreal reached their first-ever final. They would face Manchester United in Gdansk on 26 May, a day forever in the minds of Villarreal supporters. The match was not for the faint of heart. Gerard Moreno, who had climbed the ranks from the C team to the first team, scored the opening goal. Edison Cavani equalised, and the match remained tied until the penalty shoot-out. It was the longest-ever shoot-out in the history of the European cups. All 11 players took turns, and, in the end, it all came down to the goalkeepers. Argentina international Geronimo Rulli took his chance. His Spanish counterpart David de Gea did not. With that, Villarreal won their first-ever trophy. And what a way to do it.

'Whether you like or not, Villarreal has done things the right way,' says Bruno Alemany, director of *PlayFutbol*, Spain's most important radio show on international football. 'They have the backing of important companies owned by the Roigs but always searched for a sustainable policy and, in the end, it bore its fruits.' Villarreal became the club from the smallest town ever to win a European Cup. Every person living in it could have been at the local ground to celebrate the victory of the Yellow Submarine. In a country dominated by historic sides from the bigger cities of Madrid, Barcelona, Seville, Bilbao or Valencia, their success is unique. People are enjoying the experience because, especially after the tragic death of José Llaneza, they know it's all down to Fernando Roig's vision and when he too leaves the club will probably suffer deeply. What few remember now is that Villarreal was a club that got lucky. Roig was very much into buying a football club, but it was not the *Groguets* he had in mind.

* * *

'Castellón could have been Villarreal.' Sports journalist Rafael Escrig of DAZN smiles while contemplating the thought. 'Fernando Roig called upon the club's doorstep and showed a keen interest in buying but was told Castellón was not for sale,' he explains. 'So, he went on to meet José Manuel Llaneza and bought Villarreal instead.' Bruno Alemany who, like Escrig, comes from Castellón, concurs. 'Roig had met several businessmen from the area of Castellón, the club from the provincial capital and the one with the historical background. The ideas he later developed at Villarreal could have been applied at Castellón. In the end, the negotiations broke down and he went a few miles south to Villarreal with great success. In return, the years that followed were a disaster for Castellón so, naturally, the club supporters feel a little bit of envy of Villarreal's success. They think it could have been us.'

It could but it wasn't. Castellón de la Plana sits 46 miles north of Valencia and nine minutes' drive north of Villarreal, just across the river Millars. It's the provincial capital of the so-called Azahara coast, whose most recognisable site is Peñiscola, a medieval seaside town that once served as home for Benedict XIII, also known as the Antipope, and was one of the main settings for the movie *El Cid*, starring Charlton Heston and Sophia Loren. It is not a large city in comparison with its southern provincial capital sites of Valencia and Alicante, but locals are deeply rooted in the local identity and traditions, well displayed in the common use of Valenciá, a language that many mistake to be a derivation of Catalan but which is, in fact, one of the oldest romance languages remaining.

What they are also proud of is Club Deportivo Castellón. Founded in the 1920s, they debuted in La Liga in 1941, a golden era for football in the Levante. During the 1942/43 season, they even went toe-to-toe against Athletic Bilbao for the title, but the side stumbled in the last few matches and finished fourth. Despite spending the 50s and 60s moving around between the second and third tier, they experienced a short-lived revival in the following decade. In 1973 they even reached the cup final, lost also against the Basque side. The greatest moment of that cup run happened when the old Castalia, the local ground, saw the team beat Valencia in the last 16, after a goalless draw in Mestalla. It was one of the few times that Castellón outclassed their southern rivals. Then, at the end of the 1980s, the side climbed back to La Liga for a short period. Bruno Alemany remembers well the impact it had on the city. 'I recall the players visiting school, every kid just playing in the streets, wanting to wear the club's black-and-shirt. It was the moment I fell in love with the game, and I think it happened for my generation as well, we started to see football differently because our team was playing against the elite.' It was a short-lived experience. Castellón were relegated in 1991 and they never climbed back. Worse, after passing up Roig's offer, the club changed hands until they became the property of the Castellnou SL group. It was a disastrous move. 'The city was asking for more than just competing in the second tier and there was a moment when Castellón had the players to go all the way,' says Escrig. 'We were so close, but unfortunately the owners were also football agents and decided to profit from the sale of players instead. Our opportunity slipped away and now they are on trial for the sacking of the club in those years.' In 2011 Castellón were relegated to the fourth tier and were nearly bankrupt. At the same time, Villarreal were playing in the semi-finals of the Europa League. The contrast couldn't have been bigger. The Sentimiento Albinegro platform has since fought in the courtrooms to take back some of what was taken from the club, but Castellón lost almost a decade in the lower divisions of the football pyramid. Until now that is.

Haralabos Voulgaris is someone Castellón supporters were not expecting. Born in Canada to a Greek family, he ended up living the Mediterranean dream, not far from where some of the world's biggest musical acts get together once a year at the Benicassim Music Festival. He started as an ice hockey fan and moved to Las Vegas to become a successful poker gambler later to work as director of quantitative research for the Dallas Mavericks NBA franchise. After three years and two division championships, he moved on. Few could imagine that he would land in Spain, buying a third-division club that seemed to matter only to the local supporters. He saw potential in a town deeply in love with the club's colours and determined to leave the past behind. It was also a cheaper move than to enter, as so many North Americans have done recently, British football. And gave him the perfect scenario to test his way of doing things. Because 'Bob' Voulgaris is someone with a plan. 'People feel the club is in good hands,' says Bruno Alemany. 'One of the most important things about Voulgaris is that he doesn't just own the club, he lives the club. He settled in the region, understood the importance of the club for the local supporters, and adopted our way of living. The club is his and at first people were scared it would become just a toy in the hands of an outsider millionaire, especially when foreign players and managers started to arrive. Still, now they understand the vision he has for the future.'

Voulgaris decided to implement a policy that resembles the Moneyball culture that first erupted in baseball two decades ago with Oakland Athletics General Manager Billy Beane. After all, he did it in Dallas to great success. Now he has a template on how the club should be run, analysing data to the extreme, trying to do things differently to understand who he should hire as a manager or what sort of players the team will need. Everything with the clear purpose of eventually getting Castellón to become a La Liga regular. It's a bet but, then again, few in the world understand better the power of a gamble. 'I think he saw the potential behind the club,' Rafa Escrig points out. 'We are 12,000 club members playing in the third tier, can you imagine how many would join if the team went all the way up? Nou Castalia is packed week in, week out. That is why people are falling in love with him. They understand he sees potential in us and is not just trying to make a profit. The working method he has brought, the use of big data, working in similar templates from the first team to the academy but also how he deals with the marketing, merchandising and communication departments, is something nobody else does in Spain.'

They are giants amongst minnows and people are finally feeling the monster has awakened. In his first full season in charge, with the club near bankruptcy, Castellón were on the brink of promotion. One year on they finally clinched a place back in the professional league. After two decades of suffering, people took to the streets by the thousands to celebrate with the players and staff. In between, they chanted for Oscar, Voulgaris' much-beloved dog, to take centre stage. After all, he is a regular at Nou Castalia and has since become the club mascot. Just another trait of someone who looks at football and sees something different than most. And the crowd loves him for it. They might have not gotten the Roig deal, as some would have dreamed of after seeing their local rivals Villarreal triumph, but in Voulgaris they found someone to be proud of. An owner with core values, who wants to build from the backbone and understands the true potential of the club and the region in the local football pyramid. Without expecting it, they might have just hit the jackpot.

* * *

Just outside the coast of Valencia sits the Balearic Islands. They are the paradise everyone thinks of when they think 'Mediterranean'. Whether it's the exclusivity of Menorca and its high-class yachts, the provocative and crowded beach clubs where all the well-known world DJs hang out and the hippy communities of Ibiza, or the coral bluish tones of the waters of Formentera, the Balearics take you back to the days of ancient mythology, of warriors, sailors, gods and sea nymphs. But it's in Mallorca that everything comes to a head. The island that birthed one of Spain's, and indeed the world's, greatest sportsmen, tennis champion Rafael Nadal, is a place that, when you visit, you'll never forget. It can be the ravishing Tramuntana coastline, the beach clubs around S'Arenal packed with northern European tourists during the summer, or the quieter northern resorts British families have been travelling to for the past 50 years. The island has it all. It was there that Brian Clough and his Derby County players found out they were the 1971 league champions when the manager decided to take them all on a vacation while they waited for the league to end. It became a trend for football teams in England and a favoured holiday destination for players and managers. Nadal is himself the nephew of a Spanish international footballer, Miguel Angel Nadal, a local hero and former player of Johan Cruyff's Barcelona. Football is an important part of the islands but there's not much rivalry with the clubs from Ibiza, Formentera and Menorca. Indeed, Real Mallorca stands almost alone as the flagship of the region. And they have done it so in spectacular fashion. Founded in the island's capital city, Palma de Mallorca, it is one of the oldest clubs in Spanish football. They had short spells in the first division between the 1960s and 1990s, finishing as high as sixth on one occasion. In 1991 they also lost the Copa del Rey final against Paulo Futre's Atlético de Madrid. It could have been the high point in the club's history but it wasn't, thanks to one man in particular: Antonio Asensio.

Asensio was a mass media businessman and owner of the Zeta group, known mainly because of the magazine *Interviú*. It was considered the Spanish *Playboy* for its covers, usually depicting erotic photoshoots of Spanish celebrities, actresses and models, but also because of the journalistic quality of its investigations and interviews with famous politicians. When the magazine got a hold of a previously taken photoshoot of Pepa Flores, who was the most famous child actress during Franco's regime and a cultural icon when she went by the name of Marisol, they broke all sales records, reaching a million copies sold. Flores, by then already an outspoken left-wing activist, became a symbol of a new liberated Spain and so did the magazine. After that, Asensio took control of TV channel Antena 3, the first big private company to challenge the RTVE state channel. Around that time Mallorca was suffering from the mandatory transformation into a limited company and Asensio, who despite being from Barcelona knew the island all too well, decided to buy the club. He put in charge of the operations a man he had total confidence in, Bartolome Beltran, well-known in the television world and a Mallorca supporter. His management skills were key to reconnecting the club to the island's identity. Alberto López Frau, football author and analyst, explains the impact he had on the club's rebirth: 'Bartolomé facilitated buses that picked up people in different towns of the island so they could watch the home matches at the old Luis Sitjar, established deals with local companies and was responsible for the signing of Argentine manager Héctor Cúper. He, alongside Asensio, was the key to Mallorca's golden years.'

With the new manager came a legion of footballers from South America, like Carlos Roa, Gabriel Amato and Oscar Mena, and Mallorca finally got promoted to the first division in 1997. They would spend the following 16 seasons in the elite. In 1998 the side finished fifth in the league and went all the way to the Copa del Rey final, losing it on penalties against Barcelona after having two players sent off in regular time. But since Barça had already won the league, the Balearic side booked a ticket for the last edition of the Cup Winners' Cup.

Cúper's men beat Hearts, Genk and Vartkes before travelling to Stamford Bridge to meet reigning champions Chelsea in the semis. Dani opened the scoring but Tore Andre Flo levelled. It all came down to the return leg in Palma, with an Oscar Biaggini goal enough to send the *Bermellones* to the final. The match was played at Villa Park and was an intense affair right from the start. Christian Vieri opened the score for Lazio but just four minutes later Dani equalised with a clinical finish, after a combination between Dejan Stankovic and Miquel Soler, two of the side's creative players. It took a towering shot by Pavel Nedved in the dying minutes to decide the final. It was a bitter end for Mallorca, but the best was yet to come. The club moved from the old Sitjar to San Moix and Cúper, who had already signed for Valencia, was replaced by Luis Aragonés. The arrival of the likes of Walter Pandiani, Leo Franco and Samuel Eto'o took the club to third in 2000/01, fighting for the league title until the end. 'Everyone in Mallorca believes,' says López Frau, 'that if there had been four or five more games to be played, Mallorca would have ended up as champions. Samuel Eto'o's form was incredible, Aragonés' leadership was amazing and the team dynamics in the end promised so much.' It wasn't to be. The following season Aragonés was out, as he was set the task of bringing his beloved Atlético Madrid back to the first division, so Gregorio Manzano took hold. With him came another cup final and this time the club finally prevailed, beating Recreativo Huelva to claim their first piece of silverware. Rafael Nadal was about to turn pro when his uncle Miguel Angel lifted the trophy.

It was a moment to remember. Gradually, though, Mallorca became less and less competitive. Asensio had just died in 2001 and was unable to witness his club clinch the Copa del Rey. Soon the Zeta group sold Mallorca, they were eventually relegated and fell into the third tier in 2017. Many thought the club would disappear altogether. Since then, new ownership that includes famous sportsmen like Steve Nash, Graeme Le Saux and Andy Kohlberg have taken control and things have begun to change. The perfect example is the cup run in 2023/24 when a side led by Mexican coach Javier Aguirre reached the final against all odds. They were eventually beaten by Athletic Bilbao in Seville, with Nadal watching proudly from the stands, but it was a sign for supporters that the worst might have been behind them. Hours before the match, the Mallorquin music group L.A., for the past decade one of the most talented acts in Spanish indie rock and known for being one of the few Spanish bands who perform in English, took the stage in the fan zone. After playing some of their hit songs, when the chords of 'Stop the Clocks' started to sound, many wished for the lyrics to become real. This was a dream nobody wanted to end, a moment frozen in time. But as life in the Mediterranean has proven repeatedly, nothing stays forever. The waves that take something away also bring something back. It usually comes with a sense of certainty and belonging. While the sun shines on the golden beaches, time will always move differently around those shores.

GO OUT AND ENJOY YOURSELVES

A FEW moments after the final whistle Sir Alex Ferguson appeared surprisingly gracious in accepting defeat. It was the best team he had ever faced, he said. It was also probably the best team anyone has ever met. Pep Guardiola's Barcelona had just won their second Champions League trophy. It was the pinnacle of three unforgettable seasons when they became renowned as one of the greatest football teams in history. A decade on and their heritage seems even bigger. Guardiola revolutionised the game from the bench, and a group of iconic players expressed it on the pitch. That night they played at their best and it was much more than just the genius of Lionel Messi. Or the forward runs of Dani Alves, the defensive leadership of Victor Valdés or Gerard Piqué, and the attacking movements of Pedro Rodriguez and David Villa. It was essentially how the midfield trio of Sergio Busquets, Xavi Hernández and Andrés Iniesta controlled space and time. They were the flowers that had blossomed from the seeds planted by a Dutch genius. After 20 years of patient waiting, his ideas had transformed the club inside out. On that same sacred Wembley turf, 19 years before, Johan Cruyff had ended Barcelona's traumas by lifting their first-ever European Cup. Before the match against Sampdoria, he told his players to go out and enjoy themselves on the pitch. Not only did they, but also helped to establish a brand of football that ever since became the symbol of a club that always wanted to be more than just a football team.

* * *

FC Barcelona has been around for over a 126 years, yet it is easy to point out when they became the club we all know: 5 May 1988 marked the beginning of their modern era. Barcelona were by then Europe's biggest sleeping giant. A powerful force in Spanish football since their birth, alongside Athletic Bilbao the most decorated side for the first half of the 20th century – and miles away from their rival Real Madrid – they entered a state of coma after firing Helenio Herrera as head coach in 1961. The manager who had led one of the most remarkable *Blaugrana* sides ever went on to make a name for himself with Internazionale while Barcelona, without him, simply stopped winning. Since the beginning of the football league in 1928/29 – whose first edition they won – Barcelona were record eight-time winners until 1961. Over the following three decades, they would triumph only twice.

When Cruyff was announced as the new manager, Barcelona were 13 league wins behind Real Madrid. They were a deeply hurt football club, living the worst moment of their history. A few months before, the squad declared themselves on strike against the board. They had expected the club's chairman to take care of a debt claimed by the Treasury regarding payments made under the table to avoid taxes but found themselves exposed. The Hesperia Mutiny, as it became known, increased the distance between the board, players and supporters. Yet just three years prior everything seemed different. Terry Venables had just arrived and led Barça to their first league title in a decade. Maradona was sold to Napoli – one of many world-class players signed but unable to meet expectations – and in the following season, despite being unable to retain the league, Barcelona got a ticket for their second-ever European Cup Final.

They had lost their first in 1961, after beating Real Madrid in the first round, to a relatively unknown Benfica, and that moment marked the beginning of 30 years of hurt for the *Culés*. Many believed victory could not escape them, not only because the match was to be played in Seville – packed out with *Blaugrana* supporters – but also because it was against another unknown side, Steaua Bucharest. People celebrated beforehand and they should have known better. The match finished goalless and went to penalties. Venables had by then taken off the pitch their leading star figure, Bernd Schuster, who decided to take a bath and catch a taxi home before even waiting for the match to end. Romanian goalkeeper Helmut Duckadam saved three shots and Barcelona ended up on the losing side again. All the hype around Venables was soon washed away and when he left, months later, it seemed to part with all remaining hope. Football historian Angel Iturriaga believes that, had Venables won that European Cup, the club's future would have been radically different. 'Venables has not been treated fairly but he was a revolutionary, especially working aspects of the game like pressing, a radical approach for the standards of the day,' he said. 'He was well-liked by players and fans alike but that bitter defeat precipitated the end. Had he won perhaps we would never have known Barcelona's Cruyff and all that came with it.'

With Venables gone, it was Luis Aragonés, also a much-respected figure, who came in. Against all odds, he won the Copa del Rey but by siding with the players during the mutiny, he sealed his fate. Josép Luis Nuñez, a man who had won the presidential ballot almost a decade before with the support of Johan Cruyff, by then at the end of his playing days at the club, had to choose between the Dutchman and Javier

Clemente, who had recently led Athletic Bilbao to back-to-back league honours. By May he understood that Cruyff had more appeal to the fans, and an agreement was signed. The club's history changed for good, although it took a while for people to realise what was coming. Cruyff arrived at a time when the Camp Nou, one of Europe's largest stadiums, rarely had attendances as high as 30,000 supporters. He promised entertaining football and trophies, a tough task that had him rebuild the club almost from scratch. Many players left after the Hesperia Mutiny and many came in, mainly Basques, an indication that perhaps Nuñez was more inclined to sign Clemente after all. But the true star of the project was Cruyff.

A precocious genius, Johan had been one of the best players ever to grace a football pitch. His role as a shadow striker in Rinus Michels' Total Football movement changed the game. He led Ajax to three consecutive European Cup trophies while revolutionising football both on and off the pitch. He was a pioneer in bringing players closer to the commercial side of the game, working with a representative – his father-in-law – striking deals with brands, demanding money for interviews and special insurance from the Dutch federation to play for the national side.

He also had a character. After losing a vote for club captain he decided it was time to go. For years he had been travelling to Barcelona and made a few friends along the way. It also helped that Michels was by then the club's manager. Cruyff demanded a transfer in the summer of 1973, claiming he would retire from football when Ajax announced they had decided to sell him to Real Madrid instead. He got his way as he always used to, but since the Dutch federation delayed sending his registration to Spain – and only agreed to when he threatened to boycott the upcoming World Cup – he made his debut in late October. Forced to play friendlies to stay fit, when he took to the pitch for his debut against Granada,

Barcelona had just two points more than Sporting Gijón, who sat last in the table. That day, a series of influential Catalan left-wing political figures had just been arrested by Franco's regime, many with tickets for the match in their pockets. When the Dutch genius scored a brace in a 4-0 win, the crowd saw in him the liberator Barcelona so much needed, not just in footballing terms. His impact was immediate. Barcelona took a few weeks to top the league, beating rivals Atlético de Madrid on their way up.

But no triumph was as iconic as the 5-0 win at the Santiago Bernabéu. It was a footballing masterpiece and full of symbolism for Catalonia. A few days before, Johan's son was born, his wife Danny forced into an induced labour so that he would not be absent from the match. As the couple used to, they decided on an original name and went for Jordi, the Catalan version of George. They probably weren't aware the name – like all Catalan or Basque names – was forbidden in Franco's Spain, but if they were, Johan didn't care. When the family arrived back in Barcelona, Cruyff went to the public office to register his newborn and was informed that the name was not allowed. He famously replied that the boy was Dutch, not Spanish, and had been registered in Amsterdam as Jordi. If Franco didn't like it, it wasn't his problem.

The gesture of defiance made him even more popular, although it had more to do with Cruyff's rebellious character than any political affiliation. He was far from being a left-wing radical or even a nationalist and in more than 40 years living in Catalonia he never bothered to learn the local language. But that didn't matter to a group of people who saw the club as the remaining symbol against Franco's regime. Manuel Vazquez Montalbán, the celebrated local writer, coined the expression of the club being 'the weaponless army of Catalonia' and the Camp Nou was famously the only place people could talk in Catalan without the fear of being arrested. A few years before Cruyff's arrival, the club's chairman Narcís de Carrera, was the first to coin the expression of Barcelona being 'more than a club', to explain their emotional bond with Catalonia. When the *Blaugrana* won the league, at the end of that season, ending a 15-year drought, Cruyff was seen as a prophet – the herald of a new age. Nobody said congratulations. They said thank you.

A few weeks later he stormed the World Cup in the famous two-stripe orange shirt and led the Netherlands to the final. Even in defeat, he left his imprint, and many expected his return to Barcelona would mark the dawn of a new era. It didn't. Cruyff spent the following four years fighting against referees, the board, managers and himself. He only won one more trophy – the cup in his farewell season – and although he was not to blame for the ill-fated decision of replacing Peruvian striker Hugo Sotil with Johan Neskeens, the truth is that he never rose to the challenge as expected. Despite all that, however, he was never forgotten by those who saw him dance on the pitch. A generation of supporters fell in love with his footballing skills and the wit of his character, and when his return was announced, many expected him to fulfil his role as club saviour. This time, he didn't let them down.

Cruyff's Barcelona had to coexist in those first seasons alongside Real Madrid's *Quinta del Buitre,* one of the most spectacular and beloved football sides Spanish football ever produced. They won a record five consecutive league titles, the last two against Johan's men. Unable to beat Madrid, Cruyff spent his first seasons moulding his signature side. His first decision was to change how they played, pressing high. He went for two lines of three defenders and three attackers stretched wide open and with a midfield diamond. To improve his players' skills, he started a series of drills in practice called *rondos*, piggy-in-the-middle. Take the ball, pass the ball. Over and over again. Over that sort of 3-4-3, the key figure was the defensive midfielder. He had to have a peripheral vision of the pitch and be precise and creative while passing the ball around. He first tried Luis Milla in the role but when he signed for Madrid, Cruyff found in the youth ranks one who was even better: Pep Guardiola.

The young teenager's rise to the first team also marked a shift in the club's history. During his first seasons – as Barcelona had always done in the past – Cruyff built his side on signings from both Spanish clubs – Andoni Zubizarreta, José Maria Bakero, Txiki Beguiristain, Jon Andoni Goikotxea – and foreign – such as Ronald Koeman, Hristo Stoichkov and Michael Laudrup. But he had come from the ranks of Ajax and knew the importance of having a youth set-up that trained and played like the first team, so he spent time revamping the club academy alongside men of genius like Laureano Ruiz and Paco Seiru-lo. Guardiola was the prime example of his philosophy, but he was not the only one to be added to the first team over the following years. In 1991, after three seasons in which Cruyff showed he could compete in knockout tournaments by winning a Cup Winners' Cup and a Copa del Rey, Barcelona finally won the league. The sheer artistry of that team was an expression of his football ideals. They also showed character after losing captain Ronald Koeman to a season-long injury and suffering the anxiety that followed the news that Cruyff had to undergo a heart bypass after unexpected surgery. It would be the first of four consecutive league titles – a club record never equalled – although the last three would be renowned for their last-minute drama.

In 1992 and 1993 Barcelona arrived on the final day of the season a point behind Real Madrid and twice their rivals were beaten away to Tenerife. In 1994 the situation was even more dramatic after a tense title run against Deportivo, the Galician side cast as the nation's favourite. Once again luck favoured the Dutch manager, as the news arrived that Depor had failed to score a decisive penalty in the dying minutes of their home match. For a club that had been traumatised for decades, those wins brought a new winning mentality for both players and supporters. Those who had grown up convinced that there was always some mystical force operating against Barcelona now had to face a new reality. Nothing exemplifies that better than the 1992 European Cup Final.

Barcelona supporters had already celebrated an unusual comeback in the qualifying rounds when José Maria Bakero scored a last-minute effort against Kaiserslautern to book a place in the group stages. After toppling Benfica, Sparta Prague and Dynamo Kyiv, they travelled to Wembley to play Sampdoria, whom they had already beaten in a Cup Winners' Cup final. Wearing orange, the team stuttered at first with the same emotional block behind past defeats. Cruyff, however, had changed their minds as well as their game. Before kick-off, he famously told the players to enjoy themselves and, despite the uncompromising defence of the Italians and the danger posed by the striking partnership of Gianluca Vialli and Roberto Mancini, Barcelona were always in control. Yet, time went by, and the match was still goalless. It was well into extra-time when a foul in front of Gianluca Pagliuca's goal forever changed the club's history. A ferocious, thunderous free kick from Ronald Koeman torpedoed the net and Barcelona's emotional traumas. It was the single-most important goal in their history. A few weeks later the city of Barcelona hosted the Olympic Games, an event that marked a profound change, converting it from a grey and chaotic urban centre into one of the most colourful and joyful cities in the world. The remarkable USA basketball squad, comprising the best players of their generation, took centre stage and was christened the Dream Team. But the locals had already decided that if there was going to be one Dream Team that summer it would be Cruyff's Barça. So the iconic tag was born.

'Cruyff is the greatest giant in the game's history,' says former Catalan Olympic athlete and lauded author Martí Perarnau. 'He was and still is a divisive figure in Barcelona because he had to fight the typical Catalan fearful mindset, which he fought with sheer optimism. Johan put Catalan society in front of a mirror, questioned everything and proved doubters wrong, showing they had to embrace bravery and not fall under a permanent sense of fear. That was applied to football, arts, and politics as well. Because it contradicted a way of doing things, inevitably he became a love or hate figure. Loved by those who admire his trait and how he pointed the way to success and hated by those who were left wanting and thrived only by feeding fear around themselves.'

Since that iconic Wembley moment, Cruyff became more than just a manager. Even when he stopped winning, he maintained an aura of blind allegiance. In 1994 his Dream Team – with the genius of Romário added to the attack – was thrashed by AC Milan in the European Cup Final. Over the following two seasons, the inability to renew the squad and his permanent rows with key players and the board led to his sacking. His genius was there, nonetheless. He was behind the signing of Luís Figo and pushed for the club to get Zinedine Zidane while he was still plying his trade in France. In the end, he was a victim of both his character and the ever-chastising nature of the club, controlled by a hard-core group of members of the press and renowned business figures, a group he dubbed the '*entorno*'.

Yet his legacy lived on as he prepared the ground and planted the seeds of change. His revamping of the youth set-ups meant that players who would be usually discarded until his arrival for lack of height were by then being signed to train at La Masia, the now celebrated club academy. The tactical imprint of his team also left a profound memory. So big in fact that neither of his direct successors, Sir Bobby Robson and Louis van Gaal, were ever able to get full backing from supporters simply because they didn't play 'the Cruyff way'.

When a group of young entrepreneurs decided it was time to end Nuñez's rule, they did it partly because of how he treated the Dutchman after his sacking, choosing him as their guru. A group led by Joan Laporta, a local Barcelona attorney, finally won the election ballot in 2003 and the new board anointed Cruyff as special advisor. It was on his advice that Laporta hired Frank Rijkaard the following season, leading the club to new heights with back-to-back league titles and a second European crown in 2006. When the Dutch manager era came to an end – and with many boardroom members pressing for the hiring of José Mourinho – once again Cruyff's wisdom proved vital to the club's future, with Laporta choosing his protege Guardiola instead. The golden years of Barcelona were at the doorstep. After two Dutch winning managers, a local boy would be the man leading the *Blaugrana* into their most memorable era. And he did it when things were politically changing fast in Catalonia. A fight Barcelona could not avoid getting into. After all, it has been in the club's identity since its inception.

* * *

FC Barcelona was founded in 1899 by a Swiss businessman. Their most important historical figure was Dutch and throughout their history they were a club renowned for signing some of the best international players that ever lived, from the days of Ladislao Kubala and Diego Armando Maradona to the Brazilian magic of Romário, Ronaldo Nazário, Rivaldo, Ronaldinho or Neymar. Yet, despite all that foreign influence fundamental to the club's success, Barcelona remains a profoundly Catalan institution. It is what defines the club's soul. Hans Gamper might have been Swiss, but he was the one who changed his name to the local Joan after learning Catalan quicker than he ever learned Spanish. He also might have enjoyed the company of members of the British community who helped him kick-start the club, but in their first line-up there were six Catalan players already, most notably local businessman Bartomeu Terradas, who became chairman. They were the first football club in town and their arrival came at a glorious period for the city.

After the Barcelona Universal Exposition held in 1888, Antonio Gaudi's genius had been put to work and for decades helped enhance the city landscape with a set of iconic avant-garde architectural buildings. It wasn't just the Sagrada Familia church but the famed Parque Guell, the Casa Figueras and the Casa Battló as well. The revamped L'Eixample district brought Barcelona closer to the aesthetics of modern European capitals and while local business thrived, so did its culture. Football entered the arena during that golden period but the club's beginnings weren't easy.

Barcelona could have been extinct by the end of the 1910s if it hadn't been for the arrival of local hero Paulino Alcantara, a teenager who turned out to be one of the deadliest strikers in the history of Spanish football. With Alcantara's goals and Gamper's vision as acting chairman, the club survived. The inauguration of the Industria ground – with 6,000 capacity and floodlights, the first of its kind in the Iberian Peninsula – brought a new nickname for the club supporters. Those who could only afford a seat over the surrounding wall would find themselves with half of their backsides looming over the street, so they became known as *Culés*, the local slang for bottoms. The connection between the club and the Catalan identity was immediate. By 1914 they already used the local language in official documents. Three years later, when the Catalans pressed for a more autonomous regime, FC Barcelona was one of the first institutions to support the pledge.

The crown took notice, but it was on 14 July 1925 that the club faced, for the first time, the consequences of their political stance. They were due to play local rivals Jupiter, and the Royal Navy band, who were visiting the city, were invited to perform at half-time at the recently opened Les Corts ground. When they took centre stage and played the Spanish royal anthem, the crowd started to boo. Uncertain of what was happening, the band quickly performed the chords of 'God Save the King', receiving thunderous applause. News spread and the army took matters into their own hands.

Dictator Primo de Rivera ordered the ground to be shut down for any sports activities for six months and forced Gamper into exile, after compelling the resignation of the board. The reports from the local police authorities first mentioned expressions that would be repeated in the years to come, presenting the club as a place where both nationalists and opposers would secretly meet and where Catalan was preferred to Spanish. Despite all that, Barcelona were still the most powerful force in the land, winning several accolades including the first-ever league title. Football writer and acclaimed historian Toni Padilla explains that there were other relevant clubs in the city but none like Barça's. 'The way the club aligned itself with the Catalan cause made Barcelona extremely popular among the local middle classes,' he said. 'There were other clubs, more left-wing oriented like Jupiter, closer to the anarchist movement, who were also persecuted by Primo de Rivera and saw their growth crippled by the authorities, but despite that, Barcelona soon became the predominant force in the city because they symbolised everything the locals stood for.'

By 1939 everything changed. Franco's army entered Barcelona after three long years of Civil War and despite the crowds who took to the streets to celebrate his triumph, there was more fear than expectation. The club was broke, and many players had stayed behind when they toured Mexico during hostilities to find some much-needed funding. Everyone knew Franco had taken a stance against nationalism within Spain and he was quick to act. He forbade the use of regional or foreign designations – thus transforming Football Club Barcelona into Barcelona Club de Fútbol – and saw that there were no voices against the regime on the board of any football institution. 'The club was hijacked by the fascist regime,' explains Iturriaga. 'All chairmen over the following years were hand-picked, many were not even club members, positioned simply to control any nationalist impulse.' Yet Barcelona didn't suffer as could have been expected during the first two decades of the regime. In fact, they thrived. The club won several league titles and cups and got the aid of the Spanish Federation and Sports Minister to sign Ladislao Kubala, who had escaped communist Hungary and was searching for a football club to play for. Kubala's signing marked a new golden era for the club, hastening the construction of the Camp Nou. Those 'Hunger Years' of Franco's dictatorship happened to be the most vicious and cruel of his four decades in power. But the regime also wanted to quieten things down, and having regional sides like Barcelona or Athletic Bilbao triumphing on the pitch helped to ease tension. But, even silently, the Catalan national identity remained active, and the Camp Nou was, for the following decades, a safe space for those who longed for an independent state or, at least, a more autonomous rule. After the restoration of democracy, Catalonia was one of the first regions to press for an autonomous regime with institutions controlled locally. As journalist Roger Xuriach recalls, the Cup Winners' Cup Final of 1979 between Barcelona and

Fortuna Dusseldorf, just a couple of years after Franco's death, was also the greatest political rally in favour of the Catalan cause. 'That day was key to understanding the importance of the club to the politics and identity of Catalonia,' the founder of *Panenka* magazine explains. 'Thousands of Catalans were able, for the first time in decades, to go abroad freely, and they decided to march on Basel, where the match was going to be played, not showing just the club colours, but taking with them hundreds of *Senyeras*, the Catalan flag, raising the issue of the autonomy in newsrooms all around Europe. Barça's triumph that night was also the triumph of Catalonia as a nation.'

Things cooled down, and while it seemed the Camp Nou was more concerned with footballing issues than politics for a time, everything changed when in December 2012 the regional government presided by Artur Más publicly called for an independence referendum. Barcelona was by then a much-changed city. Gone were the grey days of old. The euphoria that came with the Olympic Games modernised its landscape and cultural life. The city embraced the harbour as an important part of its way of life and, after decades of living with its back to the sea, the beachside neighbourhoods became a new haven for tourists who wanted to experience the Mediterranean spirit to the fullest. From the century-old large avenues that connected the core business areas with downtown to the old medieval streets surrounding Las Ramblas, Barcelona became one of the world's most coveted tourist destinations.

The celebrated local cuisine captured the hearts of visitors from around the world as its local culture benefited from the mingling between Catalans, the ever-flowing tourists and the second-generation sons of the immigration movement that took thousands of families since the mid-1960s from Extremadura, Andalusia or Castile to live in the factory belt towns that surrounded the capital. From the cities of Sabadell, Igualada, Badalona and Hospitalet came not only famed sportsmen but also renowned artists who mixed the Spanish and Catalan identities freely, something best expressed in music. Some acts chose to sing mainly in Spanish, like Estopa, Elefantes or Pastora, as they represented the mix of those different cultures. Others, such as Manel, performed exclusively in Catalan following the example of the Nova Cançó, the protest cultural movement of the late Francoist years that brought back Catalan to arts and had Lluis Lach and Joan Manuel Serrat as their most renowned ambassadors. Each one was following a historical trend of a city that was always multicultural.

There has never been a Catalan state, as such, but there is no denying that a Catalan nation exists. That was the feeling that took thousands to the streets in 2013 to claim a political referendum like the Scots had had in the past. As expected, they met with strong defiance from the central state government and a great part of Spanish society. Ironically, at the same time, Spain was enjoying a golden age in sports mostly thanks to Catalan athletes. The all-winning national football side included several Barcelona players and was inspired by their style of football. Pau Gasol was becoming an NBA legend while drivers like Nani Roma, Marc Comas, Marc Marquez and Dani Pedrosa were worldwide stars. They were waving the Spanish flag, but many also vindicated their Catalan roots.

The Camp Nou also took centre stage in the political arena. Huge *Senyera* flags were shown during crucial Champions League matches to raise awareness of the Catalan cause and, for months, the stadium would wait for the 17th minute to shout for independence, recollecting a period during the Succession War between the Habsburgs and the Bourbons when they were promised autonomous rule by the royal Habsburg pretender who end up on the losing side. 'Barcelona as an institution has always been there when the Catalan society needed it,' says Xuriach. 'It has served as a refuge and during the years of the *Procés* the Camp Nou was vocal, even if the club is now supported worldwide, including by many people from parts of Spain who don't favour the idea of independence. But the *Soci*, the local supporter, has every right to demand the club speak for the values of the Catalan society, for all that Catalonia means for Barcelona but also for all that Barcelona means to Catalonia as well,' stresses the journalist.

In November 2014 there was a first vote where an estimated 30per cent of Catalans took to the polls and, of those, more than 80 per cent did so in favour of independence. The referendum was deemed unconstitutional by Spain's High Court. A long process of back and forth followed but everything culminated when the local parliament of Catalonia unilaterally sanctioned a definitive vote overtly against the state. All typical electoral procedures were followed but when the ballots were out, on 1 October 2017, they were met with an unseen display of violence from police authorities, sanctioned by the conservative Partido Popular government. There were several arrests, and more than 800 injured. Barcelona were due to play that afternoon at the Camp Nou against Las Palmas, and on hearing the news of the police's violent behaviour, many players asked the club to boycott the match. A warning of a severe punishment from the Football League changed their minds. They played and won but in an empty ground.

The referendum results showed massive support for independence among the voters and over the following weeks several banks and companies left Catalonia fearing the worst. Finally, the regional government decided to suspend the independence procedures sanctioned by the referendum, but it was too late. The right-wing Madrid government declared the process a high-treason case and arrested several political leaders, while others escaped the country and found refuge in Brussels. With time support faded and now, for the first time in more than two decades, the Catalan parliament has a majority who voted against independence.

Many things changed, including the city and the club. Barcelona suffered deeply from the economic crisis and the housing bubble. Tourism, once an opportunity to grow, became a severe issue, leading the local city council to apply restrictions against tourist lodgings. The shiny city has given way to a much more sombre place over the years and even artistically today Barcelona is more well-known for the success of Rosalía, a local singer who embraced fusion flamenco, the most typical of Spain's music genres, before turning herself into a global icon of Latin music than for artists who express their local identities.

The same could be said of the football club. Barça is living in a very complicated period in its history. Over the years the board, led first by Sandro Rossell and later by Josép Bartomeu, took the club near bankruptcy. A mix of poor signings and lack of ability to renew the squad while still offering players high-value contracts transformed a club once seen as the most well-run football institution in the world into an example of what not to do. Both chairmen also made all possible efforts to distance themselves as much as possible from the club's local identity. For journalist and pundit Fermín Suárez, the current situation is a clear consequence of bad management. 'The board didn't show the ability nor was able to surround itself with people who could manage the abundance Barcelona had in those years,' he states. 'Wages skyrocketed without logic, nobody bothered to find replacements for key players and everything was done simply by improvising. The

COVID-19 was the last nail in the coffin and brought the club to its knees.'

Juanma Romero, also a renowned journalist devoted to the club's life, concurs: 'It was a perfect storm, everything happening at once. The most important thing of all perhaps was the relationship between Rossell and Guardiola, which paved the way for everything that came to pass. Pep's legacy was destroyed by a board that wanted to do things differently and ended up losing complete control.'

Barcelona was the most cherished club in the world around 2013. More than a decade on few can imagine a new golden era can come soon. But if that comes to pass, it will be all about La Masia. As Xuriach points out, 'Youth players are the past, present and future of this football club. The love for a club's colours can't be bought and we see the rise of players like Lamine Yamal – the star of Spain's winning Euro 24 side – Pau Cubarsi, Fermín López, Gavi and many more who will follow and there's hope. The club might be on the brink of bankruptcy, but I haven't lost faith because I know the *cantera* is what saved the club in the past more than once, what made it great and where the Barcelona identity truly lies.' Xuriach is right. More than 15 years ago it was precisely the youth ranks of Barcelona who paved the way for the most memorable football team in the history of the game.

* * *

Few could believe it. With 15 minutes to go, a free-kick from Jonathan Pereira took the Camp Nou by surprise. Barcelona had scored the opener but, after a defeat against Numancia on the season's day one, that Racing Santander goal meant another setback. Perhaps the board had made a huge mistake gambling the club's future in the hands of a manager with no more experience than coaching the B team in the third tier. One who seemed confident enough was Johan Cruyff. He penned an opinion piece claiming that, despite the results, this was the best Barcelona side he had seen in ages. People just needed to give them time. And believe. Most didn't, to be fair. But they only had to wait another week before witnessing a miracle.

On 21 September Barcelona travelled north to Gijón. El Molinón was not the place one would choose to go to turn things around. But FC Barcelona did. The *Blaugrana* didn't simply win. They thrashed the home side. Xavi opened the scorng before the half-hour and Messi closed with two goals in the final minutes. The Catalan side won 6-1 and never looked back. Eight months later they celebrated a historic treble. At the end of 2009, they were partying at the Camp Nou after winning a record six out of six trophies. That side was probably one of the best to grace the game. They weren't just revolutionaries. They were artists. Football never looked so clean, so aesthetically perfect. A mixture of perfectly timed pressing, absolute control of space, constant movement on and off the ball and the ability to always find the right pass at the right time made Pep Guardiola's team one for the ages. Yet, that was also a team that might have never seen the light of day.

Frank Rijkaard's final days were unworthy of what he had done for the football club. After the Champions League win in 2006 everyone believed that the Deco, Ronaldinho and Eto'o trio would elevate them to new heights. Instead, complacency became the norm. Rijkaard couldn't control the partying spirit of the Brazilian genius nor the discipline needed to hold the side together and Barcelona lost two consecutive league titles to Real Madrid. Joan Laporta knew the club needed a change and many around him believed José Mourinho was the man for the job. Mourinho had been a deputy of both Sir Bobby Robson and Louis van Gaal, still had many friends there and was, at the time, the most coveted manager in the world. He also impressed many with a presentation pointing out how he would play 'the Barcelona way' while applying a much-needed discipline in the dressing room. The Portuguese manager was believed to leave the room feeling the job was his. For acclaimed writer Simon Kuper, author of several books including *Barça*, 'If Mourinho got the job as Barcelona coach in 2008 he would have been remembered as a great attacking coach, not to the extreme of Guardiola, but he would be playing a much more flowing football in Barcelona than in Madrid. He would still be the same version of himself, with the same personality traits, but we would have had a great coach with a great attacking team at his disposal.' And those traits made many mistrustful. One of those was Johan Cruyff who suggested to Laporta that he already had someone coaching the B team – on their way to winning the third division – who was not only ready for the job but would elevate the club to another level. He was also a local legend. Laporta followed his gut and appointed a then-37-year-old Pep Guardiola as the new manager.

Pep was what Barcelona had been all about since Cruyff arrived at the club. A supporter and *Socí* since childhood, he had been a ball boy at Camp Nou and the first graduate of La Masia to take centre stage in Cruyff's renowned Dream Team. He became club captain before leaving in 2001, after a couple of last seasons limited by constant injuries. He was also one of the best passers the game had ever known and, already since his playing days, a coach. Xavi Hernández, who had just won the Euros with Spain and was being coveted by AC Milan, famously said things were about to get interesting. Guardiola took the team to Scotland for the pre-season. Beforehand, he informed the board that changes were needed.

For his plan to work, the club had to part ways with Ronaldinho, Deco and Eto'o. It was a revolution many weren't expecting. The Brazilian superstar had been pivotal in bringing back Barcelona from a dark period after the traumatic departure of Luís Figo to Real Madrid but was sold to AC Milan, while Deco moved to Chelsea. Eto'o, however, was determined to prove himself and refused to leave. In the end, the squad pressed in his favour and Guardiola acquiesced. He would not repent. In his mind, though, it was all about La Masia graduates, players who spoke his football language and understood the importance of the passing game better than anyone. Xavi and Iniesta were to be the cornerstone of the team's movements and Lionel Messi the key element in attack. Off-pitch behaviour, much influenced by Ronaldinho, had taken a toll on the young Argentine, who suffered persistent muscle injuries. Guardiola took him aside and persuaded him that if he followed his advice and focused his life exclusively on football, he would become the best player in the world. Messi completely changed his routines and diet. He would turn out to be the best signing of that season.

Still, Guardiola also added to the squad the free-flowing spirit of Dani Alves on the right, the ever-presence of Seydou Keita in the middle and the hunger of young centre-back Gerard Piqué, who had spent the previous seasons at Manchester United. He also promoted two players who had done wonders for his B side, midfielder Sergio Busquets and winger Pedro Rodriguez. The squad already had the talents of Victor Valdés, Carles Puyol, Eric Abidal, Yaya Touré, Rafael Marquez and Thierry Henry, to name but a few. It was a constellation of stars who only needed guidance to express themselves. Guardiola provided that. The key elements of his game were high pressing to recover possession once lost, the constant movement of the ball and a team stretched wide so that the creative midfielders would benefit from the movement of the forward line to give the final pass or even to score against tight defences. The result was a masterpiece.

The win in Gijón was the first of 20 consecutive matches without defeat. In the meantime, the thrashing of Atlético

Madrid (6-1), Almería (5-0), Valladolid (6-0), Valencia (4-0), Deportivo (5-0) and Real Madrid (2-0) showed that once the side clicked there was no stopping them. Despite back-to-back defeats in late February, Barcelona went on another eight-game streak without losing and arrived at the Bernabéu for the title decider four points clear. By then, they were also in the Copa del Rey final and humiliated Olympique Lyon and Bayern Munich before being held to a home draw against Chelsea in the Champions League semi-finals. It was 2 May, a public holiday in Madrid, and Guardiola's men knew the season would be decided in the upcoming week.

For the Bernabéu match, Guardiola decided to deploy Messi as a false nine, moving Eto'o to the wing. It was a chess move that obliterated Madrid's slow defensive line. Although they scored first, it was a Barça show from the beginning. In one of the most memorable *El Clásico*s ever, they were merciless and sealed the league title with a 6-2 win. Piqué, the young graduate, scored the sixth and last goal of the match. Puyol, his defence partner, had scored the first. Messi and Henry, with a brace each, dominated the attacking line but once again it was the triangle of passes between Busquets, Xavi and Iniesta that knocked out Madrid. A week later, in Valencia, a thunderous performance from the side ended with a 4-1 win against Athletic Bilbao and the cup followed its way to Barça's museum.

The most memorable moment of the season happened days before. The goalless draw against Chelsea meant a place in the Champions League Final was up for discussion when the two sides met again at Stamford Bridge. It was a tense affair, full of disputed refereeing decisions against the home side and with a Barcelona team inexplicably unable to play to the best of their abilities. Essien scored early in the match and as the clock ticked by it seemed likely that the Blues would be on their way to back-to-back finals. Guardiola's Barcelona, however, had not just reaped Cruyff's tactical and technical teachings. They also inherited his personality and, sometimes, his luck. With three minutes of added time gone, the ball found itself at the feet of Lionel Messi. The young Argentinean genius rolled it over to his right where, unmarked, Andrés Iniesta fired a shot from just outside of the box right into Petr Čech's goal. The 'Iniestazo' was the moment that defined a generation. Three weeks later, in Rome, Barcelona was again at their best. Despite Manchester United's roaring start, bit by bit the clever passing between Messi, Xavi and Iniesta started to rattle the United midfield and from one of those movements the ball ended up with Samuel Eto'o scoring the opener. The forward who Guardiola had almost cast out once again proved his worth. From that moment on it was all Barcelona, Messi scoring a second with 20 minutes to go with a header.

Nobody in the history of Spanish football had ever won the treble. But it was not just about the silverware. If anything, Guardiola's side became revered not by how much they won but by how they did it. They offered a mix of Arrigo Sacchi's Milan, Rinus Michel's Netherlands, Tele Santana's Brazil and Johan Cruyff's Barcelona all in one. Football had never witnessed such a dominant side before. In a sense, the 2008/09 season was the football equivalent of the Renaissance. It didn't end there. The following season Barcelona won three more trophies to complete an unprecedented sextuple – the European and Spanish Supercups and the Club World Cup – and once again clinched the league. An Icelandic volcano and Mourinho's cunning efforts deprived them of another Champions League Final, with the signing of Zlatan Ibrahimović and the long-term absence of Andrés Iniesta proving decisive in the later stages of the season.

Ever-evolving, Guardiola learned his lesson. Out went the Swede, in came David Villa, a formidable striker who perfectly understood the playing style of the side, performing alongside many of the Barcelona players in the all-conquering national team. Villa offered mobility and allowed Messi to thrive as a deep-lying forward at a time when the Argentine was converting himself into the world's most astonishing footballer. But, most of all, the team was forced to evolve to more of a possession side. Gone were the surprising first months when nobody knew how they would play. By 2011 everyone was aware of their abilities and many rivals opted just to drop deep and wait. Barcelona's possession numbers went up, and Xavi and Iniesta became more important than ever in dictating play. Most of all, they found their nemesis.

Mourinho had earned himself the job of Real Madrid manager by beating Barcelona in the Champions League semi-finals the previous season, avoiding what would have been a catastrophe for *Madridistas*, to see their rival winning the competition at their home ground. Instead, Mourinho's Inter won it and the Portuguese cancelled his return ticket back to Italy. He found in his hands a powerful side paid for by Florentino Pérez, who had just returned for a second spell as chairman, and began the season playing enthralling attacking football, powered by Cristiano Ronaldo's hunger.

When they faced Barcelona at the Camp Nou, Madrid were leading the table and Mourinho decided to play a high line, confident his players would perform at their best. What he got in return was one of the worst defeats of his career, one that would scar him deeply. The triangulations – take the ball, pass the ball – between Barcelona players easily tore Madrid to shreds. In the end, Piqué raised his hand in celebration, showing his five fingers wide, one for each goal scored. That 5-0 win was perhaps Barcelona's finest, an exhibition of such superiority that it rocked the foundations of Spanish football.

For many observers, that season Guardiola's men played their best football ever, demolishing when attacking, exhausting when in possession. Yet 2011 would be defined by a fortnight of tense duels against Mourinho's Madrid. The two weeks that had the football world holding its breath.

After the defeat at Camp Nou, Mourinho licked his wounds, reshaped his side and returned to the ring. His Madrid side kept on winning, at home and abroad, and by March they were still fighting for the league, in the cup final and in the Champions League semi-finals. The problem was that, in all competitions, they had to face their worst nightmare. Spanish football being the cauldron of nerves and tension that it is, those weeks were hysterical. In footballing terms, however, it was a feast for the eyes. There was no memory of the world's two best sides having to play against each other so many times in so few days.

'I remember fondly those days,' says Miguel Quintana, one of Spain's leading sports journalists. 'For me that Madrid team was a better side than the one who later won all those Champions Leagues, and Barcelona was by far the best in history. It was also Mourinho's best version against a genius like Guardiola, two great generations and two of the world's most memorable players. So, it was up to us to enjoy this battle of the gods.'

The first match was also the least spectacular. Barcelona had the league almost wrapped up, and a draw – with Messi and Ronaldo scoring from the spot – practically assured them the title. A few days later, however, as they met again in Valencia, everything changed. 'It is the best football match I ever witnessed,' remembers Quintana. It was also probably the tensest ever played. The two sides locked horns and fought fiercely for almost two hours. Barcelona had more of the ball, and Madrid were always dangerous on the counter as they seemed the perfect antithesis of each other. Right near the end of the first half of extra time, a centre from the left by Argentine Angel Di Maria was met by Cristiano Ronaldo with a leaping header that would go down in history as one of the most remarkable goals ever scored. Madrid won the cup and showed they were back in the game just in time for the Champions League semi-finals.

And things were getting rougher. During the previous match, Barcelona players felt their rivals had crossed the line on more than one occasion as the more physical approach preferred by Mourinho seemed to unsettle their rivals. 'I saw Madrid being aggressive, perhaps too aggressive, playing on the limit too often, an excess I never saw again in the duels between him and Guardiola or between Pep and Klopp sides,' says Martí Perarnau. 'But it was also the apotheosis of sporting duels, a sense of duality full field, a rivalry that in the end is what gives meaning to everything,' he adds, smiling.

Mourinho decided to play one of his usual mind games in the press conference before the first leg of the semi-finals claiming Guardiola – who was one of his best friends in Barcelona and had a reputation for never complaining about referees – had criticised a correct referee's decision in the follow-up to the cup final, meaning the white knight was no more. Barcelona's way of playing, helped by the fact that the core of the side was also the heart of a Spanish national side who had just won the Euros and the World Cup, was seen by many at the time as 'the right way' to play. An idea spread not by Guardiola but by many of his players and certainly by some of the press. That didn't sit well with supporters from rival clubs, especially at Real Madrid, and Mourinho decided to embrace that duality, proclaiming since his arrival that the way his side played was not inferior but different. He accepted the role of villain, but his mission became more than winning, it was also to tarnish the impeccable reputation of their rivals.

Guardiola, sensing the players were starting to doubt themselves, took centre stage and for the first and only time in his career, fought fire with fire and put on a remarkable display in front of the TV cameras, before returning to the hotel to be greeted by an enthusiastic squad. The following day, after Pepe was sent off for an attempted foul on Dani Alves, Lionel Messi scored twice, and Barcelona sealed their place in the final. It was bitter, it was dirty, and it was spectacular. Spanish football would suffer deeply the consequences of those days but when Barcelona thrashed Manchester United in the Wembley final, a month later, nobody seemed to care. They were too busy watching a football masterpiece live. They played like kids in the park. It was mesmerising. It was also their last hurrah.

As the new season unveiled, they won the Super Cup against Madrid but both matches showed the gap had diminished. The physical abuse was still there, though. It was the infamous moment when, after a brawl between the players in the later stages of the return leg, Mourinho poked his finger in the eye of Tito Vilanova, Pep's assistant. Guardiola was getting tired of Mourinho's provocations, and despite his side still playing a very recognisable brand of football, something was missing. The manager also felt detached from the board, now led by Sandro Rossell, and after losing a decisive home match against Real Madrid at the Camp Nou, Guardiola announced he would leave the club at the end of the season. Many expected a rallying cry in the run of back-to-back Champions League titles, but Chelsea had their revenge and, after a draw in London, they went to Barcelona to claim a late winner. Barça still managed to win the Copa del Rey for a last collective celebration of Guardiola's legacy but by then there was already a sourness in the air.

Even now it is hard to believe a man as important as Guardiola never had the chance to get a proper goodbye. His team kept on winning – first with Vilanova, his successor who sadly lasted only a season in charge after being diagnosed with a fatal cancer – and later with Luis Enrique, who also won the treble with an iconic forward line of Messi, Neymar Jr and Luis Suárez. But for all accolades, no football team was as loved and admired as his and probably no other marked a shift so deep between two different periods in history. Football is an always-evolving game, regularly producing world-class players, managers and sides. What's hard is to find a team that has it all. They did go out and enjoy themselves, as Cruyff suggested. In the process, they also made everyone around them experience a sense of joy and awe. Perhaps that is their greatest legacy.

THE GATES OF TIME

TWO MEN, Júlian and Federico, dressed in 1930s fashion, move silently along closed corridors, open an old wooden door and come out surprisingly in a crowded traditional flamenco bar in Granada. While they sit and talk, another man with curly hair, a huge beard and an open shirt sits on a small stage and starts to sing his lungs out. Suddenly Federico realises the song he is listening to is a version of one of his poems, 'The Legend of Time'. Only it couldn't be, could it? At that moment, Julián, a government agent who travels through time, explains to him that they have travelled to 1979. Federico García Lorca should have been dead back in 1936 but, here he was, witnessing first-hand how Camarón de la Isla revolutionised Spain's most popular music genre with a tribute song to his genius. Franco, whose men shot Lorca during the early days of the Civil War, had just died and, in that moment, the poet realised that in the end he was the one that prevailed. Not only him but Spain, as a nation of culture and genius.

Lorca and Camarón were kindred spirits and two of the greatest cultural figures in their modern history. They were also from Andalusia, a special place if there ever was one. Sadly, they never met. This fictitious scene, from the award-winning TV Show *El Ministerio del Tiempo*, pays homage to a region where artistry, boldness, and an everlasting sense of *carpe diem* can be found everywhere. Especially in football.

The game might have become more successful in other parts of Spanish geography, but it first arrived here and, through time, developed a particular sense of itself: a uniqueness that flourished and is as alive on the pitch as within the poetry, the dancing and the singing of giants who came before but never left.

* * *

If there ever was a gate in time that could take us to the moment football was first played in Spain it would lead up to 16 August 1873 around the Rio Tinto mines. While local workers were celebrating their patron saint, some British expats who also worked in the mines grabbed a ball and started an exhibition match that didn't follow any particular set of rules. Yet their movements mesmerised everyone.

Rio Tinto is a small village north of Huelva, the westernmost provincial capital of Andalusia. A mining region since ancient history, it came under the control of the Rio Tinto Company Limited around that time and soon a British colony was settled to control operations. When a train line connecting Huelva with the mines was finally opened, trade flourished. So did football. It quickly expanded in the province and later to the rest of the region, with press reports mentioning matches played regularly by the end of the 19th century. In 1889 the Real Club Recreativo de Huelva was founded by Scottish miners, thus becoming Spain's oldest club. They are still fondly remembered by the nickname *Decano*, the Dean, although they were never truly successful on the pitch. The blue-and-whites reached a cup final only once in all their history – in 2003, lost against Mallorca – and have spent a total of five seasons in the first division. Yet, despite the lack of sporting success, Recreativo are well-loved for what they represent, the beginning of something unique. Huelva is a town on the crossing of two rivers, the Tinto and the Odiel, just a few miles from the Bay of Cádiz. Its white buildings and large parks throw us back to the day when the city was the resting point for the British merchant families while men travelled up north to work in the mines. Its origins, however, go way back to when Phoenicians and Romans ruled the world. Looking lost in time, yet profoundly alive. To the west sits the Portuguese border and moving south, following the coastline, travellers enter one of Spain's most remarkable sights: the Doñana Natural Park. A breathtaking mixture of marshes, sandy dunes and shallow streams, it is home to many endangered species and stretches for hundreds of miles. It is considered the most biodiverse national park in all of Europe and its natural reserve has been threatened for years, despite being protected by UNESCO World Heritage. It is also a reminder of what Andalusia is all about. A land of men, yes, but, most of all, a mixture of very different natural landscapes that go from its marshy west to what is Europe's greatest desert to its east, in Almería.

Moving further south still, right before the strait of Gibraltar almost touches Africa, we arrive at Cádiz. For many, it will be hard to keep travelling forward once they have reached its sunny, chaotic streets. The oldest city in Western Europe, some claim Cádiz is the emotional capital of Spain. It is certainly one of a kind. The city is but a strip of land that stretches out on what was once a small island, now connected to the peninsula by a couple of bridges and an isthmus that defies the Atlantic unashamedly. For a while, when the wind lifts and the tides change, it seems everything could vanish under the ocean like Atlantis in a matter of seconds. Almost all the houses, pearly white, are enclosed on extremely narrow streets. From the balconies, you can hear neighbours talk metres away. And you will hear them. Life is something to be shared and celebrated. If the Spanish are known for being loud speakers there is no place where that makes more sense than here. Locals particularly enjoy living outdoors. Climate helps. There's sun all year long and beaches all around. Cádiz Carnival is also well-known, a celebration where you can enjoy the best comedy shows Spain has to offer, as the celebrated Chirigotas own the show. They are groups of satirical folk singers who make fun of the hot topics of the day, especially those related to politics. With *guasa*, a particular silly grace. Franco forbade them, afraid of their influence among the locals, but they have survived and thrived.

It helps that there is no lack of subjects to talk about. Despite being one of the most beautiful cities in Europe, Cádiz is also one of the poorest. Its province, which includes other unforgettable sites like San Fernando, Jerez de la Frontera, Tarifa or El Puerto de Santa Maria, has the highest unemployment rate in the country, almost 50 per cent. Life is hard and tourism, especially thanks to the wild sand beaches that stretch either side of Gibraltar, is the only way for many to make a living. Especially now that the local fishing industry has started to decline. Yet, even despite all the hardships, people from Cádiz walk around fearing nothing. Perhaps because there is a light that never goes out, especially when you reach the Nuevo Mirandilla.

Cádiz Fútbol Club is one of the city's greatest symbols. It is a club different from any other. They are not particularly known for their wins but for their artistry on the pitch and their deep-rooted connection within the community. In June 2024 news broke out that the club, through its foundation, had decided to buy a flat downtown to make sure that Maria Muñoz, a local supporter who turned 87, wasn't evicted. The club not only bought the house where she had lived all her life but offered her the chance to stay until her death by paying a symbolic rent. In a country where tourism and foreign investors are forcing many locals, particularly those who are poorer, to abandon city centres, this has become one of the biggest social issues to tackle. The club's gesture meant the world to those hundreds who had taken the streets in the previous weeks to help Maria, but it was also to be expected. After all, they always take care of their own. Alberto Cifuentes, a club legend, explains how important the team is among the locals. 'People around here don't support the club, they feel they own it,' explains Cádiz's record-breaking goalkeeper. 'It is part of their lives as much as their families. They always give their most for the team and expect the club to give something back.' Cifuentes is not from Cádiz. He arrived at the city for a short last stop after a long career. They immediately won him over and, without expecting it, he became a pivotal part of a side coached by Alvaro Cervera who surprised everyone by jumping from the third division to La Liga in four seasons. Cifuentes, by then 41, played a single match in La Liga against Huesca before immediately retiring, thus becoming the oldest player to debut in the competition. It was recognition for more than 200 matches played. 'Football is very important for people around here,' he explains: 'Life is hard but the moments before, during and after matches offer an escape, a sense of liberation. To be part of something good. You can always lose but you know that you must give your absolute best because nobody wants to let these wonderful supporters down.' The city where the first Spanish constitution was signed never forgot how the values of righteousness and unity can translate to a football stadium. And if everywhere you can find clubs deeply rooted within the community, in this tip of southern Spain, the bond looks as strong as you can get. In a word, people are football crazy.

Cádiz are not a side used to playing in La Liga, but they had their moments. They got promoted in 1977 for the first time, went down immediately, but then became a regular for the great part of the following decade. In that period the club was a much-beloved side because of a Salvadorian named Jorge Gonzalez, nicknamed *Mágico*. Famously, Maradona, who toured the United States with him, said he was the most talented footballer he had ever seen. He was also not the best behaved. After impressing during the 1982 World Cup, *Mágico* signed for Cádiz and found the perfect city for his flamboyant nature. Capable of doing magical tricks on the pitch, he was equally famous for his enjoyment of nightlife, the closest thing Spanish football ever had to a once-in-a-lifetime maverick. Once, the Argentine manager Hector Vieira, tired of having Gonzalez miss the first hour of training, sent a local band to play in front of his house and wake him up. Unashamedly, Jorge came to the door and told the manager he would join training but only because the band performed so well. People loved him for it, and when he dazzled opponents on the pitch, in the traditional yellow shirt and blue shorts that reminded everyone of Brazil, everyone forgot about the hardships of life. Having fun is the most important thing in the life of a Cádiz supporter, and it was also the most important thing in *Mágico's* life. The Salvadorian could have signed for top European sides but preferred to stay, and his goals helped Cádiz to escape the drop in late-fashion drama four seasons in a row. When he finally left, the club went down, and hard times followed. *Cadistas*, however, stayed true, and the club was finally raised from the ashes. As they say in those parts, the fight is non-negotiable. But always with a smile. A land of survivors but also artists.

Andalusia is the beacon of Spanish culture. Everything you associate with the country brings you back to here. Even bullfighting remains as popular as it was, despite the growing critical voices on how animals are violently treated in the arena. Yet, the men who take to the bullring are still revered as heroes from another era. Even geography helps. During the 1960s the Almería desert became worldwide known as the setting for many of the celebrated Spaghetti westerns starring Clint Eastwood. It was also where, in 1966, a young schoolmaster from Madrid named Juan Carrión met John Lennon and changed how we consume music. Carrión was an English teacher who found it hard to explain to his class the meaning of many of the band's lyrics. When he found out Lennon would be in Almería to shoot *How I Won the War*, he took his car and travelled for days to ask the Beatle if the band could add the printed lyrics to their following album. Lennon was impressed by his argument and passion and, a few months later, *Sgt Pepper's Lonely Hearts Club Band* became the first album in history to print the songs' lyrics, a trend immediately followed by every label. Carrion was not Andalusían but many of Spain's greatest painters, actors or writers are. Think of Francisco de Velazquez, famous for the portrait of Las Meninas, or Málaga-born Pablo Picasso, men who revolutionised their art. Theatre and cinema are also important in the region. Spain's first Hollywood star, Antonio Banderas, is also from Málaga and he is but one of many great acting stars coming from the region such as Paz Vega, Victor Clavijo, Inma Cuesta, Paco León, Marisol, or Antonio de la Torre, the most nominated actor for the Goya Cinema Awards, who began his career as a sports journalist. The same can be said of well-known writers such as poets Antonio Machado, Gustavo Becquer or Federico García Lorca. Until this day the remains of the Granada-born poet have never been found, like those of thousands of others killed during the war. Shot by the Fascist militia at the beginning of the Civil War for his left-wing ideals and his homosexuality, Lorca remains one of Spain's greatest authors, and by reading his work one may understand why Andalusians are born with a special thing for artistry.

    Nothing explains it better than music though. Flamenco remains the genre people worldwide most associate with

Spain, mainly because Franco used it as a propaganda tool. For decades his government promoted singers and musicians as nationwide celebrities. In doing so they tried to tame a genre that had more obscure origins. Flamenco, like *copla*, comes from a mix of people and cultures that have crossed these lands for centuries and helped shape the identity of Andalusia. Occupied for more than 700 years by Moors, their culture is everywhere you look, from the architectural wonders in Córdoba, Jaen, Seville or Granada, to the artistry of its people. There is also a deep-rooted connection with the travelling gipsies' community who always found Andalusia a place to call home.

From those unexpected crossings came artists who merged genres and emotions to produce new sounds. Paco de Lucia became a worldwide phenomenon during the 1980s with his guitar, but it's how flamenco is sung that left a more profound imprint. From the days of Juanito Valderrama, Manolo Caracol and Miguel de Molina to the heights of giant female artists like Lola Flores, Rocío Jurado or Carmen Sevilla, their success helped to create a sense of national cultural identity, all part of the regime's plan to sell an idea of national unity, despite the huge differences Andalusian culture has with most of the other parts of the country. Even now, with a nation more open to accepting the complexity of its geopolitical and cultural identities, travelling to Andalusia still feels like the most genuine experience when you think about visiting Spain. Walk along the streets of its towns or pueblos, and be ready to easily forget what year you are in. The past is everywhere and can change your perception of reality. As if you have just crossed one of those gates of time.

Even when you mention those who shaped the future, the past remains ever-present. Think of the talented Camarón de la Isla, a man who reinvented flamenco as an art form, mixing it with jazz and rock music, seen by many as just another extravagant gipsy. At a time when Spain was thriving for modernity, with the 1992 Olympics reshaping Barcelona and the *Movida* days erupting in Madrid, his genius was deemed something of the past to be forgotten, not cosmopolitan enough, especially because it was the work of a representative of the poor, humble people from the south. In those days the elites only valued Andalusia for the ever-present sun and beaches, the historical architectonic wonders, or the sense of humour. Local culture was seen as something not to be taken seriously by those who wanted to set themselves apart from Franco's Spain.

Despite all that, alongside olive oil and tourism, culture remained Andalusia's greatest export. During the dictator's rule, poverty hit especially hard there, and many were forced to leave their homes to survive. Some moved abroad but many went to Barcelona or Madrid, where they were treated as second-rate citizens, living in shanty-towns on the outskirts. Andalusians had to put up with jokes about their accent or fake sense of perceived laziness. Their regional identity was all they had left to cling to, and none ever let that go. It's also why, even today, some of the country's leading artists remain Andalusian-born. David Bisbal, Pablo Alboran and Pastora Soler, to name but a few, have kept the torch well alive.

All those struggles and exploits eventually reached its footballing culture. Cádiz is but one example. The same can be said in Córdoba, Almería, Málaga, Sevilla, Jaen, Huelva or Granada. Supporters want to win, and there are great stories of winners to tell. They also expect to be entertained. Traditionally, despite its immense territory, there have only been two league champions from the region and not many world-class footballers. But there were many mavericks and entertainers. Some found it hard to adapt to another culture, even inside Spain. They are comfortable playing for their crowd, always searching for new tricks. Think of Juanito, a legend at Real Madrid mostly because he ran at defenders as if he was a bullfighter. Or Diego Tristan and Kiko Narvaez, strikers who searched for the perfect shot rather than the most effective one. Even those who did triumph elsewhere, such as Sergio Ramos, José Antonio Reyes, Fernando Hierro, Joaquín Sanchez or Jesús Navas remained profoundly Andalusian in how they behaved on the pitch. Whether it's because of their passion or their artistry, they represent the true nature of their people. They play like time-travellers, bringing to today what one may imagine were the traits of the heroes of old.

* * *

If Real Madrid are known as kings of Europe, so should Sevilla FC be, even though their kingdom lies elsewhere. No club is as successful as the Andalusian side when we discuss the other European cups that rarely get the same attention as the Champions League. In this parallel universe, Sevilla are undisputed masters. They won the UEFA Cup, rebranded as Europa League, not once or twice but seven times. They have more European trophies than any other Spanish club bar Real Madrid and Barcelona and, if you sum up all UEFA European competitions, they rank seventh. In the United Kingdom alone Liverpool have won more. And they did so in the last two decades. Before that, Sevilla was just one of many well-supported sides with barely anything to show for it.

Seville is the capital of Andalusia and its greatest metropolitan area with almost 1.5 million inhabitants. It sits on the banks of the Guadalquivir river and rose to prominence when the Catholic Kings Isabel and Fernando took the last Muslim stronghold in the peninsula. Cristóbal Colón's travels to America and the conquests that followed made it one of Europe's most important urban centres. It's a huge place, full of iconic buildings and traditions, a city of culture and religion. Known worldwide for Holy Week during Easter, when thousands of congregations take to the streets to carry the statues of their patron saints and virgins for all to see, the Catholic faith is everywhere. Not just in cathedrals or churches, like the mighty Giralda Tower, but in homes, streets, businesses or bars. People are profoundly devout and are not ashamed of it. Religion remains a big part of their lives and so is partying. Seville is, if anything, a city for the senses. As you walk from the old Triana streets into old town, smells of basil and mint take you by surprise. The way the city is spread out, with its open arms around the river, makes it the perfect place for walkers. It is beautiful in the sun and joyous in the shade. More importantly, it has a beating heart that never stops allowing you to enjoy it during the day but also well into the night. It's then and there where you can find the joyful spirit of the Andalusian, especially inside the famous flamenco bars, known as *tablaos*. The intense heat, often reaching 40º Celsius, is particularly felt during the summer but also makes people enjoy outdoor life more than anywhere else.

And that is where football enters. Sports have always been popular in the city, particularly within the large British community that had settled there. It was a group of young Scots who, in 1890, chose Burns Night to kick-start the city's first football club. Two months later, after exchanging letters with friends from Recreativo Huelva, the two sides met in Spain's first official football match. Sevilla came out as winners and, as football grew in the city, they established themselves as the most influential southern club. Their peak glory arrived when the side won their only league title in 1946 with a forward line known as La Delantera Stuka, a nod to the Luftwaffe planes that helped Franco win the Civil War. Success had been coming after a couple of cup wins and two second-place finishes in the league. A decade later they even played in the European Cup, as runners-up to Di Stéfano's

Real Madrid. Under the leadership of chairman Ramón Sánchez-Pizjuán, Sevilla became one of the powerhouses of Spanish football but his untimely death threw the club almost into oblivion. First relegated in 1968, Sevilla never again punched as high and not even the short-lived stint of Diego Maradona, in the early 1990s, or the signings of the likes of Davor Suker, Diego Simeone or Ivan Zamorano helped them reach new heights. By the turn of the millennium, they were playing second-division football again. Supporters were fed up but then José Maria del Nido was appointed chairman. He proved to be an unexpected saviour. To clear the debt, he agreed to sell promising players such as José Antonio Reyes and Sergio Ramos while hiring former goalkeeper Ramón Rodriguez 'Monchi' as sports director. His ability to judge potential and a keen eye for undervalued players allowed them to rebuild, and when Juande Ramos took the helm Sevilla's golden hour finally arrived.

Ramos preferred to play a brand of direct attacking football, with speedy wingers and two men in the box. He could count on the likes of Dani Alves, Jesús Navas, Antonio Puerta and Adriano to provide width and the talented Javier Saviola, Frédèric Kanouté and Luis Fabiano to score. In 2005/06, after again qualifying to play in the UEFA Cup, they were ready to take up Europe by surprise. The campaign was full of iconic moments, none bigger than when Antonio Puerta scored the decisive goal against Schalke 04 in the semis. In the final Sevilla put four without reply past a much-fancied Middlesbrough side. Not content, a few months later they went to Monaco and beat Barcelona 3-0 to claim the European Supercup. Out of the blue Spain found an unexpected new contender, something confirmed when they overcame Espanyol on penalties in the following season's UEFA Cup Final, thus becoming the first team since Real Madrid to retain the trophy.

José Maria Nolé, journalist, writer and local supporter, was at Monaco for the match against Ronaldinho's Barça, a game he still thinks is the most memorable in the club's history. 'They were such a good side and we put in the best performance I remember in a final,' he said. 'The season before, many of us thought that Sevilla had a shot at the UEFA Cup, but we were beaten by Parma. Signing Kanouté and Saviola was a clear statement from the board: "We want to go places." And we did.'

From unknowns, Sevilla turned into a household name in a split second. During that same season, they clinched the Copa del Rey against Getafe and almost won their second league title, a campaign in which they played arguably the best football in Spain. They were loved and respected in equal measure, but when many expected the club to leap to new heights, they couldn't. Unlike Valencia before them or Atlético Madrid afterwards, Sevilla were never able to capitalise on their success. They never again fought for the league nor ever reached the Champions League semi-finals.

Tragedy also struck hard when one of the most beloved players from the side, Antonio Puerta, passed away suddenly a few days after suffering a cardiac arrest during a league match. It was a hard blow, particularly because he had become the hero behind the two European trophies, scoring the decisive goal in the semis of 2006 and another in the penalty shoot-out in the final the following season. After that tragic incident, players and managers came and went but there was a sense of missed opportunity around the Sánchez Pizjuán. It was then that 'Monchi' hired Unai Emery.

Two events between late March and early May halt Sevilla completely. One is the *Semana Santa* [Holy Week]. The other is the famed *Feria* of Seville, a week of celebration of local folklore and traditions that has become one of Spain's most important social and cultural events. Between April

2014 and 2016, you could have added European nights at the Sánchez Pizjuán to the list.

Once again 'Monchi' proved decisive by signing the likes of Ivan Rakitić, Vitolo or Eduardo Salvio, who were joined by José António Reyes, as the prodigal son returned home. In 2014 Sevilla were on the break of elimination during a tough semi-final against Emery's former side Valencia, but a late goal from Stéphane Mbia sealed the passage to the final where they beat SL Benfica in a penalty shoot-out. Beto, like Palop before him, was the hero of the night. Rakitic was sold to Barcelona but he wasn't missed as Éver Banega proved to be another shrewd signing. Alongside Polish midfielder, Grzegorz Krychowiak, the Argentine was decisive for Sevilla as they once again booked a place in the final in the following season, won against FC Dniepr in Warsaw.

Back-to-back honours once again and a place booked in the Champions League group stage began a trend that would continue over the following seasons, in which Sevilla would fail to advance in the big European competition only to end up winning the Europa League against all odds. They did so against Liverpool in 2016, coming from behind to crush Jürgen Klopp's side with goals from Kevin Gameiro and Coke. In 2020, with Julen Lopetegui in charge, Sevilla overcame Roma, Wolverhampton Wanderers and Manchester United during the final play-off, staged after COVID-19 restrictions were partly lifted, to face Inter in the final. The two biggest clubs in the competition history met eye-to-eye in a stadium empty of supporters but full of emotions. Inter's Romelu Lukaku opened the scoring, but Luuk De Jong turned it around with two goals only for Diego Godín to tie the match, all before half-time. An unfortunate own goal by the Belgium forward Lukaku confirmed the Andalusians as the kings of the tournament. And if there were still any doubts, no season sums it up better than 2023, when a Sevilla side fighting relegation with a newly appointed manager in charge, José Luis Mendilibar, once again defied the odds to beat Manchester United and Juventus, before facing José Mourinho's Roma. The Portuguese coach had never lost a European final but not even he was capable of denying Sevilla a seventh title, their third win on penalty shoot-outs.

Sevilla FC supporters have become accustomed to winning. Colin Millar, author of *The Frying Pan of Spain*, explains. 'For Sevilla fans who were born in the mid-1990s onwards, they have only ever known success,' he says. 'It became normal to win European trophies. Only, it's not. They were not a successful club until recently and now live in a sense of momentum. At the beginning of every season, there's not one supporter who doesn't believe they can do it again.' Success has transformed the identity of the club. Long gone are the days when they fought in the second tier or scrapped for a mid-table place. The stakes are much higher now. 'That generated a feeling between self-confidence and arrogance,' adds Millar. 'Of course, this cannot be sustainable forever, and in recent years we have seen complacency in the club's hierarchy.'

Del Nido was arrested in 2014 and released three years later in connection with a corruption case in Marbella. Since then, he has been fighting his son, who acts as vice-president for José Castro, to regain control. The club has also failed in recent years to replicate their famed ability to scout and sign talented unknown players. Despite winning the 2023 Europa League, Sevilla are, for the first time in many years, living under the shadows of their neighbours Real Betis. And what a rivalry that is – probably Spain's most passionate derby.

'The Seville derby is the best in Spain because it is unique – not only in Spain but probably in Europe – for how it splits families. Brothers and sisters can support different teams. In a very basic sense, this makes the game personal –

your life is directly impacted by not only your club's results but the other team's as well. It shapes your days, your joys and your pain.' This is naturally also more 'intense' says Millar. While writing his book about the Seville derby, he realised how important the game is for everyone. 'Meeting supporters and families in this situation was eye-opening for me, but the matchday itself is something special. On derby days, the few kilometres between the two stadiums are shut down and the away fans are given a police escort to walk to the stadium. The city itself stands still for these games. You have to consider that the city has around 100,000 members/season ticket holders between the two clubs – that is around one in every seven people who live there. No other city matches this.'

Sevilla FC was supposed to be the well-to-do club while Betis were seen as the working-class side. They were deeply connected with the local British community and the wealthier aristocratic families. Their home ground sits in the posh Nervión neighbourhood. However, if social class was what separated the two sides, the passing of time has since erased all boundaries. Today the club's popularity among the poorest working-class in Seville is greater than ever. That growth also affected relationships between both institutions, which suffered its lowest period when Del Nido was appointed chairman at a time when Betis was ruled by Manuel Ruiz de Lopera. In a city that celebrates bullfighters and flamenco dancers as stars, they were forever searching for the spotlight. The two biggest egos in town, both used their clubs as weapons in their quarrels for over a decade.

Eventually, Sevilla might have thought they had gotten the upper hand thanks to the silverware won, but the city remains strictly divided. The local derbies are as intense as one can imagine them to be. If Seville is the most passionate city in Spain, so are their supporters. There have been reports of stabbings and fighting ever since the two sides first met more than a century ago. Sometimes things still get messy, although much of the rivalry is lived during the weeks before and after matches with passion and humour. Like everything else in Andalusia. It doesn't matter if the clubs are fighting for a European place or if they met in the second tier. Feeling matters more than football. And football matters more than life. That's Seville for you. A city where nothing can ever be taken for granted.

* * *

Some claim Málaga is one of the best places to live in Europe. It's hard to argue with that. The sun shines particularly bright on its coastline and the city has developed over the years to become one of the most cosmopolitan places in Spain. For decades people from Málaga have stated that they, not Seville, should be the capital of Andalusia. The province stretches out to include sites as iconic as Torremolinos or Marbella. For decades, Torremolinos was seen as the perfect summer destination, first for hippies and artists like Brigitte Bardot, then by the Spanish commonfolk and now by local celebrities and a huge British community. Right alongside sits Marbella, a place where glamour, organised crime, clubbing and exotic beach clubs set the pace. Málaga is a mix of everything. The rich and the poor. The locals and the foreigners. Inevitably that melting pot became part of the culture of their football club.

Málaga CF was only established in 1994 but football was present in the region for more than a century. CD Málaga were first promoted to La Liga in 1950. Already playing their home matches at the beautiful La Rosaleda, they quickly became the most popular club in the province. Their existence didn't last long and all the ill-thought investment that took them up came with a sour price. At the beginning of the

90s, they declared bankruptcy. Many suspected it would take forever for the city to find another club capable of competing against the greats, but in four seasons newcomers Málaga CF were back at the top. They immediately qualified for European football with a side full of talented players such as César Dely Valdés, Darío Silva and Rufete. However, as in the past, success was only achieved because the club spent more than they earned and soon they found themselves once again in trouble. Only, this time, Málaga had already become a booming city, attractive for foreign investment. Aware of that, Sheikh Abdullah ben Nasser Al Thani hardly needed much persuasion to buy the club in 2010. Spain was living its footballing golden years and Qatari oil fortunes were starting to look into European football with other eyes. Local supporters were not entirely convinced but, for a time, it seemed a match made in heaven.

Al Thani invested heavily to create a squad able to compete against the very best. He hired former Real Madrid manager Manuel Pellegrini and signed the likes of Martin Demichelis, Jeremy Toulalan, Joaquín Sanchez, Isco Alarcón and Santi Cazorla. It was possibly the most star-packed side Andalusian football had ever laid their eyes upon. The passionate supporters crowded into La Roselada and Pellegrini was able to make everything tick like clockwork on the pitch. From fighting to avoid the drop, Málaga ended the 2011/12 season fourth, their best-ever result. Champions League football awaited. Ruud van Nistelrooy was added to the squad and the *Boquerones* began the following season with high hopes. Many even tipped them to fight Barcelona and Madrid for the league. Things started well. Best debutants in the history of the Champions League group stage, they eventually overcame FC Porto in the last 16 to face Jürgen Klopp's Borussia Dortmund for a place in the semi-finals. No side from Andalusia had ever gotten this far in the competition. During both matches against the Germans, Málaga were the better side but a goal in the dying minutes allowed Dortmund to go through. Without knowing it, supporters had touched the skies. They were about to enter a spiral that would take them directly to hell.

All that money spent raised alarms and, unprecedently, UEFA decided to sanction the club for breach of Financial Fair Play rules. Al Thani decided to stop pouring more money in and the side was quickly dismantled to pay the bills. Three years later they were playing in the second division again. Worse still, in 2022 the club was relegated to the third tier, the semi-professional 1ª RFEF. It was a tough blow for supporters who, just a decade prior, dreamed of playing a Champions League semi-final. The reluctance of Al Thani to sell the club, notwithstanding, had blocked the arrival of any other investors and the club fell into a pit.

It was nothing new. Football in Andalusia has been living like this for ages. All the great sides of other provincial capitals, except Seville, have experienced a similar fate. As José Maria Nolé explains, 'Córdoba, Real Jaén, UD Almería and Granada FC all once competed in La Liga but few were able to do so regularly and none have been in the elite for more than ten years. They are never capable of sustaining any sporting project and because of that they live in a self-destroying cycle.'

They have also become easy prey for foreign investors who have little to no interest in the local community or club's traditions. Almería is owned by a Saudi millionaire, Turki Al-Sheik, but that wasn't enough to keep the club from being relegated at the end of the 2023/24 season. The same could be said of Granada. The club from the city that was once the cultural lighthouse of Andalusia, famed for the astounding beauty of the Alhambra palace, is currently run by Chinese Sophia Yang with no palpable success. Abdullah Al Zain, a businessman from Bahrain, is the chairman of Córdoba CF. Once the largest in the world, its football club is far from becoming a La Liga regular. Spanish football clubs are cheap in comparison with British clubs, and they are being run poorly. Too many times former owners are tried for misdemeanours and leave a heavy heritage for those who follow, setting back any possibility of growth. Anywhere else and the clubs would have disappeared. But this is Andalusia. The passion of local fans always prevails.

Málaga saw how that works first-hand. Despite remaining the property of Al Thani, the club is now run by a legal representative, while several charges brought up against the Qatari are pending court sentence. With the club at its lowest, supporters took matters into their own hands. Thirty thousand sold out La Rosaleda, week in, week out. One of the loudest groups was the Guiri Army, a group of supporters from the local expat British community, who have been backing the club since the 1990s. They embraced the Andalusian sense of humour since the word *Guiri* is a colloquial Spanish term used to make fun of foreigners. The club became, over the years, deeply rooted within the thousands of British residents in the Costa del Sol, making it extremely popular in the United Kingdom as well.

Matt Harrison moved to Málaga five years ago and fell in love with the place and the football club. He now goes to every match, home and away, while hosting a podcast for British followers about the club's life, *Guiricast*. 'There's a huge British community here, probably the biggest in Spain, so Málaga became the club we all support, although I think there's still much to do from the club to engage with the foreign community. Yet, for me, it was a way of connecting with the locals, who find our presence amusing. It gives a much-needed sense of belonging and I very much enjoy travelling around and experiencing the sadness and joy the club has to offer.' During the 2023/24 season, thousands took to the streets to march against the current ownership's lack of interest, and some decided to spice things up by going to the local airport to treat some incoming travellers as if they were star signings. They also prayed. A lot. And it worked. After a hard-fought season, Málaga went to Tarragona to play the decisive play-off. Hundreds crossed half of Spain and brought candles, amulets and replicas of the Virgin inside the stadium. They got their miracle. After coming back from a two-goal deficit, Málaga scored the decisive goal in the dying seconds of extra time through a 17-year-old local, Antoñito Cordero. As he had been all season, Harrison was there. 'I was one of the 500 or so lucky enough to be in the away end. It is the best night I've ever experienced watching football in my life.' Promotion brought the club back to life. People took to the streets during the night and this time it was to party just as if they had won the Champions League. In a sense, they did. To stay alive and fight another day is, for many clubs from Andalusia, their crowning glory. Like the region that has shaped Spain's identity in the eyes of the rest of the world, they are all about *pasión*. They know suffering, they know joy. They know what life is all about.

ON AIR

FOOTBALL IN Spain can be found everywhere. However, the lack of connections it has developed with the cultural world may surprise some. It is one of the most deep-rooted consequences of the fascist dictatorship. Football was not seen positively – as happened in the United Kingdom – as a working-class sport and, contrary to Italy or some South American countries, it was incapable of conquering the hearts and souls of its famed artists. Used by Franco as a powerful propaganda tool, it was undressed of any political, cultural or social significance for decades. The sporting press thrived, but only by extensively discussing the swashbuckling world of refereeing decisions, club rivalries and conspiracy theories, which brought the game closer to petty arguments in pubs and far away from the creative inner circles. Democracy brought a new fresh air but at a slow pace. Only now is the nation finally discovering the richness of its footballing culture. Fired by a vibrant generation, eager to distance itself from the past, perceptions are changing, reflecting on how the game is thought, read and talked about. A world of possibilities opened up, thus transforming Spain's football culture in a way few imagined possible.

* * *

It will be hard for anyone to find a country as in love with football as Spain. The passionate way they live the game is second to none. You don't need to wait for the weekend. It is 24/7. In the streets, schools, bars, family dinners or working breaks. People are loud and proud of their club colours and often believe themselves more knowledgeable than they are. In the country with the highest number of bars in the world, football is always shown live, and people often trade the comfort of their homes to go to their local pub and enjoy matches alongside their mates. But that is all connected with the day-to-day life of their sporting identity. Since Spain greatly lacks sporting localism – support for Real Madrid, Barcelona and, to a lesser degree, Atlético de Madrid, spreads nationwide – usually everything connected with those clubs is felt as a live-or-die issue. Whether it's a player moving in or out, a poor refereeing decision, or a new manager about to be signed or sacked. People enjoy discussing the bowels of football. Yet they rarely go beyond that. Ultra groups may be right- or left-wing oriented – and you have both – but with few exceptions, they seldom take the opportunity to publicly stand in favour or against much if it is not directly connected with their clubs. Football is only a reflection of society and the lack of communal spirit and fighting for the right causes is yet to be addressed. The cultural world is partially to blame.

For decades, football was seen as a minor spectacle, unworthy of the attention of the cultural groups. Franco had something to do with it, of course. As the much-admired football author and historian Toni Padilla explains, 'The fascist regime used football as one of its main propaganda weapons, alongside folkloric singers and the sun and beach tourist locations, and that made all who stood against Franco take a dislike to football, especially around the cultured left-wing movements. Many thinkers or writers believed that just the fact they even discussed the game was serving the purposes of the regime.' As in many other fascist dictatorships, sports became an influential tool used to appease crowds. People were encouraged to talk about the match but not to think about the game. When the 'Hunger Years' were over – and in Spain, rationing was a reality until the early 50s – the government used the state-controlled cultural industries to exploit football in their favour, as they did with bullfighting and flamenco by promoting several films where singers and bullfighters were presented as mass heroes. So it happened with football.

In 1953 Francisco Rovira, one of Spain's greatest filmmakers of the day, directed *Once Pares de Botas*, a dramatic triangle love affair between the daughter of the chairman of a fictional club and two squad players. The movie served as a pretext to reinforce the values defended by the regime and was famous for including cameos of real-life icons like Alfredo Di Stéfano, Ladislao Kubala and sports pundit Matias Prats. Kubala and di Stéfano, by then, the leading figures of Barcelona and Real Madrid, starred in movies approved by the regime, using football to laud the accomplishments of Franco's policies. Kubala had the fascist regime to thank for his professional career, as Franco's government did all in their power to reverse the sanction imposed against him by FIFA when he escaped the communist Hungarian dictatorship and wandered around Italy playing nothing but friendlies. The Hungarian genius, by that time probably the best player in the world, always felt indebted and agreed to star in *Los Ases Buscan la Paz*, recounting a fictionalised version of his own story and how Franco's Spain served as a beacon of hope to those who were up against communism. Around the same time, Di Stéfano played himself in *Saeta Rubia* and *La Batalla del Domingo*, two dramas that exploited his popularity to convey a message of a modern Spain.

However, those were the exception, rather than the rule. The technical issues ofm filming football matches meant real-life footage was usually used, at a time when only the government news bulletin service, *No-Do*, showed some of those clips from matches before movie sessions. But if music, bullfighting and later tourism offered an escape, football was always seen as a suspicious world and soon enough movie production took its attention elsewhere. Around that time, the Divine Left cultural movements in Barcelona and Madrid started to denounce the role reserved by the regime for the game, shaping an emotional gap that took decades to close. There was so much contempt that even a famous *Blaugrana* supporter, Manuel Vazquez Montalbán, opted to hide his love for Barcelona in his youth so he wouldn't be seen as an apologist for the regime.

'It was a very different reality from the one lived in the United Kingdom, which was always a democracy and where the game had a profound working-class ethos,' says Aitor Lagunas, founder and director of *Panenka* magazine. 'Even myself, born during the 1980s, grew up accustomed to seeing no cultural references to football anywhere in cinema, music or literature. Franco had been dead for more than a decade but enough time hadn't passed for the cultural world to change its perception. People who aspired to be taken seriously usually bought the respected *El País* alongside *Marca* or *As* and then would hide the sports newspapers inside to read it, just for the fear of being judged.' Cinema never again took football into its arms, although there was a short period at the turn of the millennium when the game had a moment of cultural relevance on screen. In 2000 *El Portero* was released. It was an emotional drama that told the story of a former first division goalkeeper who, after the Civil War, wandered from village to village showcasing his abilities against the locals in return for a few coins. Football was the excuse to tell the tale of how life was hard in those years after the war and how the Máquis resistance movement tried to survive persecution. It helped that Gonzalo Súarez's movie counted on three of

Spain's greatest actors of the time, Antonio Resines, Carmelo Gomez and Maribel Verdú, to gain critical acclaim.

It was to be a one-off. A few years later two comedies starring Fernando Tejero, by then a national icon thanks to his role in the acclaimed TV Show *Aqui No Hay Quien Viva*, once again used football as a metaphor for the social tensions of the day, but both *El Penalti Mas Largo del Mundo* and *Dias de Fútbol* were light-hearted approaches more than anything else. Even when Daniel Sanchez-Arevalo, then the rising star of Spanish cinema, used the final of the 2010 World Cup, won by Spain, as a background for an emotional family get-together in the masterpiece *La Gran Familia Española*, football was only mentioned lightly and shown in the background. It was not just an issue with the big screen. Television shows hardly touched it as well. When they did, the tone was usually condescending. Carlos Marañón, son of RCD Español's record goalscorer (who was known simply as Marañón) and director of the movie magazine *Cinemania*, believes the issue is not just with football but popular culture. 'Social elites in Spain always disregard anything to do with 'pop culture' and football is a part of that,' he says. 'There are cultural productions, but they hardly find a market to expand and remain closed in niches, like Sergio Oksman films. We haven't broken the barrier between loving football as a game and enjoying it as a cultural experience.' For TV showrunner and screenwriter Javier Olivares, there were exceptions, but he agrees that the popularity of football has made it almost a sort of kryptonite for cultural movements. 'There's a contempt for anything popular, and few things are more so than football,' he says. 'It is also true that shooting a football match technically is very hard and, we can't forget, football is already everywhere you look so, in a sense, that exposure ends up limiting the way you look at it from a cultural content creators' perspective.'

Olivares is also part of those exceptions. His acclaimed TV show *El Ministerio del Tiempo* – which he co-created with his brother Pablo – has touched the emotional side of football more than once. The showrunner's affection for Atlético de Madrid becomes clear in more than one episode during the four seasons aired. Often one secondary character is depicted reading the same sports newspaper over again, which throws him back to what was, then, the celebrations of the last league title won by the *Colchoneros*. But not even in a show where a group of ministry agents travel through time to avoid any disturbances in the history of Spain is football seen as important enough to become a central plot for a full-scripted episode. 'We had so many things to tell in so little time that we didn't get the chance,' Olivares says with regret, 'but the goal scored by Marcelino in the Euro 64 Final would have been a good subject for a chapter. Or the figure of Luis Aragonés who was a contra-cultural genius, but most of all the stories related to football during the Republic or the Civil War period.' But then there's also the passionate side of the game and how it is lived. People are so in love with their club colours that they often resent any reference to rivals or protest if their side is not depicted as they expect them to be. 'Football in Spain offers a particular limitation; people are so club-fanatical that it is hard to be creative and not bother a part of your audience while making others happy,' says the showrunner. And that is one of the biggest issues: polarisation. The game has been lived for so long as us versus them that creative artists prefer not to mess with the masses. Passion has been the driving force in Spanish football since its heyday, but it also became one of its limitations.

Audio-visual productions are not the only cultural areas where football has been ignored. Music and literature have also been worlds that historically turned their back on the game. Recently popular musicians have turned to football for inspiration, but it is still hard to find the game as the subject for pop hits. The same happened within the literary world. It wasn't until the 1970s that Vazquez Montalbán became the first Spanish author to openly embrace the passion for the game and write about it with a flair and talent possessed by the very few. He opened the doors for others to follow but it took time. Eventually, newspaper articles by men like Jorge Valdano, Alfredo Relaño, Juan Tallón, Enric Gonzalez, Manuel Jabois or Enric Ballester started changing how the game was discussed. For Oscar Abou-Kassem, alongside Diego Barcala a founder of the quarterly magazine *Líbero*, the Argentine's role was particularly key

'Valdano helped to change things,' he said. 'His connection to Argentinian football, where the cultural establishment was proud of its attachment to the football culture, paved the way for a new approach. The way he talked about the game, and the role models he drew upon, inspired a new generation of writers and journalists who were no longer afraid to talk about the game differently.' As Abou-Kassem pointed out, these names gave football heart, substance and identity, escaping the old-school terminology and embracing a more creative speech that connected with a newer generation. At the turn of the millennium, football slowly entered the publishing world. Small short-story collections such as *Hooligans Ilustrados*, where well-known writers explain how they fell in love with their clubs' colours, the travelling narratives of Axel Torres and Toni Padilla, the tactical and historically knowledgeable books of Julio Maldonado 'Maldini' or Martí Perarnau, paved the way for a new generation of authors to finally remove the emotional shackles that seemed to separate writers from football.

Everyone felt a need to make up for lost time. 'I think we can say that it was a feeling of, yes we turned up late for the party, but we are finally here to have a good time,' says

Roger Xuriach, one of the directors of Panenka, a project that began as a football magazine but eventually expanded to become also a publisher. 'We live now in a time when people who started writing about football have become celebrated writers. People like Galder Reguera, Nacho Carretero or Miki Otero. We knew we had to be on the frontline of this generational change. That's why we move among several genres: poetry, short stories, novels, travel chronicles, essays or historical books. What's important is that there are many stories to tell, and we want to tell them,' explains Xuriach. Of course, literary creation in Spain is still far from what we find in countries like the United Kingdom or Argentina, but times are changing. There is an increase in published works dedicated to clubs, international football or the historical and tactical side of the game. Younger authors are starting to make a name for themselves and they have arrived at a time when football culture is changing fast in Spain. That has mostly to do with how the press has evolved as well.

* * *

The Spanish sports press is a juggernaut incomparable to other European nations. While in the United Kingdom sports usually can be found in the last pages of newspapers and football supporters have a plethora of dedicated magazines to read, Spain is quite the opposite. There are more than half a dozen daily sports newspapers nationwide, with many more regional publications as well. They are among the most-read in the country and their social and political relevance cannot be understated. In comparison, Spain only has a single monthly football magazine nowadays, *Panenka*, and a quarterly publication, *Libero*. Both take a very different approach to newspapers, similar to *11Freund*, *So Foot* or *When Saturday Comes*. They are the exception. Football in Spain is read in newspapers and listened to and watched mostly on talk shows. They are usually melodramatic and passionate. At least the most successful ones.

Excelsior was the first newspaper exclusively dedicated to sports in Spain. Printed in Bilbao, it sold almost 20,000 daily copies between 1924 and 1931 and opened the gates for many more that eventually didn't survive the test of time. One that did though, was *Marca*. Also founded in the Basque Country, in this case in the Francoist-occupied San Sebastián, during the Spanish Civil War, it began as a weekly publication but after 1942 started to print daily. By then it was already seeded in Madrid, and over the following decades became the most important symbol of the Spanish sporting press. It sold more than half a million copies the day after Spain won the Euro 64 edition, but when the private Prisa group launched its main competitor, *As*, it began to lose its dominant position.

Both newspapers printed in Madrid have since their beginning been linked closely to Real Madrid the same way *Sport* and *Mundo Deportivo* – printed in Barcelona – and *SuperDeporte*, published in Valencia, found their way into the hearts of supporters by aligning themselves with the local clubs. That is one of the main traits of the Spanish press, the closeness with local football identities. Newspapers and, indeed, journalists, are not shy of openly supporting club colours. Johan Cruyff coined the famous expression of the *entorno* [literally 'environment'] to describe the group of influential journalists who tried to shape the way Barcelona were perceived in Catalonia. The same can be said of Real Madrid and, to a much lesser degree, with Atlético if you read the Madrid press. That is clear not only through the daily covers or the dozens of pages dedicated almost exclusively to the clubs their readers are affiliated with but also on how they construct a sense of reality and memory.

Marca has since evolved to include a more sporting identity, going beyond football, but the core idea remains the same. Football is a vehicle for passion, and it needs to be told in a way that readers feel more than they understand. In Spanish society, it is almost impossible not to take sides, regardless of the matter in discussion. Football can't be any different. A Real Madrid supporter would never buy *Mundo Deportivo* and a Barcelona fan would hardly be seen with a copy of *As* in their hands. Not because they don't write about their club but because they do. And they do it with a biased vision. Any Madrid reference in a Barcelona newspaper will probably be negative and the same can be said the other way around. However, that doesn't mean they are not proper newspapers. The quality of match reports, the pieces signed by their well-renowned chroniclers and even some investigative works are among the best in Europe. You simply can't expect impartiality.

That old-school mentality that started in the written press soon moved elsewhere. Radio, like anywhere else in Europe, became central during the 1950s. At that time in Spain, listeners had two options, the regime broadcaster Radio Nacional de España or the privately owned Cadena Ser. The later *Carrousel Deportivo* became the favoured sports show nationwide. It would not only cover football matches but also other sports like cycling or boxing. Entire generations grew up listening to it over the weekend and many of Spain's greatest sports journalists started their careers there. Although television became a more affordable commodity during the late 60s, football was mainly absent except for the occasional league match or some continental cup displays, often featuring Real Madrid, who benefited greatly from that exposure to become a nationwide club. Indeed, *Los Blancos* appeared in the first-ever televised match in Spain, against Racing Santander, back in 1954. Football shows appeared much later and *Estudio Estadio*, the RTVE show inspired by *Match of the Day*, was only broadcast for the first time in 1972. It remains the most fun-loving football television show although now it's more of a talk show, than a weekend highlight event. Paco Caro has become the latest in a long lineage of sports journalist icons to host the show, following the likes of Pedro Ruiz, Matias Prats, José Angel de la Casa and Juan Carlos Rivero. For the RTVE journalist, the historical relevance of *Estudio Estadio* cannot be underestimated. 'When the show first started, football matches were rarely shown live so for years people only saw how football was played by watching *Estudio Estadio*,' he said. 'Everything they knew about teams, players and stadiums, they got from those weekly highlights of each match. It united people and helped define a collective mindset around how the game was played and watched. Now football is everywhere but for many years we were the torch bearers that kept the flame alive.'

Caro belongs to a long list of iconic voices that have narrated major football events for decades. Alongside the likes of Andrés Montes, Antonio Estevá, Carlos Martinez, Iñaki Cano, José Manuel Díaz, Sixto Serrano, Miguel Angel Román and Paco Grande they created an emotional blueprint for supporters, as we entered a world dominated by television broadcasts. Many also turned out inspirational heroes for a new wave of match commentators and pundits such as Fran Guillén. For the DAZN journalist, 'When football was shown live, both by state- and privately-owned companies, a new way of communicating all those emotions from the matches became popular. To people like myself who ended up working in television, those years shaped who we became and inspired us to raise our game. At DAZN we take things very seriously on how we prepare each broadcast but also try to adapt our language to these new times.'

Football was aired live and on open air until the end of the 2000s and has since become almost exclusive to cable broadcasters where the likes of Guillén capture the zeitgeist of the moment. Yet, more than the live broadcast matches, it was the quality shows and documentaries first produced by Canal Plus, such as *El Día Después, Fiebre Maldini* or *Informe Robinson*, hosted by the much-beloved former Ireland international Michael Robinson, that elevated the relationship between football and television in Spain. Still, despite all, radio ruled supreme. And it had its kings as well.

After the removal of the censorship shackles that followed Franco's death, a new generation of men started to take a more hardcore approach to radio journalism, on a permanent quest for breaking news with a taste for the exotic. Hence José Maria Garcia. Like many others, he started at Cadena Ser and in 1982 moved to Antena 3 Radio, where his show, *Supergarcia*, became a blockbuster. He turned out to be one of the most powerful figures in Spain. Garcia ruled the waves mercilessly. Even the chairman of the Football Federation wasn't spared his public wrath. He was said to have the power to sack managers and decide presidential elections. His late-night broadcasts became cult classics with a war-mongering style that reflected a period when even club chairmen were not shy of verbally and physically assaulting rivals. It wasn't pretty but it was popular.

Soon enough rivals started to appear, people who had once worked for him or knew his methods well. Such was the case of Ramon de la Morena, a groundbreaking journalist who, in 1995, eventually managed to overtake him in the rating charts. By then rivalries had gotten personal as both broadcasters used airtime to attack one another while fighting for exclusive interviews or breaking news, most of the time bordering on what was ethical. They also produced good journalism, though, fighting injustices and denouncing the corruption in the football pyramid. Heroes and villains alike. The nature of shows like *Supergarcia*, De la Morena's

El Larguero or the late-arrival Josép Pedrerol's *Punto Pelota* became the blueprint for the same style of shows broadcast on cable television networks at the turn of the 2010s. Many old-time radio stars converted themselves into television icons, yet their style remained the same. De la Morena and Garcia had by then said their goodbyes but Pedrerol, alongside top professionals like Dominguez Castaño, Paco González, Manu Carreño, Jesús Gallego or Manolo Lama, kept the radio spirit alive, remaining highly respected and popular names throughout the years. For a while, almost every media company had their newspapers, radio and TV shows and used to crossover their star figures to compete for ratings at a time when Spanish football was enjoying its golden age, and the rivalry between Barcelona and Madrid was at its peak. It was also the moment for a changing of the guard. It all started with a group of friends who decided to publish the magazine they had wished existed when they were younger.

* * *

'In 2011 sports journalism was still anchored in the old ways, the bar culture, very masculine, with little to no margin for introspection or analysis. We thought there was a void that needed to be filled, knew about other projects in Europe with whom we shared a common spirit and went for it,' says Aitor Lagunas, director and founder of *Panenka*. The Barcelona-based magazine became the paradigm of a new Spanish football culture. Fourteen years on they are still alive and kicking, having expanded from a monthly magazine to a book publisher, podcast content creator and a university for the journalists of tomorrow. 'We always looked for something different from what we were used to' adds Roger Xuriach, also from the magazine. '*Panenka* always went for stories that weren't told, not only from other countries but inside Spain as well, because the way journalism was done meant only talking about Barcelona and Madrid. We wanted to tell them with a different visual imprint and fight for causes we believed were right. That's why we are still here; those who began this path with us are not just readers, they are part of a community that shares the same principles.'

Panenka became a symbol. For decades, *Don Balón* had been the only football magazine in Spain, but they were by then on a low and would soon disappear. *Líbero*, founded around the same time in Madrid, lasted a few years as a monthly magazine, soon transforming itself into a quarterly publication. But if they became the beacon of a new era, the internet was the playground of the names that command the revolution of tomorrow. At the beginning of the 2010s, several different projects came to light. Axel Torres and Toni Padilla were at the helm of *Marcador Internacional*, a radio show dedicated to international football that soon became a webpage from which many of Spain's greatest reports of today have come. In Cadena Ser, Bruno Alemany kick-started *PlayFutbol*, the most important international football radio show in Spain. Football tactics were beginning to be a subject of interest especially when the project *Ecos del Balón* came to light. Fernando Asenjo got together a group of young journalists with an appetite for a radical approach on how to analyse the game, focusing more on tactics, concepts and identities than searching for breaking news or discussing referees' decisions. Miguel Quintana, Abel Rojas and Alejandro Arroyo, among others, became household names for a generation that grew up with tactical simulators like Football Manager. More focused on the day-to-day and the historical background, both *Kaiser Magazine* and *Sphera Sports* served as the Oxford and Cambridge for future sports journalists, many of whom are now leading pundits nationwide. None of those names and projects wanted anything to do with the classical journalistic approach that had reigned supreme for decades. Together they changed the rules of the game but also suffered a backlash against the old-school journalists, who saw in the rebellious youth a menace. One of them, Roberto Gomez, mockingly started to call them 'Panenkitas', taking the magazine as a reference for what was wrong, in his view, with this new generation of football hipsters turned journalists. Many believed he had just started a cultural war. But did he?

'I don't see it as a cultural war, no,' says Miguel Gutierrez, a key figure in understanding the evolution of sports journalism in Spain for the past two decades. His project, *La Libreta de van Gaal*, has been an uncomfortable mirror for journalists and supporters alike over the years, highlighting the contradictions of the sporting press. 'What is clear is that the old-time journalists have found that there are professionals who are trying to do things differently, and, since they don't understand the purpose, they have decided to mock them. They are just afraid of a generation that is more well prepared, more self-demanding than they ever were.' For Bruno Alemany, who always worked for Cadena Ser but has an approach closer to the newer generation, it's all a question of perspective. 'I feel like John Travolta's meme,' he says. 'I grew up wanting to work on the radio because of people like Paco González or José Garcia but I also wanted to take a more modern approach to it. Then I realised what I like to do differs to what they did. But there's room for both. In Spain, you have a group of people who like to consume football that way and another one that started a few years ago who demands something different.'

But there is also tension in the air. 'I don't believe there's a need to have a clash between them but it's also true that some of the elements of the old guard have tried to drag the newcomers through the dirt, because in truth they don't like nor understand the game, they are in it for the show. And the newer generations have been clever enough not to engage and to keep doing what they do for their audiences,' adds Alemany.

The internet was the entrance gate for many newcomers, providing a freedom that doesn't exist in mass media. Borja Pardo lived it first-hand, having worked at *Don Balón* and radio station Cadena COPE just before he kick-started *Sphera Sports*. The project born in 2012 has become a reference point ever since, a digital media that could adapt to the successive changes in the way younger audiences communicate. 'We understand that digital is a world where nothing stays forever,' he says. 'We give a lot of relevance to the visual side of communicating, through our front pages, and our presence on social media and, at the same time, we always offer quality content.' They have since begun their podcast, extending the influence of the *Sphera* brand to audio as well.

The same could be said of *Kaiser*. When Juan Arroita, Guillermo Gonzalez, Andrés Cabrera and Ignacio Velazquez started the project, they had no idea that a decade later they would be part of one of the most recognisable brands in Spain and South America. 'I knew there was a great generation of young writers who had no platform at their disposal, the traditional media were closed to any outsiders and, with the help of social media, we were able to create a popular and quality project,' explains Arroita, the main man behind the project.

Kaiser became the first digital medium to trade text for image, as they converted themselves into the first successful generation of sports YouTubers in Spain. Their audio-visual project was an instant hit on both sides of the Atlantic, paving the way for the new platform to serve as the perfect way to communicate with Generation-Z supporters, who no longer regularly watch television or listen to the radio. Rafa Escrig, who now works in television, also began his career with a YouTube channel dedicated to his travels around Spain to show a younger audience there were more tales to tell than just Barcelona and Madrid. 'Until the 2000s everything was the same as it had always been,' he said. 'The newspapers printed the match report, and you caught the highlights on the television and listened to the match on the radio. The internet paved the way for a change. We found out football could exist without that war-like mentality and stopped being just consumers and became creators of the content we would have liked to follow. And the newer generations now don't even want to work in the old media, they want to use TikTok or Instagram to tell stories and, frankly, they are much better prepared and knowledgeable than everyone ever was back then.'

The future was up for grabs, and no one understood it better than Miguel Quintana. Already a renowned figure thanks to his analytical work in *Ecos del Balón*, Quintana took a gamble and started his own YouTube channel. Seven years on he became the leading figure of sports journalism in Spain. He still reigns supreme on the digital platform, but now also appears on DAZN broadcasts, is a match pundit for the channel and has also become a well-loved radio voice, hosting *La Pizarra* alongside Adrian Blanco and Nahuel Miranda for Radio Marca. 'Those who are starting now are moving away from journalism and searching for a more show business-like mentality,' he says smilingly, sitting at an old-school Madrid bar during a short break between air casts. 'We grew up with those old-school figures and a way of doing things and wanted to do it differently, but deep down we were still journalists at heart. The new content creators are something else, but in the end I believe there will always be room for everyone.

'The internet provides you with a sense of freedom that you can't find anywhere else. I now work in a radio station and television, and I have freedom, of course, but also a responsibility to know there are different publics.' Quintana was able to cross over like no other. He has brought a younger generation back to the radio thanks to his afternoon show, and opened the doors of the digital world to those who only knew him when they heard him on the airwaves. That's no meagre feat. Like Garcia before him, he understood well the needs of the public, the perfect combination of both worlds. There is now a world where younger supporters know all about not only Madrid or Barcelona but also Ipswich and Como, and no aspiring writer is ashamed of telling the world that football is probably the best way to understand how society works. And a place where even pop stars now proudly take the stage wearing their favourite football shirts. A world where a footballing culture is finally gaining momentum in Spain. A brave new world.

LADY MADRID

IT IS striking how easily forgotten Madrid is when ranked among the most beautiful of Europe's capital cities. It may not have the glamour of the likes of London, Paris or Rome but walk through its streets, dive into its hidden secrets, and it's impossible not to fall in love with her. What was once an ambitious political project to establish a capital around a small medieval town, right in the geographical centre of the Iberian Peninsula, has since become a reflection of how Spain sees itself. For those who don't live there, the city represents the asphyxiating essence of a centralised state, with all its flaws. In truth, by being Spain's capital for almost half a millennium now, Madrid turns out to be exactly the opposite. A place that grew used to welcoming people from everywhere, that belongs to all rather than a few. It always has been a haven for artists, lovers, travellers and dreamers. Perhaps because it has such an open heart, the *Madrileños* feel different from anyone else, and that sense of specialness has crossed into the backbone of its football culture.

* * *

It's almost midnight. It pours in Madrid, one of those typical spring storms that wash the first signs of the heat that the summer will soon bring. You can already smell the petrichor in the air. And yet, the lightning thunders in the sky are muted by the crowd inside the Vicente Calderón stadium.

More than 50,000 people are soaking wet, jumping up and down and singing the club anthem. Players and coaches watch in awe from the turf while the earth shakes. People are celebrating despite their team having just lost. They not only lost, but they did it against their greatest-ever rival. A club against whom they partially define their very existence. And yet, while the victors walk almost silently back home, with a mission-accomplished gaze in their eyes, the losers stay and sing. 'Derrochando coraje y corazon'. Spilling guts and heart. Losing against Real Madrid and still celebrating the passion for their colours. They knew they would soon be moving to a fully covered modern arena and yet many already missed the rain and wind. 'Yo me voy al Manzanares,' they chant. It would be the last time they went to the old ground that kissed the waters of the Rio Manzanares on a European night and thousands decided no one would ever forget that moment. Because that's what Atlético de Madrid is all about: moments.

'Atlético Madrid is a team with a particular identity. It is the biggest club in Europe never to win the Champions League. We are the only ones who lost three finals, none in regular time and twice against our city rival. But we are also the only side that won an Intercontinental Cup without a major continental trophy. That is something only Atlético would be capable of doing.' Juan Esteban Rodriguez is a college professor and author of several books dedicated to the club. After the death of Bernardo Salazar, probably Spain's greatest-ever football historian, he is the most knowledgeable figure in the history of Spain's third-greatest club. A team that, many would be surprised to know, was born as a local franchise of Athletic Bilbao and ended up mirroring their city rivals Real Madrid throughout their history to a point where one cannot understand their very own nature without thinking of the other side of the capital. 'It is hard to separate Atlético from Real Madrid,' says Rodriguez. 'It's a duality that is everywhere. Streets, bars, popular culture... more than half of the *futbolines* – table soccer – in Spain depict a white set of Real Madrid players against the *Rojiblancos*. If you are from Madrid nobody asks what's your club. They ask if you support Madrid or Atlético.'

It is not easy to be the neighbours of a club crowned as the best in the 20th century. Real Madrid is a giant, more than a club from the city, a club from the world. It was not always like that, of course. Its legacy owes much to the genius of Santiago Bernabéu and his idea of building the biggest stadium in Spain. And, of course, the signing of Argentine Alfredo di Stéfano. When, months after a new competition called the European Cup was born, the set was complete and Real Madrid went into a galaxy of their own. But Atlético stayed true to their origins. Although they are a national club – alongside Real and Barcelona the only ones that can claim it – their core of support remains in the region. Walking around Madrid you can feel the *Colchonero* spirit ever present, whether you move in the working-class neighbourhoods of Tetuan or Lavapies or the poshest areas of Chamberi. Atlético supporters think they are special, and they may be right. It is not easy to support a club in a city shared with a colossus. But it's precisely that spirit that allowed them to prosper.

Atlético was born only because a group of Basque students from the Engineering School of Madrid felt insulted by how the Real Madrid supporters behaved when they faced Athletic Bilbao in the 1903 cup final. On their way back from the match, walking the streets of Rios Rosas, they decided to establish a version of Athletic Bilbao in the capital city. The club was originally branded Athletic Madrid and wore the same blue-and-white Blackburn-inspired colours of the Bilbao side. When Athletic changed their kit to a red and white striped shirt after a club representative's trip to Southampton, the side from Madrid did the same. As mattresses – *colchones* in Spanish – were usually covered with a red stripe the club became popularly known as *Colchoneros*. Originally, they expanded within the well-educated university student groups. By the 1930s their rivalry with Madrid became bitter because of how *Los Blancos* were already becoming the biggest force in town. 'The rivalry comes from early on and it's not only because of Real's success or the political and economic background,' explains Juan Esteban Rodriguez. 'It began when Madrid used their muscle to financially ruin smaller clubs from the city, by signing their best players at a bargain price. Clubs like Moncloa, Español de Madrid and Racing de Madrid. So, many of the supporters of those sides, angered by the Real way of doing things, turned to Atlético instead and joined the cause.' But even that was not enough for them to be spared a similar fate. In 1936 Atlético, one of the founders of the football league, was relegated for the first time in their history. The club was bankrupt, and many believed it had no future. Only they did and have a war to thank for it. Ironically, for an institution that has proudly presented itself over the years as the only opposition to a club they consider to be almost state-sponsored, it was they who were once the favoured side of a political regime. Or, at least, a club that only survived and prospered because of the fascist rulers that came out victors of the terrible Civil War that tore the country apart.

During the armed conflict, a group of Franco's soldiers from the air force started to play exhibition matches in the occupied territory around Salamanca's airbase, later moving to Zaragoza, where the decisive battle of the Ebro was fought. When the war was over the popularity of the team and their hunger for more led some of the higher-ranked officers to request a joint venture between the air force and a football league club. They tried Real Madrid, but it was with Atlético they merged. It was a lifeboat for the *Colchoneros*, who found themselves twice lucky. Once the league started again, in 1939/40, they should have played in the second division, but Real Oviedo's ground was in tatters and the club asked for a year's license to rebuild. The vacancy should have gone directly to the Madrid side but the important role of Navarra's paramilitary forces, the Requetés, led Osasuna also to claim the vacant spot.

The regime, trying not to raise too many waves, arranged a play-off between both sides. Atlético, now named Club Atlético Aviación, won. A few months afterwards they were league champions. They won it again the following season, thanks to a muscled group of players, many of them former militaries, coached by Spain's greatest football legend of the day, Ricardo Zamora, a man ideologically close to the new regime. From bankruptcy to becoming Madrid's leading force and one of Spain's greatest teams. And all with the close support of the air force, a connection that lasted until the end of the 1940s. It didn't end there. Not only did the club become extremely popular among the military, but it was also the army connection that allowed them to move to their most iconic ground. During those winning seasons, Atlético had been forced to play in Vallecas because of the damage the war had left to their stadium. But the Metropolitano was getting smaller by the day, and the accolades of a side coached by Helenio Herrera and led by Africa's first football superstar, Larbi Ben Barek, made it clear Atlético needed a new ground. The then club president, Javier Barroso, used the influence of his brother, a highly ranked military, to buy some land that belonged to the army over the banks of the river Manzanares at a bargain price. It would be there that the club would settle.

The Manzanares stadium was opened by Barroso's successor, Vicente Calderón, and would eventually receive his name. By then Atlético had already won their first European trophy – a Cup Winners' Cup – and they could have also been the ones ending Real Madrid's iconic European run of five consecutive trophies in 1957/58. Forced into a play-off for a place in the final, set to be played in Zaragoza, they accepted instead a Real Madrid offer of the entire gate receipt in exchange for the match to be played at Chamartin, Real's home ground. It proved fatal for their aspirations as *Los Blancos* came out victors.

When Atlético de Madrid settled on the southern side of town they found a new spiritual home and a very different group of supporters. Madrid is a city full of nuances. Despite being mostly known for its beautiful parks, museums and iconic avenues, it is also proudly working class. If you pass by the southern neighbourhoods, you won't see glamour or 19th-century mansions but red-bricked tower blocks and small bars with typical terraces and balconies. Places where people from every single part of Spain, South America or places as far as Asia or Africa ended up in search of a better life. Those are the streets of Usera, Carabanchel, Lavapies or Embajadores where *Madrileños* are poorer, warm-hearted and passionate. When Atlético arrived, they were enlisted to the cause and became hard-core fans. From those streets came many of the far-right radicals that populate the ultra group Frente Atlético and also the critical left-wingers who saw Atlético as a rebellious club, the last stand against the establishment. And there were still those long-lasting club members from the previous decades who took the metro up north, in the more well-to-do streets of Chamberi, and then walked down the Paseo de los Melancolicos, an appropriate name if there ever was one if you were going to support the *Colchoneros*.

In a sense, Atlético became the club that better defined Madrid because everyone felt represented there, regardless of social condition or political ideology. And since they never won much, especially compared with their local rivals, each triumph tasted special. They also became a fundamental part of Madrid's cultural life, remembered in the works of folk songwriter Joaquín Sabina, new wave band Nacho Pop, pop act El Canto del Loco and indie rock duo Péreza. In books or TV Shows *Colchoneros* are always presented as suffering but honest, hard-working people. Juan José Montero is a content creator and club fan. He also feels the club represents Madrid in all its glorious complexity. 'We are the club of the people, drawing support from those who want to take a stand against the powerful, even if the mayor is a well-known club supporter nowadays. But that sense of resistance, to be different from Madrid, has shaped our identity.'

Taking advantage of a sense of disbelief that had begun to crawl into the club's identity after the 1970s, a shady constructor named Jésus Gil y Gil entered the stage in 1987. He had served jail time for involuntary manslaughter when one of his buildings collapsed, killing 58 people. Gil was originally sentenced to five years but only served 18 months, thanks to a governmental pardon signed by Franco himself. To win that year's presidential election Gil promised to sign Paulo Futre, recently the winner of the European Cup with FC Porto, to put the club back at the top where it belonged. Atlético had been Real's greatest rival during the previous decades but they were now on a low. Gil initially connected well with the fans. He had a wildness reflected in the confrontational culture triumphing in the Spanish footballing world of those years, mainly fuelled by a sporting press who loved him. Yet the lack of footballing knowledge, his political ambitions – he also became mayor of Marbella and tried to form a party to enter the national parliament – and tendency to sack managers at the first sign of trouble boycotted the club's growth. Sadly, he also used the new legislation that made it mandatory for clubs to convert themselves into public limited companies to take full control. In a manoeuvre that ended up in court, Gil took the club's money to buy the necessary stocks but registered them as his own. The current owners are still his son, Miguel Angel Marin, and his then-partner, film producer Enrique Cerezo.

Many have opposed him ever since, establishing supporters' trust groups like Señales de Humo and when, in 2000, the club was relegated and put into administration, many of Gil's secrets came to light, shattering his relationship with supporters. The memory of the epic 1995/96 season, the *doblete* year – when he finally won the promised league title and the Copa del Rey, the only time Atlético achieved the double – had by then become a symbol of what could have been but wasn't. Gil arose as a prophet and ended up as the doom of the club. But while ownership remains an issue, supporters never stopped longing for larger-than-life figures. And they got it not only once, but twice. They only had to look to the dugout instead of the presidential balcony.

Luis Aragonés is the most beloved and important figure in the club's history. The wise man of Hortaleza was *Colchonero* through thick and thin. In 2001, when the club failed to get promoted at the first attempt, he came to the rescue. A star player in the late 1960s and early 1970s, he had coached the side to their Intercontinental trophy triumph almost 30 years before. Aragonés also won the league and cup as manager in his first stints in charge, before becoming a much-respected journeyman coach in Spain. He was in Mallorca when the cries for help from the love of his life came. He couldn't say no. In his first season back, he took Atlético to the second division championship, with a packed-out Calderón beating all sorts of record attendances for a second-tier club. More importantly, perhaps, he trusted in a young local teenager whom he took under his wing, like a son, and helped to transform into one of the deadliest strikers of his time. His name was Fernando Torres.

Aragonés returned Atlético its lost pride. The year they climbed back to La Liga the club sponsored a TV ad where Argentine goalkeeper German Burgos famously climbed from a manhole in the Gran Via, Madrid's most famous street, with the tag: 'Here we are'. Things weren't easy though. After several seasons where he outperformed everyone around him, 'El Niño' Torres had to be sold to Liverpool in 2007 to balance the books, as the economics of the club were still suffering from the relegation and the period in administration. Despite winning a Europa League trophy under the tenure of Quique Sanchez Flores, with an iconic striking partnership in Diego Forlán and Sergio Agüero, the club was drifting once again when on 23 December 2011 Diego Pablo Simeone was appointed as manager.

It was the best Christmas gift possible. Himself a club heroe, part of the *doblete* side, Simeone reshaped Atlético as no one had done before. He also connected deeply with a new fighting spirit brewing in the streets of Madrid in the awakening of the public demonstrations against the European Union's harsh economic measures imposed on Spain. On 15 May a group of people got together at the Puerta del Sol, the iconic central plaza of the city and Spain's self-proclaimed mile zero. They had been vocal against austerity measures applied by the right-wing government of the Partido Popular on different social media platforms. On the day that Madrid celebrated its patron saint Isidro, they took to the streets. People slept in tents, held committees to discuss all sorts of subjects, occupying the square and the iconic commercial streets around it, and, as the local musical group Vetusta Morla – Spain's greatest musical band of this century – would later sing in *Atraco Perfecto*, showed they still had a voice to be heard. Eventually, the gathering was disbanded after a month, following inevitable clashes with the police.

Initially, the movement of the *Indignados* seemed to have failed in its attempt to reverse the austerity policies. In truth

At the turn of the millennium Galicia was home to some of the best football in Europe as both Celta Vigo and Deportivo touched the sky.

Unionistas Salamanca represents the spirit of the Accionariado Popular football clubs to perfection. From the bottom of the football pyramid, they now dream of reaching professional football.

No Spanish side connects with their local community more passionately than Rayo Vallecano, the perfect working-class football club.

Rodri winning the prestigious Ballon d'Or is a testament to the Spanish holding midfielder and their impact on the game over the last decades.

The oldest ground in La Liga, Mestalla is home to Valencia CF, one of the greatest and longest-suffering Spanish football clubs, from their twice Champions League final defeats to the supporters' fight to keep the club alive.

A goal to end all traumas. Ronald Koeman's free kick at Wembley paved the way for Barcelona's first European Cup and the success of the blueprint left by Johan Cruyff.

The love story between Sevilla and the Europa League knows no rival. In the most passionate city in Spain lives the other king of Europe.

José Maria Garcia was the master of the airwaves, a symbol of the sporting press's power and of how they set the standards of Spain's football culture.

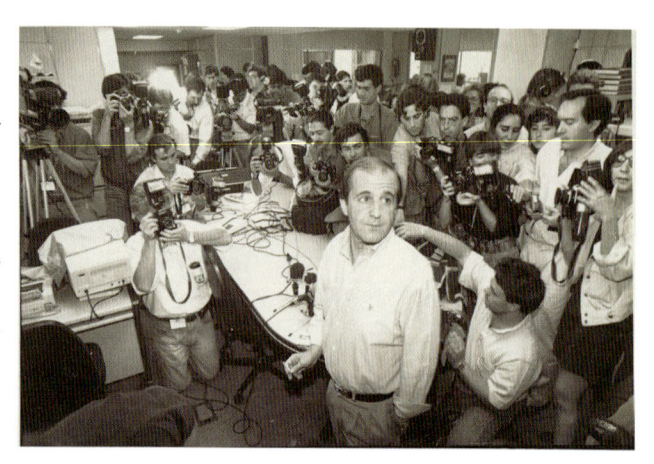

'Proud not to be like you'. Atlético Madrid supporters forged their identity as opposition to their city rivals. Nobody loves their club colours quite like them.

Bars are the heart and soul of the Spanish football culture and the futbolín, a popular table soccer game invented by a Galician in the 1930s, is always present.

The tense rivalry between Pep Guardiola and José Mourinho epitomised the El Clásico spirit at a time when Spanish football was at its peak.

The spirit of the Basque managerial school thrives thanks to the likes of Unai Emery, a four-time Europa League winner.

One of the smallest grounds ever to host first-division football, Eibar's Ipurua defines the nature of northern Spain's rock-and-roll football.

The goal that changed everything. Fernando Torres's effort in the Euro 2008 final puts an end to decades of hurt as La Roja enter their golden age.

Top of the world. Vicente del Bosque celebrates Spain's triumph at the World Cup Final in 2010.

From Andalusia to the world, Real Bétis is the second favourite team for most football fans. A feel-good club whose die-hard supporters know all about suffering and unconditional love.

More than a million Athletic Bilbao supporters gathered around the city's riverbanks in April 2024 to celebrate the first trophy in 40 years as the Gabarra, *carrying the squad, passed by.*

The impossible win. Nayim's last-minute goal against Arsenal in the Cup Winners' Cup Final crowned Real Zaragoza's golden generation.

Zinedine Zidane scores the most beautiful goal in the history of Champions League finals, the tournament that came to define Real Madrid.

they set the ground for a revamp in Spanish politics, bringing new political forces on the left to centre-stage, thus ending the historical bi-party rule of socialists and conservatives. It also showed Madrid, despite the ill-famed link with Franco's regime, still maintained a strong fighting spirit against oppressors, similar to the mentality Simeone brought to Atlético – although it was not Brussels or the right-wing government they were targeting at the Calderón, but the duopoly of Madrid and Barcelona.

More than a decade has passed since then. Simeone has become the longest-serving manager in Europe's top leagues and made Atlético a continental powerhouse. He also took the fight to the establishment powers, like the protestors in the Puerta del Sol square rallies would do in the following elections. In the press room, during his presentation, Simeone made clear what he was all about. Dressed impeccably in a dark suit, a sort of James Bond figure, he promised hard-tackling, hard-pressing, counter-attacking football: tactical concepts that people always associated with Atlético in the past. Most of all, he promised a team that would hold their ground and look right into the eye of every opponent. He wasn't showing off.

In his first season in charge, Atlético won the Europa League, fuelled by the goals of Radamel Falcao, beating Athletic Bilbao in the final. It was an iconic moment as the club who began as a franchise from the Basque side showed how they had overcome their patrons. The following season, not only did Atlético seal a Champions League spot – the beginning of a series of 12 consecutive seasons in a competition where they had only managed to play eight times in all their history – but they also won the Copa del Rey at the Bernabéu against José Mourinho's Real Madrid. It was not the first time they had beaten their rivals in a cup final at their home ground – they had done it memorably in 1960,

1961 and 1992 – but it ended a 16-year spell without national silverware.

What nobody expected was that they would go one better. Against two superpowers such as Cristiano Ronaldo's Real Madrid and Lionel Messi's Barcelona, the squad coached by Simeone won the league on the final day of the 2013/14 season. And they did it in style, by holding Barcelona, who were still in the title race, to a draw at Camp Nou with a late Diego Godin goal. 'To put Simeone's achievement into context,' author Euan McTear explains, 'in the four seasons before 2013/14, no club outside the duopoly had finished within 20 points of each season's champions. The financial gap was simply too huge. On the day when Atlético won the title at Camp Nou, their starting XI cost the club less than €45m. It was a spectacular feat.' 'To compete with the Barcelona of Messi and Neymar or the Real Madrid of the BBC front-line was supposed to be impossible,' McTear adds. 'They did it, beating not just one Goliath but two. Years later, when Atlético won another league title in 2020/21, the financial gap had lessened, but only because Simeone's success had helped the club build more solid foundations. Winning a second league title proved to the world he was not a one-hit-wonder.'

He wasn't. In the aftermath, Atlético played their second Champions League Final. Ironically, their opponents were their old foes, Real Madrid. They scored early and took control of the game right until the end. With two minutes of added time to go, Atlético conceded a corner. Luka Modrić crossed, and Sergio Ramos appeared from nowhere to head the equaliser. Just as had happened in the dying seconds of their previous final against Bayern Munich when a desperate shot from centre-back Schwarzenbeck bounced off the hands of goalkeeper Miguel Reina into the net. In extra time Madrid scored three more and clinched their tenth European Cup.

It was emotionally devastating, but by then Simeone had left an imprint on the club ethos. The 'win, win and win again' of Aragonés had been updated to a 'one match at a time' philosophy. There were no impossibles for his side and two years on Atlético were once again in the Champions League Final. And Real Madrid were their opponents, again. A dubious goal from Ramos opened the scoring, but Atlético showed grit, led by a stellar Antoine Griezmann, and levelled. The match went to penalties. Juanfran failed with his shot, and Cristiano Ronaldo did not. But even in the face of defeat, there was a sense of pride in the Atlético supporters' hearts. They had always been faithful to the club's colours, more so perhaps than any other club in continental football. 'In the future Simeone's work will be put in perspective because I don't believe we are aware of what he has achieved so far,' says Juanjo Montero. 'He converted a lot of kids to the cause, children who are now proud to walk the streets of Madrid with their Atlético shirt on.'

For showrunner Javier Olivares, he is the key figure. '*Atléti* remains a top side thanks to Simeone,' he says. 'Because of his work, even with his mistakes, for his sense of belonging. And while he is doing all this, the club is going in a different direction. It seems the people running the club don't like very much the people who, like myself, love the club.' It has been a difficult time for Atlético supporters. In March 2017 the club, without consulting supporters, decided to buy Madrid's Olympic stadium, now rebranded as the new Metropolitano, from the city council. Sitting on the eastern side of Madrid, the area had no connection with the club whatsoever. The reason was that the land where the Calderón sat had a huge market value and the owners took the opportunity to sell it for a fortune. A new set of luxury compounds in an area rebaptised as Madrid Rio will be built in a place where so many emotions have been spilt over the years. If there was ever a stadium that explained the ethos of its supporters, that was it. A true South American ground in the very sense of the word, both in its architecture and spirit, with the crowd chants and *tifos* mimicking the Argentinian clubs. Around the same time, unilaterally, the club changed the old-school crest for a new logo, removing iconic elements that rooted the club to the city's traditions. In 2024 supporters got it back, but only after years of public pressure. 'Football isn't what it used to be,' says Olivares, 'it's all just a business now and in Atlético we see that. There's no sense of belonging from the owners, no pride in the club's history and tradition, no plan for the future. Those at the top have no love for the club.'

And yet Atlético fans remain faithful. The new Metropolitano was as far away as possible from the Calderón and still the stadium is always packed. Atlético won a third Europa League in 2018 and another league title during the COVID-19-constrained 2020/21 season. They are a regular top-three side and part of the Champions League elite. Despite the lack of investment from the owners, Simeone has been able to sustain the ship in high waters. He has done it mainly by going back to its original identity, a club that feels proud to bother the more powerful, where people are more interested in belonging than in winning. If some clubs count themselves as relevant for the silverware they collect, Atlético de Madrid belongs to that very limited group of clubs who know they are great because of the love they inspire. And there is no late goal that could ever change their DNA. It's not just only because they have grown accustomed to suffering. It is because they don't know how to be any different. Guts and hearts, all the way.

* * *

Madrid is more than a city. It's a whole political and geographic institution.

When Franco's regime ended there was genuine panic that another civil war was on the way. A complex and turbulent period called *Transición* followed. One of its high points happened when the different regions within Spain started to extract some sort of autonomy ruling from the state. Not quite the federal nation many hoped for, but far from the highly centralised days of the previous regime. However, no one knew what to do with Madrid, a place with its own identity but too close to the central government to be mistaken for the very notion of Spain. Since none of their neighbouring regions wanted to include a city as big and powerful as the capital in their territory, it became a region of its own. On 26 June 1982, the official document was signed at the Mendoza castle in Manzanares el Real.

The location couldn't have been better suited. Manzanares is not only home to the impressive La Pedriza, one of Spain's most iconic natural reserves, but also served during the 1960s as one of the main shooting sets for Hollywood productions in Spain. Franco had decided the region should become the equivalent of Rome's Cinecittá and, despite being a small village at the bottom of the mighty Sierra de Guadarrama, it welcomed some of the world's most famous actors. In that same castle, Charlton Heston and Sophie Loren shot MGM's *El Cid*, while in the rocky mountains above, several westerns and sword-and-sandal epics were filmed, none as famous as Stanley Kubrick's *Spartacus*. Not far to the west another iconic location by the foothill of the mountains served as the starting point of the idea of a national capital in the region. Felipe II built an impressive monastery that would serve as his residence. He chose El Escorial and erected one of Europe's most remarkable buildings.

Madrid was, at that time, still a small town to the south but his decision planted the seed of having a capital in the geographical centre of the peninsula. Until then the court would move around the country, establishing the capital wherever they went. Felipe, the instigator of the Spanish Armada, changed all that and with it the fate of a region. To the city began to arrive the best artists and thinkers Spain had ever produced in a period known as the Golden Century, the days of Lope de Vega theatrical plays, Francisco de Quevedo poems and the absolute genius of Miguel de Cervantes. Born in Alcala de Henares, a dashing city well known since the Roman period that is home to one of Spain's most important universities, Cervantes was a soldier who fought in the naval battle of Lepanto, losing mobility in one hand. Thankfully it was his left and he could use the other to write one of the greatest works ever published, one that still defines the very nature of Spain's identity: *Don Quixote*.

Probably the best novel of all time, *Quixote* was also a landmark at a time when the Spanish empire was at its height and Madrid started to get noticed. The cultural grip of the city has never faded since. They were in the vanguard in the late 19th century and again in the Roaring Twenties, serving as the meeting point for some of Spain's greatest-ever geniuses, from Antonio Machado, Pio Baroja and Ramon Valle-Inclan from the acclaimed generation of 1898 to Federico García Lorca, Luis Buñuel or Rafael Alberti 25 years on. It was the first bastion of republicanism and women's rights, mainly thanks to groundbreaking women who defied the norm and fought for the right to vote. They became known as *Las Sin Sombrero*, the Hatless Women, and in many ways pioneered women's rights in Europe.

If later Madrid became known as Franco's capital, associated with the fascist movement, it was actually the last standing ground of the republican cause against the rebellious army. For three long years, the city was surrounded, bombarded and forced to stand alone until the very last breath of war. Barcelona may have become associated with the opposition to Franco but it was Madrid that led the resistance until the bitter end. That identity survived the four decades of fascism and was reborn during the 1980s, a period known as *La Movida*. During those years in the small, tight streets of the central neighbourhood of Malasaña, a group of avant-garde artists broke cultural and social boundaries. Powered by the punk and electronic sounds of the new wave, they brought Madrid back to the vanguard. Out of that group of artists came filmmaker Pedro Almodóvar, singer Alaska and Mecano, whose first hit single 'Hoy No Me Puedo Levantar' tells the story of an epic hangover after a night partying in the bars around Fuencarral Street, the epicentre of the movement. It became the soundtrack of a generation. *La Movida* also paved the way for the public recognition of the LGTB+ movement, which made the nearby streets of Chueca their safe place, transforming Madrid into one of the world's capitals of gay rights. For a city that had just been ruled by fascists for decades, it was a bold claim to make but with support from the socialist mayor Enrique Tierno-Galván, alongside its contracultural and cosmopolitan spirit, change became irreversible.

Football, of course, remains pretty much an important part of Madrid's life and identity but if Real Madrid, Atlético de Madrid and, in a lesser way, Rayo Vallecano, all left their imprint within the city, they aren't the only sides around the region with a story to tell. Madrid is one of Europe's metropolitan areas with most football clubs registered and it boasts up to nine football divisions, from professional sides to local amateur teams. For the 2024/25 season, the region of Madrid boasted five clubs in La Liga. Impressive numbers, considering how geographically small it is. There are many more. In the semi-professional competitions run by the Spanish Football Federation, 27 others play at national level. Add the 508 sides from the regional leagues and you have one of the biggest rosters in Europe. It is a world on its own with many wonderful stories to tell.

In the southern working-class neighbourhood of Carabanchel, for instance, lies the oldest football ground still in use in the city, the centennial Campo de La Mina, property of Real Club Deportivo Carabanchel. It's one of those clubs that have survived in the lowest divisions supported by the local communal spirit. A *castizo* identity that serves to remind you that Madrid is about much more than the glamour of its biggest clubs. The same can be said of the Manzanares el Real football side, which competes in the lowest division on the football pyramid. They are a must-visit, with the small local ground of Las Ermitas boasting a splendid view over the Santillana lake, where some naval battles were shot for Hollywood productions, although in footballing terms they play as low as you can get. In comparison, the B teams from Atlético and Real Madrid compete in the 1RFEF and have played before in the second tier, the highest level they are allowed. Madrid's second team, known as Castilla, even faced West Ham United in a Cup Winners' Cup clash in 1980. They got there because Castilla went all the way to the cup final of that year, a match played in the Santiago Bernabéu against ... Real Madrid. It was one of the most memorable moments in the history of football in the city of Madrid and a ludicrous event that prompted the Spanish Federation to veto B teams being allowed to take part in the cup.

Madrid's economic muscle has also allowed several sides from the areas surrounding the capital to dream of becoming first-division sides someday, as has happened with London. AD Sanse, from San Sebastián de los Reyes, are currently on an upward trajectory that could take them as high as the second division in a few years. Rayo Majadhonda, from a posh municipality on the outskirts of Madrid, played at that level for some years, without ever accomplishing the much-awaited promotion to La Liga. In places like Alcala de Henares, Torrejon de Ardoz, Alcobendas, Collado Villalba, Tres Cantos or Las Rozas, some projects are looking to reach as high as the professional leagues shortly. Local investors, the signing of promising players that fail to triumph in the youth set-ups of the bigger sides in the capital and the incoming arrival of local supporters who are fed up with how professional football is being run nowadays have empowered these smaller clubs to the extent that many analysts believe Madrid will end up being the most representative region in professional football. One clear example of that scenario is Union Adarve.

Originally just a small club from the working-class neighbourhood of Barrio del Pilar, a place densely populated and known for its tower blocks- and closeness to the neighbouring Plaza de Castilla hub, Adarve became known as a club dedicated almost exclusively to its youth set-up. Here everyone believes the most important team is the under-15s, as they represent the ethos and future of the institution. But with time, the quality of their work moulding the players of tomorrow in a northern area of Madrid, where the shadow of Real looms large, they ended up producing a very competitive senior side and are now on the brink of reaching the top of the semi-professional football pyramid, something few believed possible a few years ago. 'Adarve is a special club,' says DAZN reporter Rafael Escrig. 'They invest mainly in their *cantera* but are harnessing the benefits of that policy over the years and now they face a situation when they realise that the club can grow even more. They are very aware of their limitations but remain a self-sustained club, with a small structure. A club that now has achieved the most difficult task, to connect with the neighbourhood in a way that it is extremely hard to do in Madrid.'

For newsman Miguel Quintana, connection is also the key. 'Clubs depend less and less on the numbers of their supporters. They depend on the financial strength of projects and institutional stability and, in the end, I think it is inevitable that Madrid will have a bigger presence in time because the region receives each year more people, more jobs and more money and that ends up sparking football projects,' he says. 'But, at the same time, for the moment, most of those projects don't have a strong local identity yet, they are more about the money than the people.' His airwave partner Adrian Blanco concurs. 'I am not surprised if it happens,' says the Radio Marca journalist, 'but those projects will also need to establish themselves and for that they need time. They need to put their eyes on what Getafe and Leganés have done in the past.' Madrid is rising, that much is clear. But at a different pace. And it was on its southern working-class belt that the revolution began, 20 years ago.

* * *

South of Madrid lie the most populated cities in the region if you exclude the more than three million people who live in the capital itself. They almost form a perfect circle, that starts west on Alcorcon and Móstoles and circles the area now known as Madrid Sur, passing from Fuenlabrada to Getafe and Leganés. They are so close to the capital that only a highway separates them. Small villages until not long ago, over the years they became entrance points for poor emigrants from the south and, more recently, the port of call for thousands forced to leave the city centre due to the rising housing prices. They are not Vallecas, with its long-standing cultural and social identity, but there is a sense of belonging perhaps stronger than in other parts of the region. Football helped create that. Of the five main cities to the south of Madrid, four host clubs that have played regularly in the top two professional leagues over the last three decades. Fuenlabrada and Alcorcon have just been relegated to the third tier, but Leganés were promoted once again to La Liga, where they spent much of the last decade. They are a club that everyone seems to like. Their social media is among the best in Europe and their local ground of Butarque usually boasts some of the best sunset views in all Spanish football. But one of the most curious aspects of Leganés is the long-standing rivalry with their eastern neighbours from Getafe. After all, it's the only rivalry in Spanish football where both sides have met face-to-face in every division of the football pyramid.

'We are separated by a single street and our stadiums are not a mile and a half away from one another.' Fran Iborra is a well-known Getafe supporter and the author of *Sueños de Primera*, a book about the recent history of the club. A history of success. A lower-league side until the late 90s, Getafe got promoted to La Liga for the first time in 2004. It took them 20 years from the time they first started to compete to go from the lowest regional league to the first tier. Over the past two decades, they have been relegated once but climbed back immediately. The *Azulones* also played two consecutive Copa del Rey finals. The first, in 2007, was lost against Sevilla after the side overturned a four-goal deficit against Barcelona in the semi-finals. The following season they were also unable to beat Valencia. Yet, Getafe played European football with significant success as well, drawing against mighty Bayern Munich in an away tie back in 2008 only to be beaten by the away-goals rule in extra-time at home. A few years on they went to Amsterdam to humble an Ajax side who had just recently reached the Champions League semi-finals.

During that time they become a household name for Spanish football lovers. Angel Torres, their iconic chairman, has always shown a good eye for managers. Bernd Schuster, Michael Laudrup and Quique Sanchez Flores practically started their careers at Getafe and he even offered Pep

Guardiola the job when he took his coaching badge. 'Getafe, as we know it, is an Angel Torres project,' Iborra explains. 'He has built the club from scratch, putting in his own money, improving the ground facilities and shrewdly signing managers and players that have allowed us to stay in La Liga for so long. In a way there are entire generations who have never seen Getafe more than the odd season outside of the top.'

In between all those exploits, Getafe and Leganés have met regularly. 'It's one of my favourite rivalries,' Rafa Escrig explains. 'People don't talk enough about it. It was played in six different tiers, and it reflects what I believe a derby should be like, a rivalry between two pueblos that goes way back in time when they would fight for absolutely everything on a day-to-day basis, now transferred to football.' Getafe have come out on top more often than not. The Coliseum, a beautiful stadium that belongs to the city hall, has become used to more happy nights than their neighbours. For Fran Iborra, 'one of Getafe's greatest landmarks is to remain a very familiar down-to-earth club. Inside the dressing room, among the fans. We are proud to be known for having a sound atmosphere during matchdays independent of who comes by. It kicks off hours before the match, drinking *cañas* and eating *tapas* in the pubs around the stadium alongside away supporters.'

Thanks to the tactical leadership of José Bordalás, Getafe has become one of the toughest bones to crack in La Liga and many hope things will get better. There are plans for a new stadium and aspirations for more European football. For a club that didn't exist four decades ago, they represent not only the economic and demographic growth of the southern area of Madrid. Above all, they show that the sheer presence of the towering landscape of the capital has allowed them to compete and beat historical sides from much bigger cities.

The days when many believed Madrid was all about the rivalry between Atlético and Real are long gone. Felipe II made it the centre of the world. The region now aspires to dominate Spanish football as it already does in business or culture. Few doubt they can. After all, Madrid has proved over the centuries to be as addicted to success as the people who are drawn to it. Walking down the Gran Via by night, surrounded by neon lights and memories of yesterday, Lady Madrid still casts a shadow larger than life.

THE DREAMERS

TWENTY YEARS ago, few supporters could name three or four world-class Spanish managers. They were invisible to the eye. Supporters knew the teams and the players. They could even probably recall the names of some high-profile chairmen. But not those in the dugouts. Today, they are everywhere. Spanish gaffers have crowded the Premier League and have won major trophies in Germany and France. And don't forget they also boast this century's most influential football figure. For decades underrated mostly because of their perceived lack of glamour, language skills and a common tactical school, the Spanish football manager has become the most respected figure in his trade. Current success results from a long lineage of men who endured hard times when Spain was still at odds with itself. Without any of those dreamers, things might have turned out rather differently.

* * *

Black suit and tie, immaculate hair, and a huge smile. On 17 June of 2008, Josép Guardiola was living the most exciting day of his new-found life. For a man who had won everything as a footballer, it was hard to believe that things could become even more interesting. Things might have turned out spectacularly wrong, but there was a man used to defying all odds and coming out victorious. He survived oblivion in the Barcelona youth set-up and ended up hand-picked by

Johan Cruyff himself to become a regular first-team starter. A year and a half later he counted the steps of Wembley while walking to collect his European Cup medal. Back home he offered the trophy to the ecstatic local supporters by remembering the iconic speech of the returned exiled nationalist leader Josép Tarradellas: 'Citizens of Catalonia, we finally have it here.' For him, Barcelona and the nationalist Catalan cause were always one and the same. After persistent injuries, a decade later he quietly quit without a fuss and emerged in Italy, where he was forced to fight in court for his innocence, when wrongly accused of doping. It was there that Pep began a tour that would have him travel the world to prepare for that moment. The moment when he felt alive again. Guardiola was 37 years old and by that time nobody could imagine that football, as everyone knew it, had just become something of the past. He was to take all of us into the future.

Born in Santpedor, a small pueblo in the interior of Catalonia, the third son of a humble family, nobody ever expected to see him change the world. Much less so in the grey late days of Franco's rule, a dark period for those, who like the Guardiola family, were profoundly Catalans. At 13 he joined Barcelona's La Masia, a youth academy inaugurated a few years before under the patronage of Laureano Ruiz. He was first scouted at Manresa by Oriol Tort, the man behind many of the shrewd youth academy signings that shaped Barcelona's history. Pep was a shy, slim boy, forced to live away from home in pursuit of a dream. He loved playing like Michel Platini but his lack of physicality was always an issue. He served as a ball boy and the first time the world saw his face was when he hugged a celebrating Victor Muñoz the night Barcelona beat IFK Gothenburg to clinch a place in the ill-fated European Cup Final of 1986. Come 1990 Guardiola could have felt that his playing days were going nowhere.

But then something magical happened. Luis Milla, who was playing in the newly designed holding midfielder position, signed for Real Madrid, and since Barcelona had no money to bring in Jan Mølby, Johan Cruyff's first choice, he was forced to improvise. The Dutchman had heard from his assistant Charly Rexach nice things about a kid in the reserves who could play and decided to take a look only to be surprised that he wasn't in the starting XI. He ordered the reserves coach to play him and, after observing the slim midfielder, took no time to promote him to the first team. Pep debuted against Cádiz in January of 1990 and, although he didn't play much that season, he received his first champions' medal.

From the following season onwards, he would become a stalwart for the club. Fast forward almost two decades and Guardiola was back home. He never hid his wish to become a manager. His team-mates remember he was already one on the pitch, never shutting up, always commanding. Travelling the world to meet influential figures such as Juanma Lillo and Marcelo Bielsa, he famously shared an *asado* with the Argentine that lasted until the following morning, while discussing tactics by using vases as players. Guardiola first took on the Barcelona B team, who languished in the third tier, and quickly had them promoted, a side that included Sergio Busquets and Pedro Rodriguez, whom he also took with him to the following pre-season in Scotland.

What Guardiola did during his first season as Barcelona's manager went down as one of the greatest works of art in the history of the game. It wasn't just the wins but the how. Inspired by his mentor Johan Cruyff's football philosophy with add-ons from many other geniuses he met along the way, Guardiola transformed the game. 'If Cruyff put the ball in the centre of everything, Pep did the same with passing,' says Martí Perarnau, the man behind a fantastic trilogy of best-selling books on the career of the Catalan manager. Thierry

Henry, arguably the Premier League's greatest player of the 2000s, famously said that only after he met Guardiola did he fully understand how the game was played. He wasn't the only elite footballer who described Pep as a perfectionist, so great is his obsession with going around every single detail.

He had his haters, none more famous than Zlatan Ibrahimović, whom he signed in 2009 only to later repent, unable to integrate the ego of the Swedish forward into the team ethos he had built at Camp Nou. But Ibrahimović was the exception, rather than the rule. Guardiola had played with some of the best talents in history, but also knew the importance of team play, especially when he needed the collective to put his idea into action. Or ideas. Because despite all the backslash, especially by the Madrid press in Spain, Guardiola has proven time and time again that he is always looking for something new rather than to enclose himself in what was negatively called 'tiki-taka' football.

'Pep is far from being the orthodox figure many imagine, quite the contrary,' explains Perarnau. 'He is extremely eclectic, likes to add things he studies from other sports and has always evolved from one season to another. All Guardiola teams have identical principles, yes, but they play differently each season and that is why, after 15 years, he remains an influential figure.' Guardiola is not only one of the greatest winners in the history of world football, he's also the first to be in the elite for so long. Only Herbert Chapman could claim to be as influential. Since his debut season in 2008 until 2025, except for his sabbatical year, Pep has beaten every single manager he came across, from José Mourinho and Alex Ferguson to Jürgen Klopp. Looking back on the career of some of the game's greatest managers, many lasted no longer than a decade at the top. He has now started his 17th season, and no one expects him to stop winning soon. Tactical analyst Michael Cox believes he is the perfect blend of success and legacy. 'I find it difficult to imagine there has been another coach both so successful and so influential. And I think sometimes we forget about the first bit, successful, now there is such an emphasis upon being influential. Sacchi is often held up as one of the greatest coaches ever but he won one league title! Guardiola has ticked both boxes,' says the author of *Zonal Marking*.

In 2013 Guardiola left Barcelona with a unique legacy. That side ranks as almost everyone's favourite club side of all time. His footballing philosophy became pivotal for how the game was played, whether someone was trying to imitate or counter him. The revival of a more defensive-minded football by José Mourinho or Antonio Conte was as much an answer to questions he posed as the rise in popularity of the German school of *Gegenpressing*. While facing him, some preferred to sit deep and hold the lines to work on the counter while others chose pressing and speed. But everything was done to counter a Barcelona side who mastered like no other a free-flowing passing game, with constant pressing, high tempo and forward thinking.

Guardiola had the pass at the centre of everything, but he also demanded his players find quick solutions once they got the ball and to get it back immediately after they lost it. To have the ball just for the sake of it became a trademark for the lesser managers who imitated his work but had nothing to do with Guardiola's way of thinking. By the time he left the Camp Nou, as much because of his tiresome rivalry against his old friend José Mourinho as due to the dark-alley manoeuvres of the then club chairman Sandro Rossel, the Santpedor man decided to do the unthinkable and took a sabbatical year. He moved to New York, spent time with his family and friends, learned about sports, cultivated new language skills and returned renewed. For months he had heard how his success had more to do with the genius of

Lionel Messi or the talented squad at his disposal than with his ideas. He decided to prove everyone wrong by taking his trade to the two nations that traditionally represented the opposite of what he stood for. What happened next, more than his early success, was proof of his uniqueness.

Being Cruyff's protege, it looked a shocking move to see him taking the reins at the club of the Dutchman's greatest rival, Franz Beckenbauer. Even more so because he accepted the job long before the Bavarian side went on to claim a historical treble under Jupp Heynckes. Over the following three seasons, Bayern Munich would become the most dominant force in German football history. He accustomed supporters to celebrate winning the league as soon as March and never finished a season less than ten points clear of the runners-up. With him at the helm, Bayern became one of the most well-oiled football machines in the world. He exploited Arjen Robben's and Frank Ribery's ability to play on the wings but evolved the side progressively to a more possession mindset in the end, with players like Philiph Lahm, Joshua Kimmich, Xabi Alonso and Thiago Alcantara gaining more relevance as time went by. What he was never able to deliver was the Champions League. Every single season he reached the semi-finals. Every single time he was beaten by a Spanish side. First, it was Ancelotti's Real Madrid, who played brilliantly on the counter to get a 4-0 win in Munich, and then Barcelona who came out on top with Messi and Neymar running the show. When in 2016 Bayern were playing their best football ever, they were beaten by Diego Simeone's Atlético de Madrid, on the away-goals rule. It was the only trophy missing to complete a full revamp of one of the most traditional clubs in the world.

It wasn't always easy. Guardiola had feuds with the medical staff, part of the local press and some former Bayern players but he also enjoyed the full support of the board and found in the dressing room a group of players eager to learn. His impact in the Bundesliga was also immediate. Seen as the most important of the less important football leagues, while he was in Germany the Bundesliga became fashionable and his tactical adjustments anticipated a profound change in how the game was played there. He also had to adapt. The football philosophy of his early days as manager was there for everyone to see but his Bayern side was also much different to that Barcelona team.

Then, in 2016, Guardiola took up the final challenge. For years many believed he could never impose his passing football in such a demanding and intense setting as the Premier League. All that despite his sides having successfully beaten English opposition time and time again in the Champions League. When his old friends from his early Barcelona days, Ferran Soriano and Txiki Beguiristain, came knocking at his door to have him guide the Manchester City project to the next level, he could hardly say no. He would have been the perfect choice to succeed Sir Alex Ferguson but at City, despite the league titles already won by Roberto Mancini and Manuel Pellegrini, there was no legacy. It was the perfect scenario for Pep to create his own and do what no other Spanish manager had before him: to win the most important football league in the world.

When Guardiola arrived in England there had only been six Spanish managers in English football. Roberto Martínez at Wigan and Everton, Pepe Mel at West Bromwich Albion, Aitor Karanka with Middlesbrough, Quique Sánchez Flores at Watford, Juande Ramos at Tottenham, and the iconic Rafael Benítez. He had been the pioneer, more than a decade earlier, but for all his ability and accolades, the Premier League title eluded him. Benítez came from a very different background than Guardiola's. Not a professional player, he came up through the ranks of Real Madrid's youth set-ups coaching alongside Vicente del Bosque and later went on a solo career that took him in 2001 to Valencia. There he made a name for himself, winning two leagues and a UEFA Cup in three consecutive seasons with a no-nonsense team that rarely played spectacularly. In the summer of 2004, after failing to get José Mourinho, Liverpool went for the Spaniard and his emotional connection with the Kop sparked immediately. Benítez returned the club to their glorious European nights and, after beating his Portuguese nemesis in the Champions League semi-final, his famous half-time team-talk was behind one of the most remembered comebacks in football history. Liverpool's spectacular win in Athens against AC Milan crowned the Reds as European champions for the fifth time.

The Spaniard installed a new sense of purpose to the club that would play another Champions League Final two years on. He also was close to taking Liverpool to their first-ever Premier League trophy when they fought neck-to-neck with Manchester United in the 2008/09 season. It was his moment but, despite Steven Gerrard, Xabi Alonso and Fernando Torres's efforts, the Reds came up short. Benítez would move on to Chelsea, where he would also win the Europa League, and later to Newcastle, becoming a much-cherished figure. He had also been the first Spanish manager to triumph abroad before the international side and Barcelona's success made them fashionable. Yet, much like Mourinho or Wenger, he proved unable to adapt to the new days heralded by his home nation's triumphs. His pioneering role must never be forgotten but, by the time Guardiola landed in Manchester, he was a thing of the past. Pep, on the contrary, arrived to shape the future.

The Premier League is known for its competitiveness. There had always been sides favoured to win but one of its main attractions was the idea that, among the top sides, anyone could clinch the title. During Guardiola's first season in charge, 2016/17, tradition was held. Chelsea won the league while City finished a very distant third. It was the first time Pep's debut season didn't end with a trophy parade. Many of his long-standing critics were quick to express their negative views yet Guardiola was learning fast. Over the following seven seasons, he lost the league once. A tyranny never seen in English football was about to take shape. Ilkay Gundogan, John Stones and Gabriel Jesús had been notable add-ons in his first season, and the following summer Ederson, Bernardo Silva and Kyle Walker joined in. The likes of Sergio Agüero, Kevin De Bruyne, Vincent Kompany and David Silva were already part of the squad and became apostles of the Guardiola style of play.

In 2017/18, Manchester City won the League Cup in February and ended up beating all Premier League records by reaching 100 points while conceding only two defeats. They did it again the following season, adding an FA Cup win to celebrate the club's first-ever treble. Showing an extraordinary ability to adapt, much as he did in the Bundesliga, Pep took some of the most resonating aspects of the English game and made them his own. While moving pieces on the board, he revamped the idea of football tactics up to a point that in the end the pyramid was inverted once again, as City became the first side since the 1940s to play with a 2-3-5, with his full-backs now converted to supporting midfielders. Asphyxiating with the ball, relentless without it and clinical in front of goal. They also had found their nemesis by that time.

If Guardiola's stint in Barcelona had been pretty much shaped by the presence of José Mourinho, his tenure in Manchester would become forever intertwined with Jürgen Klopp. The two had played against each other fiercely during Guardiola's days in Munich but it was in England that their feuds would become the stuff of legends. Klopp, unlike

Mourinho, presented a challenge to Guardiola because he was never content to sit deep and wait as the Portuguese had done. The German was in the process of reconstructing Liverpool into a dominant force and the two trains were bound to collide. Klopp took first blood by beating City in the quarter-finals of the 2018 Champions League, but the Citizens remained dominant in the national arena for one more season. In 2019/20, however, the recently crowned European champions finally won their first league since the Kenny Dalglish days. It was a strange season, shaped by the COVID-19 pandemic, that only ended at the end of July after a three-month halt.

However, Liverpool's success only fuelled City into another glory run. They have since won all Premier League editions and, in 2023, after several failed attempts, including a lost final against Chelsea in Porto, the club won its first-ever Champions League. It was a special win for Guardiola, who had been taunted for years for his inability to win it since he left Barcelona. Success had been coming but with Rodri and Erling Haaland added, the Manchester side finally lifted the only trophy missing in their ever-expanding cabinet. Many would expect Guardiola to call it a day, but he decided to remain. For a manager who had served no more than four complete seasons at one club, this relationship remains an anomaly, but the structure of the club and the challenges posed by Premier League football have proven to be motivation enough.

There are still critics who look at the dark side of his blue moon, especially regarding accusations of foul play with regard to Financial Fair Play rules and how the money poured into the club by the Abu Dhabi royal family provided a shortcut to success. There are still others who claim that Guardiola hasn't proved himself in a club of smaller dimensions, as if any successful manager needed to win titles with lesser-known sides to be recognised. Martí Perarnau explains that his nine years in English football have been a surprise to Pep himself. 'He never imagined himself coaching for so many years, less so being in England for almost a decade. No one knows what will happen next, except for the fact, because he told me so, that he wants to coach a national side and experience what it's like to live a World Cup or the Euros as manager.' Also, by staying so many years at the top, Guardiola has begun to say goodbye to his rivals. Ferguson and Wenger are now long gone. Mourinho is out of elite football and Klopp has said his farewell for the time being. But that a new generation of young Turks is coming to get him might be the motivation he especially needs. Particularly because, among them, some started their trade alongside Guardiola himself.

Over the years Pep has not just been a winning manager like there has never been. He also set a trend of followers, most of whom have begun to draw inspiration from the same fountain of knowledge, the figure of Johan Cruyff. None of those managers have truly been successful because they have embedded themselves in theoretical knowledge while lacking Pep's genius. A different matter is those who have directly worked with him and now present new challenges. Ironically, Guardiola's success, alongside Spain's international honours, also opened the doors for Spanish managers to become highly sought-after by some of the greatest clubs in the world. Men who, in the past, would have been forgotten are now leading the way for a new era. It is hard to believe that any will ever reach the heights of Guardiola. Yet they are showing that there is more to the figure of the Spanish manager than his Messiah.

* * *

Look around and they are everywhere. On any given Sunday in the Premier League, you will easily find two Spanish managers facing each other. From almost unknowns, they have become some of the greatest exports of Spanish football. Rafael Benítez might have been the pioneer and Pep Guardiola the man who showed the way but there are now several coaches who have made a name for themselves abroad.

It wasn't like this at the turn of the century. Like footballers, Spanish managers rarely crossed the Pyrenees. There was a permanent issue with linguistics. Spaniards are not particularly good at speaking other languages rather than their own. Everything on cinema or television is voiced over and the fact that their language is second only to Chinese in the number of worldwide first language speakers has created a feeling that there is no need to learn another. Culturally it was always hard for them to adapt outside of home, especially in countries lacking sun exposure and a Mediterranean diet. As La Liga was forever seen as one of the strongest in the world, there was also a lack of ambition to move elsewhere when there was already prestige in winning trophies at home. Despite the important influences from abroad, Spanish managers always found a way to thrive. The impact of the British was immense until the 1930s, as well as the Hungarians or Czechs during that time. Men like Fred Pentland, William Garbutt, James Bellamy, Patrick O'Connell, Robert Firth or Lippo Hertzka were among the first league champions.

The Civil War changed everything. The triumph of the Fascist faction meant foreigners were no longer welcomed and national managers thrived in their absence. Until Franco's death, there were only another five European managers who won the league. There was an influx of South American coaches, facilitated by the lack of a language barrier, allowing the likes of Helenio Herrera to thrive. But essentially, those were the days when the local manager was seen more favourably. Old football legends like Ricardo Zamora, Ramón Encinas, Josép Samitier and, above all, Miguel Muñoz, not only won trophies but guaranteed that the spirit of *La Furia*, much valued by Franco, remained alive.

No tactical school was backing their success. Since they didn't travel abroad nor face foreign managers regularly, inevitably the game stalled, depending gradually solely on the players' abilities. Even the likes of Luis Molowny, Luis Aragonés and Vicente del Bosque, who triumphed later, were more indebted to that generation than to any foreign influence. But with the new democratic regime came change. Between Leo Beenhakker's Real Madrid title win in 1987 and Louis van Gaal's back-to-back triumphs for Barcelona in 1999, no Spanish manager won the league. But that didn't mean there was a lack of talent at the time. Benito Floro made minnows Albacete into European contenders and later moved to Real Madrid, playing a pressing game that resembled Arrigo Sacchi's tactical approach. Victor Fernàndez was making a name for himself at Zaragoza following many of Cruyff's principles. And then there was Juanma Lillo.

The man who now sits alongside Pep Guardiola on the Manchester City bench was once the most prominent mind in Spanish football. Whenever you see any side in modern football playing a 4-2-3-1, know that they owe something to Lillo, who initially devised the tactical system while coaching Cultural Leonesa and then Salamanca. At 27 he became the youngest ever to earn his coaching badge. He already had toyed with the idea of reshaping Sacchi's idea of a 4-4-2, mixing some concepts of the Dutch school along the way, when he arrived at Salamanca.

For Lillo, the most important aspects of the game were the control of space and time, and the associations players could forge on the pitch. He moved several pieces on the board, transforming the second striker into a creative midfielder with the freedom to roam, and two wingers who could link up play with midfielders rather than just stretching out the field. As football analyst Alejandro Arroyo points out, 'Lillo's idea allowed the Spanish manager to be more flexible and made them able to compete against continental rivals because it allowed for an asymmetric approach, combining different profiles in many positions on the pitch. The following generations of Spanish managers became more tactically rich and prepared for different contexts thanks to his groundbreaking work.'

His experiment thrived at Salamanca as the club reached the top tier, making him the youngest manager ever to do it, just before he turned 30. He then moved between Real Oviedo, Tenerife and Zaragoza but, by the turn of the millennium, his idea had already been adopted by many. Both Deportivo la Coruña and Valencia won the league playing a conservative version of Lillo's tactics and soon the model was exported worldwide. But why wasn't he the one leading the charge? For writer Martí Perarnau, the cultural barriers once again proved to be an issue, as they had been in the past. 'If there was a Serie A or a Premier League side in the 1990s who would have wanted to sign Lillo, they would have had a hard time since he didn't speak any of the languages,' the author explained. 'That impacted his career and how he is perceived outside the Spanish-speaking world. That mentality also prevented many talented managers from moving abroad like our Portuguese neighbours, who are well versed in different languages and adapt easily, were able to.'

And Lillo is a man who likes to express himself. He probably remains the most fluent communicator in football terminology ever to grace the game. After Spain, he moved to Mexico, where he was joined by Guardiola, who only went there to learn from him first-hand. It is easy to understand why they now work together in Manchester. A manager who valued possession and passing before it became fashionable but who always contended that having the ball was just a means to an end and not a concept, paved the way for a series of ideas around pressing or the passing game that were key for Spain's golden era. The focus was that the best shortcut to winning was simply to play the game to the best of the abilities of the footballers.

Those successful years at the end of the 2000s allowed a new generation to break an invisible wall by trying life abroad. After Benítez moved to Anfield, so the likes of Juande Ramos, Julen Lopetegui and Quique Sanchez Flores began coaching in Portugal, Ukraine and the United Kingdom. None had the success that Unai Emery experienced though. A precocious manager – he coached Almería and Valencia in La Liga while still in his early 30s – Emery signed for Paris Saint-Germain (PSG) in 2016. He became just the third Spanish manager to win a top league abroad, by guiding the Parisian side to the 2017/18 title, but his stay at the Parc des Princes was taunted by an unexpected comeback from Barcelona in the return leg of the Champions League last 16.

His tactical genius, however, was there for everyone to see, and he was eventually chosen to succeed Arsène Wenger at Arsenal. In London Emery experienced both the cultural hardships of any Spanish manager abroad, mainly the language barrier, and also the weight of following in the footsteps of a legend. He led the club to the Europa League Final – his fourth, after having won it three times with Sevilla – the first continental final for the Gunners in more than a decade. Defeat against Chelsea and a poor start to the following campaign brought an end to his spell at the Emirates, but after reinventing himself at Villarreal, winning his record fourth Europa League, Emery came back to the Premier League as Aston Villa manager, guiding the Birmingham side to Champions League football for the first time since 1983.

At Villa, the Hondarribia-born coach proved again to be the perfect example of the modern Spanish manager. His tactical acumen and ability to elevate players to the best of their abilities made him one of the most accomplished managers in the league. He was also the last name of a long dynasty of Emerys who had been deeply rooted in Spanish football. His grandfather and several of his brothers were key players for Real Union Irún and Arenas Getxo, two of the most important sides in 1920s Spanish football, as were his father and uncle years later. Emery finally decided to buy Real Irún where his brother now sits as chairman, and many would expect that if they ever climbed back to the first division that he would be tempted to try and win them some silverware.

Emery arrived at the elite on the back of trophies won in Spain. Success was, for Martí Perarnau, the greatest reason why the world started to take notice of what managers were doing there. 'There was always a cultural backslash in Spain and a certain fear to leave their comfort zone, both for players and managers, but success at the international level started to shake things up. Nowadays, when clubs think about signing Spanish managers, they think about how they play the game, that passing philosophy so cherished now, but at the beginning they were only looking for winners and these were the most successful men available.'

Emery's success on the international stage also paved the way for others to follow, like Luis Enrique, who also won Ligue 1 while coaching PSG, or Andoni Iraola. The Bournemouth manager was the last name to join the list and a perfect example of a new trend that has proven that times have changed. As a footballer in the new millennium, Iraola belonged to a different generation, one that could embrace a cultural shift that included breaking the language barrier.

He's not alone in this. Both Mikel Arteta and Xabi Alonso, best friends during their youth years at Real

Sociedad, have come to represent better than anyone this new generation. Both Guardiola's disciples are now seen as two football managers tipped to rule the world in the years to come. They have learned a lot from the Manchester City coach – Arteta worked as his deputy while Alonso moved to Munich to play for him just like Guardiola had done with Lillo – but they have moved beyond positional play as their sole tactical ideal. They also had an immediate impact on their first stints as professional managers. Arteta arrived at Arsenal with the difficult task of returning the Gunners to the top and after four seasons he has done so, the first time in over a decade that the London club has been able to put up a fight for the Premier League. Alonso, on the other hand, returned to Germany and applied his football principles to Bayer Leverkusen, a club that had never won the league and was mocked by rival supporters with the 'Neverkusen' tag. He arrived with the team dangerously close to relegation and a year and a half later won the double while playing the first European final in the club's history in two decades.

'They are different characters who share similar principles,' says Perarnau, who knows both well from his travels while following Guardiola. 'Xabi is perhaps more serious, Mikel is more passionate. But in footballing terms, they share the same ideas, not as orthodox as Guardiola toward positional play, and more able to adapt to their players and to new ideas.' And perhaps the future is theirs for the taking. They represent the very best of the Spanish manager and the fact they played abroad before embracing a coaching career made them more able to adapt than previous generations. Both also drank from the magical cup. Arteta worked alongside Wenger and Guardiola, and Alonso famously did so with four of this century's greatest living managers: Benítez, Mourinho, Ancelotti and Guardiola. Like Emery, Iraola and Lopetegui, they also represent Spain's most influential managerial school.

Only you would probably never have heard about it. There is a reason for it.

***

No place in Spain has birthed so many talented and successful managers as the Basque Country. It has been so since the game first arrived on the peninsula, and it remains today. Perhaps it's their working-class ethos that remains alive, even long after many of its industries were shut down. It could be the stern, disciplined yet extremely cooperative identity of the Basque people. Or simply it was just because they understood the nature of the game better. Euskadi – the local name for the region – was where football first evolved in Spain. Green pastures, rocky cliffs, high mountains all around. Nature has shaped its people and the uniqueness of their language, and their traditions have bound people together. That expresses itself in how they play and coach. The link with the United Kingdom was also decisive, mostly thanks to the merchant ships that connected Bilbao and Southampton or other British ports regularly. Ideas flowed freely as well as footballs, kits and a competitive identity that made the Basque school very similar to the British for decades. As writer and football historian Javier Roldán points out, 'The popular concept of the *Furia* was also inspired by the players, most of them from the area, who comprised the national side that went to Antwerp to play in the 1920 Olympics.' By then the legacy of José Angel Berraondo was well established.

Berraondo was born in Donostia – or San Sebastián for Spanish speakers – and became the most important figure in the early days of Spanish football. He had a role to play in the birth of both Real Madrid and Real Sociedad and was one of the best footballers of his day. He was also the first Spaniard to play abroad, appearing regularly for Brentford during his schooling days in London. Upon his return, he brought new ideas on how to play the game that he quickly put into practice, guiding Real Madrid to their first golden era before taking Real Sociedad, his hometown club, to two cup finals. He then served as manager of the national side and was also a founding member of the Royal Spanish Football Federation. Berraondo even served as a match official, wrote regularly in the sporting press and became a stalwart of the values later embraced by the Basque school, ideals followed by José Maria Mateos, Pedro Vallana and Benito Díaz, three wise men who kept the torch alight.

Díaz was the most remarkable of them all. A regular traveller since his playing days with Real Sociedad, he was the first to use Herbert Chapman's WM tactical system in Spanish football. Like Berraondo, whom he assisted with the national side, he came from Donostia and as a player learned first-hand all about the Danubian school thanks to the teachings of Hungarian coach Lippo Hertzka, who recommended him for the job when he departed. During the Civil War, he moved to Bordeaux, taking the locals to regional glory. When the Nazis arrived in France, Díaz decided it was better to return home. He once again took the helm in San Sebastián where he stayed for almost a decade, famously coaching a promising goalkeeper who, after sustaining an injury, would abandon football to eventually become one of the world's most celebrated sculptors: Eduardo Chillida.

While Berraondo and Díaz triumphed in Donostia, in Bilbao the British influence of the likes of Fred Pentland and William Garbutt was greater and caused a profound impact on Patricio Caicedo who, as an Athletic Club manager, became the first Spanish coach to win La Liga. For the following decades, the Basque school impacted the local game like no other. Thirteen Basque managers won the Spanish cup and six were league champions. Among those with most official matches to their name in the top ten rankings, six come from

Euskadi. Men like Javier Irureta, who won the league with Deportivo in 2000. Or Javier Clemente, who guided Athletic Bilbao to back-to-back league titles before becoming national manager, without forgetting Ernesto Valverde, both league champion with Barcelona and cup winner with Athletic Club. And of course, José Luis Mendilibar, who won consecutive European competitions with Sevilla and Olympiakos.

The list of noted managers spreads out through time, from the glory runs of Jacinto Quincoces, Rafael Iriondo, Juan Urkizo or Baltasar Albéniz between the 1940s and 1970s, to the 21st-century success tales of Miguel Ángel Lotina, Imanol Alguacil or Jagoba Arrasate. Never mind those who have thrived abroad like Emery, Alonso, Arteta, Lopetegui, Iraola or Lillo. Spain's most celebrated triumphs might have come from managers from other latitudes, like Madrid-born Luis Aragonés and Miguel Muñoz, Salamanca's Vicente del Bosque or Santpedor's favourite son Pep Guardiola, but in numbers there is no other region that boasts such a greater influence. And there is one man who unites them all.

Born in Lasarte, in 1946, Mikel Etxarri is responsible for creating a blueprint for local managers to follow religiously. He has become the beacon of wisdom and knowledge in the region, leading the coaching courses for the Basque Football Federation for more than four decades. A school originally founded by no other than Benito Díaz back in 1960. Over the past 40 years, all the great coaching names born in the region were once seen in his classroom. There, the focus is not necessarily on football tactics or, at least, on a common tactical approach. The Basque School is not like the Dutch or Italian, in the sense that creates a lineage of thinkers with the same tactical principles. What it does is transform coaches into shepherds of men. The human touch is the most prized asset the Basque has to offer. Some may have preferred a more defensive approach – like José Maria Magueregui, who became known in Spain for inventing the concept of 'parking the bus' that Mourinho picked up while there and made worldwide famous – while others were more offensive-minded. What they all shared, though, in Etxarri's classes, were the values of teamwork and collectiveness. The *cuadrilla* spirit, as they say around those parts where traditional sports still thrive, and the idea of team play has always played a key part in society. Etxarri is the man who has guaranteed that the likes of Xabi Alonso or Mikel Arteta are following the same path as Javier Clemente or Ernesto Valverde. One of Etxarri's most successful students is also one of the less talked about when one thinks of Basque coaches, though his work revolutionised a small country in South America.

Xabier Azkargorta was a promising forward born in Azpeitia with a career cut short by injury. He followed medical school but, at the same time, decided to take his coaching badge in Extarri's classes and was called up by Espanyol to be an assistant coach when he was just 29. When the board sacked the manager, the squad asked for Azkargorta to be promoted. He stayed for three seasons, laying the foundations for a side that would reach the UEFA Cup Final. Short spells in Valladolid, Seville and Tenerife followed, and in 1993 Xabier received an approach from the Bolivian Federation. They wanted to sign him for the following Copa América and the qualifying stages of the World Cup. With nothing to lose, Azkargorta crossed the ocean and changed the identity of a nation forever. He found a group of talented footballers who suffered to work together, and implemented all the Basque principles of team play while getting the best out of individuals like Erwin Sánchez or Marco Etcheverry.

Against all odds, he was the first manager to defeat Brazil in an away World Cup qualifier, guiding the national side to their first World Cup in almost half a century. Bolivia lost against holders Germany in their first match but drew with

South Korea next, only to be defeated by Spain, coached by his neighbour Javier Clemente. Guardiola scored one of the goals. It was of no consequence. *El Bigoton*, a nickname derived from his huge moustache, became such a celebrity that he was offered the position of Sports Minister. He politely declined before moving to Chile, Japan and Mexico, later returning to Bolivia. Few managers have represented so well the ethos of the Basque school as him and his exploits are perhaps only surpassed by the man who inspired Etxarri himself by elevating French football to new heights.

In 1939, aged just 16, José Arribas was forced to board a ship destined for France alongside a thousand others. They were all fleeing the Luftwaffe bombers who brought death and mayhem as Pablo Picasso depicted in the world-famous painting, *Guernica*. The vessel ended up in Nantes and, after experiencing a short-lived career as a footballer, the boy who fell in love with the game by watching Athletic Club play started to coach at Saint-Malo. He became one of the first managers in Europe to adopt the Brazilian 4-2-4 and later claimed to be greatly influenced by Bill Shankly's leadership skills. His exploits impressed Nantes Atlantique, who hired him in 1960. Arribas returned to town and while there he not only took a trophyless club to three league championships but left an imprint that would become synonymous with artistic football: *Le Jeux à la Nantaise*.

Essentially Arribas applied the Basque mentality of playing fast football as a unit at a time when football was still seen as a game of individuals. He preferred a high-tempo passing style and his down-to-earth approach made him a well-loved figure in France. The way his side played shaped the template of French football from the 1980s onwards, influencing the likes of Michel Platini and Zinedine Zidane. One of his pupils, Raynald Denoix, would continue his legacy as a coach, and not only by shaping the career of iconic players such as France's future World Cup winner, captain and national coach Didier Deschamps. In 2001 Denouix was signed by Real Sociedad and brought Arribas's philosophy back home. There he almost guided Real Sociedad to an unexpected league title in 2003 and was responsible for the breakthrough of a young midfielder with a bright future: Xabi Alonso.

From Berraondo to Alonso, from Arribas to Arteta, the Basque managerial school has played a huge role in the history of the Spanish game. The days of the *Furia* are long gone but their emotional leadership ethos is more alive than ever. Spain's success at the latest Euros under the guidance of Luis de la Fuente, another of Etxarri's pupils, has guaranteed that whenever someone thinks of Spanish managers, they will always have a Basque in mind even if they don't know it. With a spirit of togetherness, down to earth and passionate, the Basque manager is forever the face of the past, present and future of the Spanish gaffer.

ROCK YOU LIKE A HURRICANE

THE LAND is everything. Northern Spain breathes a different air, pushed by the Atlantic winds that shape its shores. Tides dictate time while a landscape of high mountains stretches the horizon, setting it apart from the rest of the country. Everything about modern Spain started there but, while the country geographically and politically moved south, the north stayed true to its origins. A land of fishermen, shepherds, miners and soil workers, a world where courage and bravery are more important than anything else. Football thrived not because it bred flourishing artists but because of a sense of togetherness and commitment. From the principality of Asturias well into Navarre, these lands have always been a place of resistance to foreign invaders, and their football grounds became heirs of that fighting spirit. Expect no poetry or philosophical stances. This is the land of die-hard punk fandom. Of heavy-metal football. Of hurricanes of emotions spilt on muddy pitches and concrete stands. A place you can only understand with your hands' dirt from the ground.

***

The first-ever La Liga edition boasted ten teams. Five came from the country's northern shore. Almost all were from the eastern Basque region. Then, there was Racing Santander. They weren't supposed to have been there in the first place.

The ruling authorities invited all nine former cup finalists to the inaugural season. Still, a free spot remained, so they started a qualifying tournament with ten other sides to fill the vacant slot. Santander came out the unexpected winners, after beating much-fancied sides like Valencia, Real Bétis and Sevilla. Well, at least that's how it looks now, but Racing was all but a minnow back in the day. The club comes from the capital city of Cantabria, an autonomous region that boasts a particular identity hard to decipher even for Spaniards. The Altamira cave pre-historic paintings from 36,000 years ago show how the area has always been an attractive site, yet, historically, they were never seen as fondly as their neighbours.

A land of breathtaking beauty, birthplace of iconic golfer Severiano Ballesteros, Cantabria mixes what remains of the rural Spain of old with the memories of the maritime industries that were thriving when the football league started. Back then, bucolic sites like Comillas were the perfect holiday destination for the wealthier families in the kingdom, with their salty waters and chilly Atlantic winds. A few miles to the east, Santander rises proudly along the Sardinero Bay, the setting of Racing's home matches. Fred Pentland, the British manager who revolutionised Spanish football, arrived there in 1921 and planted the seeds that a decade onwards would bring the local club into the country's elite. In 1931, coached by Birmingham-born Robert Firth – who would later win the league with Real Madrid – they tied Athletic Bilbao for the league title, only losing it on goal average.

It was as good as it got. For the following decades, Racing Santander became an up-and-down club, never staying too long in the first division to cause an impact but always long enough for people to remember how hard it was to play on a chilly, windy night at the Sardinero. During the late 90s, Racing became a regular feature once again and eventually played European football, thanks to the striking partnership of local hero Pedro Munitis and giant Serbian forward Nikola Žigić. Like the region, however, Racing's fate also suffered from the closing of shipyards and local canning industries, a trend that almost wiped out from the elite the football culture around the Cantabric coastline. A lack of investors and a failing local economy sentenced them to fall into the shadows once more. More than a century has passed since Fred Pentland made them a national power and supporters are aware those days are never coming back. And still, despite all the pain and suffering, the Sardinero is proudly packed every home match. Like their neighbours to both east and west, Cantabrians' pride matters, and football remains the perfect excuse for locals to boast about their love for the land. It is a trait that came to define the entire northern region and no place explains it best than Asturias.

While you drive west from Santander into Asturias, along highway A-8, at first you see no significant differences. Geographically they are the same. Left, the mighty Picos de Europa mountains separate them from the rest of Spain. A wildlife paradise, where wolves and bears are still part of the landscape, the Picos have come to define the very essence of its people's grit. Their highest peaks can still show snow even during the summer months, a sight you can contemplate while sitting on your beach towel. Because, if you like the sea, then look right. There are few places as appealing as the Asturian shores, from the sandy small bays like Torimbia or fishing villages like Cudillero. The sea and the mountains – the duality of all northern Spain moulded their everyday life. But if Cantabria is a place that has never been fully recognised as having an identity of its own, no one can deny Asturias's singularity. Not least because they are proud to be the starting point of what we now know as Spain. A distinction you find in their principality status and, like with Wales, in the given name to the crown heir, the Prince or Princess of Asturias. Never fully tamed by the Romans or the Visigoths, and fiercely proud of their local heritage, it was in Asturias that the Christian Reconquista movement started in the years following the Muslim invasion. The local lords and those who fled the invading army mounted a resistance movement that took shelter in local geography and shaped what the Iberian peninsula would become, a sum of Christian-ruled kingdoms of which Asturias came as the first. What sets them apart from their neighbours is their duality. A part of the land lives by and for the sea while others thrive rooted in the land. There are common cultural elements to all, like their love of cider or popular dishes such as the local *fabada*, the *cachopo* or the well-known Cabrales cheese. But although there's a clear Asturian sense of belonging, nothing expresses that division better than the allegiances to the region's greatest cities, Oviedo and Gijón. A rivalry that has converted the local football derby into one of the most passionate in Europe.

Oviedo is the capital city, a place of art and culture, powered by an economy that relies on agriculture and mining. Gijón is bigger and sits by the sea, a working-class city of fishermen, sailors and those who search the attractiveness of its beaches. They couldn't be more different. A centuries-long rivalry has come to define their footballing identity. Despite neither of the sides having ever won any silverware, there are few places in Spain where tradition and belonging are seen as more important than sporting success. Sporting Gijón has probably the better on-pitch story but Real Oviedo's fight for survival is one of European football's greatest-ever fairy tales.

True to their city's origins, Real Oviedo was founded by well-to-do students who had returned from their studies in England, where they first played the game, while Sporting Gijón came to be so that local kids were able to play against the

British merchant sailors who harboured in town. Sporting's connection with youth has forever become their identity. The club always counted on homegrown players to thrive, and Mareo, the local academy, is on a par in Spanish football culture alongside Barcelona's famed La Masia. World-class players such as David Villa and Luis Enrique came from their youth ranks at a time when Sporting were still a regular first-division side. For more than a century, Sporting played almost as many seasons in the first as in the second tier and during 1978/79 they became Asturias's most successful side ever by challenging for the league title.

During that season El Molinón, the oldest football ground in Spain, enjoyed some of the best football played during those years. A side coached by Vicente Miera and powered by Quini's goals went neck-to-neck with Real Madrid until the last days of the season, confirming the centre-forward as Spain's most remarkable player of his day. Quini was born in Oviedo but arrived at Gijón Academy at an early age and became a local legend, winning the league's golden boot on five occasions. After 12 years playing for Sporting he signed for FC Barcelona in 1980, but never managed to win the league despite collecting several honours with the *Blaugrana*. As a Barça player, he was famously kidnapped before a decisive title decider against Atlético Madrid by an electrician who pretended to be part of a right-wing movement that wanted to prevent the Catalan side from winning the competition, but in truth was only after the ransom. Released weeks later, after Barcelona also dropped points in another couple of matches, Quini never spoke ill of his captor. He retired in 1984 as one of the most-loved players in La Liga but a call from his former club had him reconsider his decision and he went on to play three more seasons for the club of his life, helping Sporting to qualify for European football once again.

The forward embodied everything Sporting stood for. Brave, fierce, talented and profoundly local. His brother Jesús, who played alongside him in goal, was also a fan-favourite and lived by the same principles, so much so that he tragically died after rescuing two young children from drowning. The Castro brothers were symbols of a golden age but as happened with Santander, Gijón suffered from the dismantling of the once proud northern maritime industry, and while the city reinvented itself as a popular summer destination, Sporting never again flew as high, dropping to the second tier where they have been for the great part of the century, safe for a short period when Manuel Preciado, a much-admired manager, briefly brought the side back to La Liga. Preciado's Sporting mixed the traditional style of play with a more creative approach and for a while El Molinón became once again a fortress.

It was short-lived. Sacked during the 2012/13 season Preciado passed away shortly after, the victim of heart failure. His memory is remembered in the statue placed at the doorsteps of the stadium. Sporting was relegated that same season and have never again climbed back since, paving the way for something that down in Oviedo many were waiting for: the return of the Asturias derby.

Oviedo sits on a hilltop, eighteen miles away from the coast. The setting of Woody Allen's *Vicky Cristina Barcelona*, a statue of the New York filmmaker can be seen in the city centre, in a place full of iconic buildings that remind visitors of the importance of the place. The Picos de Europa mountains paint the surrounding landscape and not far away sit the mining basins where, for centuries, many locals worked. When football came to town it was brought by well-to-do middle-class students, but its popularity spread fast and by the 1930s Real Oviedo had become one of the strongest teams in Spain. It owed much to Isidro Lángara, an astonishing striker who, alongside the supremely talented Herrerita, led the so-called Delantera Electrica, a forward line that guided the club to two first-division third-place finishes. As with many, the Civil War took a toll on Oviedo and the local ground ended up destroyed by bombing, which prompted the club to ask for a leave to rebuild their facilities.

By then their star forward was in exile after taking part in the international tour comprised of Basque players to raise awareness of the Republican cause. Lángara, alongside Pichichi and Zarra arguably Spain's greatest-ever goalscorer, played in Mexico and Argentina where he became the first footballer to score more than a hundred goals for three different sides, a record equalled only by Romário, Cristiano Ronaldo and Neymar. It took the club five decades to reach similar heights but, while Sporting were on a low, in the 1990s Real Oviedo briefly enjoyed a successful spell, playing European football and signing quality players like Robert Prosinecki, Marius Lacatus, Viktor Onopko and Peter Dubovsky, who tragically died during a summer trip to Thailand aged only 28, a player the streets of Oviedo will never forget.

The changes to a renewed Carlos Tartieri stadium and all the money spent to keep the side competitive had their price. Two seasons after dropping from the first tier, the club was successively relegated to the fourth tier. Many believed it to be the end, and the mayor promoted the creation of a new football club, called Astur. Yet, unlike what happened in other parts of Spain around the same time, Oviedo supporters stood firm beside the club as more than 20,000 supporters followed the side in their fight for promotion. The popular front of support was enough to make the city hall change its mind and Oviedo survived its first match point. But it didn't get better. In the summer of 2012, the club was again on the brink of closure. They had to sell 1.9 million euros in shares in two weeks to avoid bankruptcy but needed to cash in more than four million to keep everything running.

Most football clubs claim their highest moment to be a cup or league triumph. For Real Oviedo, it came when the world united to save them from extinction. British journalist Sid Lowe had travelled to Oviedo as part of the Erasmus students' programme in 1996 and fell in love with the football club. He became a regular during that season, and when he later moved to Madrid, where he ended up as *The Guardian*'s sports correspondent in Spain, Lowe kept following them whenever they were in town. In 2012, he met Juan Ramón Torla, a member of the Supporters' Association that was trying to save the club. 'I was aware of the situation,' he recalls, and found in Torla 'the kind of person you would follow to the end of the world. A rare kind of supporter, who had both the heart and the brains to save the club. So, I asked what I could do to help.' The answer was to spread the word. Over the following days, Lowe was massively important in getting the story out through social media. He also had an ace up his sleeve. During that season three of the most beloved players in the Premier League were also Oviedo graduates. Santiago Cazorla – who in the later stage of his career returned home – and Juan Mata were forced to leave the club in their teens. Michu played for them in the third tier and famously refused to sign with Sporting Gijón, who were then playing first-division football, to stay true to his club colours.

'It's something that doesn't happen often, having three players as good as Mata, Cazorla and Michu who were also Oviedo supporters and former players,' Lowe explains. 'So I started to tell people, especially in the United Kingdom, here's a football club that needs your help and by helping them you are supporting your idol's team. There will likely be no return but the eternal gratitude of supporters and football lovers alike.' It was enough. The three Premier League star players quickly joined in, bought shares and acted as guardian angels to their former club. To make it easier for anyone who wanted in, the club facilitated a PayPal account and soon money started pouring in from around the world. More than 20,000 new shareholders from 60 different countries saved the club.

At the same time, the hard work done by the likes of Torla, Toni Fidalgo, Pedro Zuazua and the ultras group Symmachiarii was decisive in mobilising everyone else in town. 'The feeling of doing your fair share to save a football club motivated many people in the United Kingdom and indeed around the world, thanks to the appeal of the Premier League,' says Lowe. 'Some became hardcore Oviedo supporters in the end, but you can't forget that in Asturias many who couldn't afford to buy shares used their savings anyway so their club didn't disappear. That makes Oviedo a special club.' Eventually news spread, helped by the journalists Paco González and Marcos López, and, aware of the popular wave of support, Mexican billionaire Carlos Slim finally came to the rescue and bought a majority stake. The club was saved and, although more than ten years have passed by and Real Oviedo are still playing in the second tier, nobody will ever forget the fortnight when thousands of supporters from all around decided to save a part of football's soul. In a sense, they became a universal club. When Oviedo finally played the Asturias derby against Sporting after a 15-year gap, it ended in a draw. Both clubs had had their share of glory and bad luck. Both are aware these are not the best of times. Yet, proud Asturians as they are, Real Oviedo and Sporting Gijón are still fighting back against all the odds. And with them, one of the best football rivals remains well alive.

**

It's a magical place, the Basque Country. Nobody knows why but there's an energy in the air that takes us back to days long forgotten. It's part of Spain but not anything like the Spain everyone talks about. True, the landscape might not look much different than their eastern neighbours, a mix of misty mountaintops and defiant rocky shores that surround small hidden treasures like the coast of Zumaya or Gaztelugatxe, now two well-known settings thanks to the popularity of the *Game of Thrones* TV show. However, unlike Cantabria or Asturias, it ranks among the wealthiest regions in southern Europe, despite being home to just about two million people. Even if they don't look like southern Europeans to begin with.

Nobody knows where the Basques come from and even their language has no known patterns that could be linked to any other. Unlike the rest of Spain, they still live mainly in small villages, making its three biggest cities look small in comparison. What they have in abundance is a sense of national identity. It's everywhere. People talk about Euskal Herria – the name for all lands Basque, which includes parts of the south of France as well – as a stateless nation. Euskera is the usual language you catch in street conversations and local rural sports are still highly popular. The urge for independence has always been there, although many already consider they live separate lives from their compatriots. The Basque region is one of the most decentralised in the world, with a self-governing status sanctioned in the 1978 constitution.

Yet, for some, that wasn't enough. In the 1960s, a group of left-wing nationalists pressed for the secession of Euskadi from the rest of Spain. Forced to live in hiding due to political persecution, a small group thought their political actions were not enough and resorted to violence. In 1968 they killed a police officer. It was the first of 829 murders carried out by one of the worst terrorist organisations operating on European soil. ETA tainted life in the Basque Country for decades. During the days of fascist repression, the movement became popular among left-wingers, particularly when they had Franco's touted successor Admiral Carrero Blanco killed in a car bomb in Madrid. However, after the end of the fascist regime, they kept on killing police officers, military, politicians and civilians in a cry for independence that tore Basque society apart. Ironically, those were also the days when Basque football was at an all-time high.

Politics and football are well alive in the region. The sense of belonging made the game the perfect excuse to express the nationalist cause, as when Real Sociedad and Athletic Bilbao captains carried the Basque flag – the Union Jack-inspired Ikurriña – out on the pitch during a derby in 1976. Franco had been dead for weeks and the flag was still forbidden, as with all nationalist symbols. Now it's everywhere. Visit any Basque ground and it's all you will see. It is also why the national side never plays there, nor are cup finals hosted in any of their beautiful stadiums. When Basque teams reach the final, it is also common for their supporters to boo the national anthem. It's a no-compromise territory. Their core values are mainly rural but that concept of being different can also be found among the coastal fishing community or the factory workers that have populated the area for the past century. It is also reflected in their traditional folklore, although, during the 1980s, as their greatest football sides were conquering Spanish football, the region became known as well for their punk rock cultural movement. Local rock has always been punkish and when La Polla Records – literally Dick Records – started to play in local pubs, the Basque Radical Rock movement was formally set. With hardcore sounds and provocative lyrics, the genre became popular, offering an escape to those who opposed the new democratic constitution, with many bands openly supporting Herri Batasuna, the political party attached to ETA. That was also why the movement didn't stretch out outside the Basque country, but that didn't mean Basque rock was not popular nationwide.

In 1984 Mikel Erentxun started Duncan Dhu, a more pop-rock band that gradually turned out to be one of the most successful of the decade, setting the trend soon followed by the likes of Fito y los Fitipaldis or La Oreja de van Gogh, well-beloved Basque hit-makers at the turn of the millennium. Erentxun was also a hardcore Real Sociedad supporter and had been a regular at their Atotxa stadium alongside his father during the previous seasons. The crowd's roar made it one of the most feared away visits in the league, powered by a rebellious atmosphere, at a time when the small football club from Donostia ruled the land.

Few places in the world are as beautiful as La Concha Bay around where Donostia was built. It began as a summer resort for the royals during the late 19th century but quickly developed into one of the most attractive cities in the world. It's a small place with just 200,000 inhabitants but, in time, came to be considered one of Europe's most important cultural cities. Its film festival is known worldwide and its ravishing streets, a mix of old and new, have been home to many iconic writers and artists. Despite all the foreign influx, it's also proudly Basque and so is its football club. Founding members of La Liga, an important club during the first decades of Spanish football, Real Sociedad plunged into an up-and-down existence right up until the moment they signed Alberto Ormaetxea. A club legend as a player, Ormaetxea brought the club back to life when appointed head coach in 1978.

At that time Real Sociedad still practised an all-Basque policy, meaning the club only signed players from the region. Many were homegrown, and with a squad that sprung unexpected talents like Luis Arconada, Jesús Satrustegui, Jesús Zamora, López Ufarte and Periko Alonso – Xabi's father – the club became a title contender during the 1979/80 season, fighting Real Madrid until the very last hour. The following year they went one better and won their first-ever league title. It was one of the tightest-ever La Liga seasons and four teams still had the chance to claim the title in the last couple of fixtures. When Atlético Madrid flunked, it paved the way for another showdown between Real Madrid and the *Txuriurdines*. The Basque side only needed a draw at Gijón in the last fixture but were losing 2-1 entering stoppage time. In Valladolid, the winning Real Madrid players mistakenly were told the match was over and started to celebrate. With just ten seconds on the clock, Jesús Zamora shot desperately at goal and the ball managed to cross the line, taking the thousands of away supporters into ectasy. It was one of the most unexpected title deciders ever but Ormaetxea's men weren't done yet.

The following season, Real retained the league title, winning on the final day once again. Playing direct attacking football following the English template of the day, that Real side is still ever-present if you visit Donostia and find yourself in one of the locals' typical *pintxos* bars. Later in the decade, the signing of Ireland international John Aldridge caused a scandal as the board decided to go against tradition and sign a non-Basque. Since then, they have never been as competitive as they were, although in 2003 they finished runners-up.

By then ETA's killing days were almost over. The democratic regime worked hard to soften the relationship with the Basque Country's main political parties and, under the inspiring socialist prime minister José Luis Rodriguez Zapatero, the terrorist organisation finally ceased its activity. Donostia had become one of the poshest cities in Europe and the Basque Country thrived economically, with many starting to see no point in seeking formal independence. It allowed for a new generation to rediscover their identity afar from the political trenches. Real Sociedad took a similar path. The club suffered with the move from the old Atotxa to the Anoeta stadium and a relegation in 2007 sounded the alarm. Since then, they have moved forward, becoming, in the words of Sid Lowe, 'the club I would want my club to be'.

Like Brighton, they are currently perceived as a model for the perfectly run football club. Many talented young football analysts, such as Abel Rojas, were signed to revamp their scouting and analytics department. Known now for their shrewd signings and a renewed trust in academy graduates, the gamble paid off. Appointing Imanol Alguacil in 2018 also transformed how the side played, moving to a more possession-based attacking football that brought immediate results. They never finished below sixth in the league, played Champions League football and won their first silverware in over 25 years by beating local rivals Athletic Bilbao in the 2019/20 Copa del Rey final. The match was due to be played in April 2020, but the COVID-19 pandemic forced a postponement to the following year.

Why it took too long helps to explain how Basque clubs think differently. Both sides asked the Spanish Federation not to stage the match until supporters were allowed back to the stands, claiming they wouldn't want to deny them a chance to enjoy such a hard-fought moment. Eventually, it was still played in an empty ground, as it was considered unsafe by the authorities. Real won with a goal by Mikel Oyarzabal, one of the academy graduates promoted by Alguacil, the same striker who, three years later, would score the winner in the 2024 Euros. A moment of pure joy for a club that understood the need to move forward to keep the past alive. At a time when Anoeta is starting to feel more like the old passionate Atotxa and so many club graduates are turning out to be world-class players, many believe anything is possible. Walking by the sea of the Concha Bay on an autumn sunset one might feel something big is on the horizon.

* * *

It seems far away now but there was a time when Basque football ruled supreme. The commercial connection with the United Kingdom allowed the region to become the first power in Spanish football at the beginning of the 20th century. British influence was everywhere. The aesthetics of the football grounds, style of play, influential managers and even kit colours. The ships that moved between both countries provided a permanent flux of ideas and innovations and made it easier to spread the game's popularity along the coastline, where mining and metallurgic industries thrived. Even the popular expression still used today to celebrate winning a trophy, *'alirón'*, came from 'all iron' sung by British mining workers when they got extra pay. Athletic Bilbao was already the powerhouse but minnows like Arenas Getxo and Real Irún also became noteworthy sides, both winning the cup and taking part in the league's first editions.

Arenas come from Getxo, the industrial harbour of Bilbao. The club provided several of Spain's first internationals during its early decades but eventually their success wasn't sustainable as professionalism started to spread. After seven seasons at the top, Arenas were relegated, never to return. Real Irún have an even more illustrious background. The town where they come from sits right across the French border and the side excelled for three decades mainly thanks to the managerial genius of England international Steve Bloomer. The club won four Spanish Cups and played in the first seasons of La Liga. However, by the mid-1930s the economic and tactical gap with the rest of Spain had diminished as the game expanded nationwide. Many Basque clubs just peaked too soon. Irún was one of them, although many high-profile players of the day did spend their playing time at the Gal stadium. Some belonged to the Emery family. For generations, they passed the torch from father to son, up until now when manager Unai Emery decided to buy the club precisely because of his family connections.

Early success was established around the coastline but then the economic landscape of the Basque Country changed and gave a chance for clubs from the rural interior to shine. Deportivo Alavés, who come from the Basque non-official capital city of Vitoria-Gasteiz had occasionally played first-division football, yet their golden hour came in 2001. Coached by Mané, the team surprised even their supporters, first by qualifying for the UEFA Cup and then by reaching the final, beating the likes of Inter and Kaiserslautern. At the Westfallenstadion the side faced Liverpool in one of the most thrilling finals ever. The Reds came out 5-4 winners in extra time but only after defender Geli deflected a Gary McAllister free kick into his own net. Since then, they have played a cup final and become first-division regulars for the first time in their history. Yet they are a club from one of the provincial capitals of Euskadi, so success was to be expected, at least.

The same cannot be said for Eibar. The town sits in a small valley on a crossroads on the A8 highway that connects Bilbao to Donostia. Blink and you might miss it. It's greenish, misty and rainy. The town is quite small but, while on the highway, if there is something you can immediately spot it's Ipurúa. The stadium belongs to the local club, SD Eibar, one that entered the spotlight for all the right reasons a decade ago. 'At a club like Eibar, people know the success of the football team can truly put them on the map,' explains author Euan McTear, who wrote a brilliant book on their rise to the top. 'That is priceless and at the heart of the strong connection between the fanbase and the team.'

Eibar had never played first-division football when they earned one of the two top spots in the second division in the 2013/14 season. It meant back-to-back promotions for Gaizka Garitano's men and turned them into the minnows of La Liga history. Their ground was the smallest ever to host a La Liga match and became famed because of the two tall tower blocks behind one of the stands, which allow for a great view from the balconies. For a city that depended much on its industry, Eibar suffered greatly with the 1980s economic crisis and football became the sole solace for locals, who were used to being wakened by the sound of a siren from a local factory. When it closed down, the club bought it and now it serves as a call-up to supporters a couple of hours before each home match. Not that they needed much reminding.

Part of the fantastic story of SD Eibar is their core supporters. And not only the locals. After clinching promotion, the club was warned by La Liga that they needed to comply with a rule that stipulated a share capital of more than two million euros, more than double what they had. It made no sense, especially because they were one of the very few debt-free clubs, perfectly well-run and established within the community. There was fear that all they had achieved on the pitch had been for nothing. This being the Basque Country, everyone stuck together and fought back. A campaign dubbed 'Defend Eibar' was launched with the backing of other Basque rival clubs, local media and former players such as Xabi Alonso. For many, it came as a shock that the football league went after a club run like all clubs should be.

News eventually spread worldwide and supporters from more than 40 countries joined the crowdfunding campaign and bought shares, helping to reach the goal. Eibar were allowed to join the 2014/15 La Liga and stayed up for an incredible seven seasons. A town few had heard of gained notoriety thanks to its football club, especially when Real Madrid or Barcelona visited.

'I think Eibar managed to strike a perfect balance between staying true to their Basque roots while opening up to the rest of Spain and even the world,' adds McTear. 'In Garitano and José Luis Mendilibar as coaches, and Fran Garagarza as sporting director, there was a true Basque influence in how they recruited and played. They also realised they couldn't compete with the other three bigger Basque clubs in attracting Basque talent and looked further afield.' Eibar lived a fairy tale for almost a decade, proving that a sound club could compete against sides with bigger fanbases. They set the example of how to run a small football club and be successful in the process, first during Alex Aranzábal's stint as chairman and then with Amaia Gorostiza. They never overspent, stayed true to their roots and valued belonging more than winning. While historic clubs were being relegated with huge debts, Eibar proved another kind of football was possible. A familiar spirit representing the true ethos of Basque football.

* * *

The Spanish Basque Country never existed as an independent country but that doesn't mean Euskal Herria didn't. Their kingdom was once one of the most feared in Southern Europe. Only it was called by the name of the province that sits immediately south of Euskadi: Navarre.

The very essence of being Basque is often found not in their coastline lands but rather in the area around Pamplona, one of Spain's most remarkable cities. A place so different to any other that Ernest Hemingway fell madly in love with it and came back often. The American writer was particularly fond of the locals' partying spirit, their love for wine and food and the spectacular celebration of San Fermín. In the second week of July, the whole city gathers around for a series of parades, the running of bulls through the old town streets, and many folkloric events. It attracts thousands of visitors each year who, like Hemingway, always find a reason to come back. Pamplona is a place where Basque culture is lived to the fullest. It was never an industrial site like Bilbao or a popular summer destination like Donostia. Here the spirit of the old rural Basques lingers proudly.

The kingdom formed around the eastern lands that resisted the invasion of the Goths, Arabs and Franks. Quietly Navarre became a powerhouse in Spanish politics for more than half a millennium. It was the last independent kingdom added to what we now know as Spain, but its singularity remained alive and well. Yet, despite all its Basqueness, the truth is the south of the province couldn't be more Spanish. Landscape changes from the mountainous, greenish north to the yellowish prairies and with it also its culture and values, more connected with the national idea of Spain. There is only one thing that brings all Navarrese together: Club Atlético Osasuna.

No football club better represents an entire region in Spain than Osasuna. Their story is well rooted in a never-say-die attitude that has found a way to express itself from the stands of El Sadar right up to the pitch. 'Osasuna is like the national side of Navarre,' says Carlos Cuellar, a local legend. 'You feel it from day one, a club that lives as if it was a family, with core values that represent not only the city but the entire region. A place where people will support you, play well or not, if they see you give your all. If you show that you are willing to die for the club you have won their hearts forever.' Cuellar is a well-known centre-back who played for Aston Villa and, before, Glasgow Rangers, where he became the first defender voted player of the year in Scotland. Yet, before all that, he was part of Osasuna's most memorable side. The club is only one of four professional sides in Spain that is still owned by its members, and was founded in the early 1920s. No other club suffered as much as them during the Civil War, with many several players and staff members of Osasuna murdered for their political beliefs over the first weeks of conflict.

Hard times followed. While the club remained a historic side, much beloved in the region, success was scarce up until the 2000s, barring a short stint in the late 1980s when Irish international Michael Robinson became a local legend and guided them to European football for the first time. Then Javier Aguirre arrived. The Mexican manager, the son of a couple of forced Basque immigrants because of the Civil War, provided a turning point for the football club. In 2005 Osasuna reached the cup final for the first time. They were eventually beaten in extra time by Bétis but in the following season Osasuna finished fourth and qualified for Champions League football.

Cuellar was part of that side and recalls those days fondly. 'It was an incredible time. You trained and then went with your team-mates to a local pub, and you saw how people were proud of what we were doing. That only motivated us more. Then, on matchday, El Sadar just came to life, 20,000 singing for 90 minutes. That always gave us an extra push and that's why teams knew they couldn't relax because we drew or won many a game in the final minutes. When I moved to the United Kingdom, I realised there's no ground in continental football as British as El Sadar. There's no place quite like it.'

Defeated by Hamburg in the Champions League play-off, Osasuna went all the way to the semis of the UEFA Cup that season, only to be denied by Sevilla for a place in the final. Aguirre had left and so did many key players like Cuellar himself, and the following seasons were tough. So much so that the financial situation became dramatic, and Osasuna were on the brink of back-to-back relegations. On the final day of the 2014 season, they had to draw with Sabadell just to avoid the drop to the third tier, something that would likely mean the club's end. The Catalan side went 2-0 up and only a late comeback saved Osasuna from disappearing.

The diehard rebellious attitude that had been there throughout their history had saved them once more. It also served them as a reminder of what they were rather than what they were trying to become. Slowly, CA Osasuna went back to basics, a club rebuilt for and alongside the local community, more Basque and earth-minded than ever. Money from player sales and then from TV rights after returning to La Liga was used to clear all debts as the Tajonar Club Academy became the main supplier of talent for the team.

In 2018, while back in the second tier, they signed Jagoba Arrasate as manager. It was a game-changer. Capable of embodying all the ideals expected from a local Basque manager, Arrasate understood the club better than most and immediately rebuilt a working-class ethos that went along with the spirit of supporters and the sort of player available in the youth set-ups. He gradually promoted several youngsters and achieved promotion to the first tier in his first season in charge. Gradually Osasuna re-established themselves as a first-division side, with revamp works on El Sadar making it one of the most modern grounds in the league. The reward came in 2022 when the side reached their second-ever cup final, played in Seville against Real Madrid, a much-detested club in town as it is seen to portray the core of Spanish values as opposition to the Basque mindset that Osasuna represents. The side from the capital came out as winners but only after Osasuna put up a good fight. In a way, that's what they do best. Like many famed clubs from the north, if you look at trophy cabinets, they are mostly empty. Yet, their supporters carry a long-standing devotion full of memories. In a land where the connection to the elements of the earth and the sea is stronger than anywhere else, hard-fought moments are worth more than silverware. Like old rockers, they live for the moment. The purpose is not to win but to never give up.

BAND OF BROTHERS

TWO TEENAGERS smiling, playing rock-paper-scissors, it's not what you expect to see when the final match of the Euros is done and dusted. But that's the new Spain for you. Multicultural, youthful, relaxed. During their golden years, Spanish players were known for their impeccable behaviour, a moral code stressed time and time again as a pillar for their success. Now, they also seem to enjoy themselves and, because of that, a whole country again fell in love. Spain won the 2024 Euros with a thunderous display. People enjoyed watching them move around like they were still kicking about at the local park. Football is all about winning and Spain knows that better than most as they are the most decorated nation of the 21st century. Three Euros and a World Cup in just under 16 years is something never heard of before. Yet, more than winning, Spain always valued the how. Whether the supreme passing skills of a group of world-class playmakers or the dashing attitude of a new generation, their triumphs conquered admirers all around.

It wasn't always like this though. For decades, Spain always seemed to disappoint, on and off the pitch. A country permanently divided and frustrated. Left or right, north versus south, historical nations against the central state. Football turned out to be the answer. When the national side started to win regularly, Spain learned to band around one common cause. The 2024 victory took things a step further, opening the door for a new multicultural generation of players who represent a diversity that was lacking. Finally, they have embraced their national side as something for everyone.

* * *

Lamine Yamal and Nico Williams. A 17-year-old descent of Moroccan immigrants living in one of the poorest neighbourhoods around Barcelona and a 22-year-old son of a Ghanaian couple who walked the Sahara Desert to cross the Mediterranean before ending up in Bilbao. Those are not your typical Spanish heroes. Until now that is. Over the last three decades, Spain has become a multicultural nation. Millions of South and Central Americans, Africans, Asians and Eastern Europeans have settled silently, mostly around the outskirts of the biggest urban centres. They have come to represent almost 15 per cent of the nation's population. Walk the streets of Torrejón de Ardoz or Mataró, and you will see them, going about their day. Look closer and they remain invisible, rarely featured on television shows, running for office or teaching in local schools.

They aren't just immigrants. They are poor, and condemned to take the jobs no one wants, for pay few would accept, living in areas nobody cares about. Although amongst the most admirable people you could ever meet, all remain outcasts, especially for the millions who vote for far-right political parties. Except during the Euros, that is. Many have been judgemental of second-generation sons of immigrants such as Yamal or Williams, yet everyone celebrated their goals and assists. Football broke barriers for those who were left wandering in the shadows. And the players are aware of it. Lamine – who only turned 17 the day before the Euros Final – celebrated his fantastic goal against France in the semis by showing the camera the numbers of the postal code of his hometown, Rocafonda. It is not an easy neighbourhood and remains mostly inhabited by immigrants, like many around Barcelona or Madrid.

The Barcelona youth star grew up there and knows that, unlike him, many with whom he played will never get the chance to become heroes. Or even to have a decent life, for that matter. Nico Williams, whose older brother Iñaki now plays for Ghana, grew up in Pamplona without knowing how his mother, pregnant with his brother, and his father crossed the Sahara Desert, hoping to find in Europe an escape from poverty. He knows now and, while he is still young, clearly understands that his success represents hope for the sons and daughters of those immigrants and is also a tribute to the many thousands who each year die trying to follow them, drowning in the Mediterranean while Europe's political leaders look the other way.

The Spain that conquered the 2024 Euros was the first to embrace its multicultural nature. There had been players from other parts before, of course, but it was never a trend. Not like now. This was also the first time in many years that the national side felt exactly that: national. When Spain won a treble between 2008 and 2012, most internationals played for Barcelona or Real Madrid, while some were Premier League stars. The side that beat England in the final in Berlin had only one player each from Real Madrid, Barcelona and Atlético de Madrid in their starting line-up. The majority were Basques playing for Athletic Bilbao or Real Sociedad. Looking at the rest of the squad there were also Andalusians, Canarians, Valencians and Galicians. Acclaimed sports journalist and *On the Continent* host Andy Brassell felt that 'although there's a lukewarm feeling for the national team in the Basque Country for many political and social reasons, the fact you have a lot of Basque players coming through and enjoying playing for Spain is really important and adds to that sense of a side that stretches over more than just Barcelona or

Real Madrid'. The triumph of the idea of a country united around a group of young and ambitious players coming from all around.

While many pundits expected other nations to rock the Euros, Spain arrived as underdogs. Since their 2012 win, things hadn't turned out the way the country expected. The last two tournaments under Vicente del Bosque came out as disappointments and the generation of players who were touted to replace the likes of Xavi, Iniesta or Torres never fully delivered. There was hype for the 2018 World Cup in Russia, but then the newly elected chairman of the Football Federation, Luis Rubiales, decided to sack national coach Julen Lopetegui a week before the finals only because he had already signed a contract with Real Madrid for the following season.

Rubiales, of course, was then later suspended by FIFA after an investigation following his assault on one of Spain's women's internationals, Jenni Hermoso, during the celebrations of their World Cup win in 2023. By that time Luis Enrique, the man chosen to succeed Lopetegui, had said his goodbyes as well after two bitter defeats in penalty shoot-outs during the Euro 2020 and the 2022 World Cup. Spain's blueprint of possession football, established during the Luis Aragonés days, was still alive but something was missing. There was no joy around the side and supporters had begun to accept that what they had experienced at the turn of the 2010s was a once-in-a-lifetime occasion.

Only it wasn't. Many in the Federation were aware that the youth set-ups had been brewing hugely talented players over the years and a new generation was ready to take charge. Against all odds, they went for Luis de la Fuente, a former national manager in all categories in the youth set-up, as Enrique's successor. A man who had never coached at a senior level but who understood better than anyone the potential he could unleash. He went on to do exactly that. 'De la Fuente is due enormous credit,' says Brassell. 'He's a Gareth Southgate of sorts, someone who is not a glamorous choice for the job but understands young players and that understanding is important in a national team and that enables him to lean on young Basque players.'

Spain retained the ability to pass the ball like no other football nation but added other traits lost over the years, such as a high pressing line and a more vertical approach that had been missing. They finally had in players like Williams or Yamal the right men for the job. The absence, because of sustained injuries, of influential players such as Gerard Moreno, Isco Alarcón, José Luis Gaya or the young Barcelona starlet Gavi, also meant no one expected much of them. They were about to be surprised. Spain routed Croatia in their opening match and then came Italy, the reigning European champions, with, once again, De la Fuente's men much the superior side. De la Fuente had opted to partner Rodrigo Hernández, from Manchester City, with Fábian Ruiz, a deep-lying playmaker who had been under the radar at PSG. The two connected perfectly, and while Spain dominated the game in midfield, the dazzling movements of Yamal and Williams caught the eye. Yet the team had proven to be much more than that. Alvaro Morata wasn't scoring but his silent leadership and defensive work was key and full-back support from a much-experienced Dani Carvajal on the right and surprise choice Marc Cucurella on the left meant the opposition always faced multiple threats.

Nobody panicked when Georgia surprisingly scored the first goal during the last 16 match. It was clear for all to see that Spain had the mental grip as well as the talent to take on any challenge and they proved it not only that night but also against the home side in a tense quarter-final played in Stuttgart. Germany were still favourites to go through, but they only outplayed Spain when De la Fuente took a gamble by removing both Yamal and Williams from the pitch. The match went to extra time and, proving those who doubted the squad's strength wrong, substitutes Dani Olmo and Mikel Merino provided the goals, with the latter celebrating the same way his father did when he scored on that same ground in a European match for Osasuna, 30 years before.

By the time Spain faced France in the semis, nobody was laughing anymore. In a dour tournament full of disappointing performances, *La Roja* were outclassing them all. Fast, skilled and always seen smiling, they were having fun. The squad made theirs that summer's hit tune 'Potra Salvaje' by Isabel Aaiún, who was also an unknown artist. A song that was the perfect representation of what they were all about: underdogs, vibrant and youthful. France, however, counted on worldwide superstars and were known for hardly losing when scoring first. Many wondered if Spain's run had ended as they saw Kylian Mbappé's cross meet Kolo Muani's perfect header for the opening goal. Only a team with great self-confidence could do what the Spanish were able to. Instead of losing composure, they threw themselves at the French and, in four minutes, turned the score around. Yamal reminded the world of Pelé when he belted his first goal in the tournament with a cracking shot from outside the box, and Olmo, who had by then replaced the injured Pedri, netted his third in the competition.

Suddenly, the conversation was not about the possibility of Spain winning the tournament. It was on where to rank them historically if they did. In the end, England proved to be their toughest opponent, mostly because Gareth Southgate decided to short-circuit their fast-passing moves by man-marking Rodri out of the game. The plan almost worked but then the Manchester City midfielder was forced out by injury at half-time and without him Spain looked a more comfortable side. Yamal and Olmo combined to assist Nico Williams for the opening goal just at the restart, and although Cole Palmer brilliantly equalised, Spain never looked on the brink of losing control. It was substitute Mikel Oyarzabal who ended up as the hero of the night by taking advantage of Cucurella's perfect cross with four minutes left on the clock. De la Fuente's much-questioned tactical plan not only worked but proved Spanish football was much more than just a side that could pass the ball around. A side that entered the hall of greats, like their past versions of 2008 and 2012, alongside Zidane's and Platini's France.

What separates them is the fact all those winning sides were fully experienced squads with several renowned players. Spain's current generation is just starting up. Many of their key players are under 24, and looking to the youth ranks of Spanish football you can easily see many who can soon make the jump to the international level. A few weeks after the Berlin final, Spain's under-19 side won their Euros. A few days later their under-23s also won the Olympic Gold medal for only the second time in their history. Winning isn't everything though, and De la Fuente knows it. He has been part of a structure of coaches who have devoted their lives to not just raising football players but responsible citizens as well. There is a team ethos that has proven to be stronger than any tactical shape or individual performance. A sense that Spain work when everyone is rowing in the same direction. Players from different generations and backgrounds can leave behind club rivalries and political stances for the greater good. The 2024 win not only meant *La Roja* were back in contention. It was also a reflection of Spain embracing multiculturalism and how different national identities are perceived in a context where Pedro Sánchez's years in government also allowed for a left-wing coalition to move forward with social advances that Spain badly needed. A sense of a common national identity is hard to find in a country that is a sum of different nations. Providing it was this side's greatest achievement, one that had been failing Spanish football for decades.

* * *

1982 was supposed to be Spanish football's golden hour. It turned out to be a nightmare. Although hosting that year's World Cup had been granted during Franco's rule, by the time it took place Spain was finally ready to embrace a new democratic regime. The dictator had died six years prior and, despite a failed military coup in 1981, all of Adolfo Suárez's efforts to take the country closer to their Western European neighbours prevailed. At the end of 1982 socialist Felipe González won a landslide election, paving the way for Spain to join the European Union. The World Cup was supposed to be an event that would bring together a nation divided, showing the world how the country had evolved. Yet Spain was still incapable of looking itself in the mirror. The idea of what Spanish football was all about didn't help either.

The national side had always been considered one of Europe's greatest underachievers. There was a time when Real Madrid ruled the European Cup, but 15 years had gone by without a single Spanish side winning the most coveted continental trophy. Barcelona were miles away from what they would become and football success, at that time, was centred in the Basque region. Real Sociedad had just won back-to-back league titles for the first time in their history and Athletic Bilbao were on course to emulate the feat. The Basque football identity had always been a crucial part of the national side's style of play and, for many, a reason why they regularly failed. The first time *La Roja* attended an international tournament it was mainly comprised of Basque players.

It was during the 1920 Olympics, that the *La Furia* nickname was born, as players behaved more like charging bulls rather than footballers. The Fury was set as the national template for decades. Players were expected to be tough, hard-tackling and uncompromising. Football in Euskadi was essentially played like in Britain with players more prone to excel under a direct style than the more talented and creative footballers from the sunny western and southern regions. Even Franco, who loathed the idea of a Basque national identity, was known to press for the national side to follow their no-nonsense attitude.

Spain turned its back on its most talented players and as time went by it also became a victim of the constant internal feuds between Real Madrid and Barcelona. For one reason or another, they never delivered. Exceptions happened, of course. They famously beat England in the 1950 World Cup but then ended last in the final group stage. Spain would not take part in the following two tournaments, and when their most talented side ever arrived in Chile for the 1962 edition, issues between national coach Helenio Herrera and most of the all-star Real Madrid players, alongside Alfredo di Stéfano's late injury, meant they were out in the group stage, beaten by eventual finalists Brazil and Czechoslovakia. Over the following four World Cups, Spain would qualify twice, never progressing from the first round.

There was a sign of hope in 1964 with a triumph at the second edition of the Euros. It was a tense political affair. The team had walked out four years before because Franco refused to play against the Soviet Union. When the two nations qualified for the 1964 final four, many within his government urged him to do the same. It was a period when Spain was starting to open itself more on the international stage and tourism was already an important economic sector, so Franco listened to his most prudent advisors and allowed the tournament to proceed. They hosted the finals and won against the Soviets in Madrid, the perfect opportunity for the fascist dictator to gloat. It would be a one-off though. By the time the 1982 World Cup was approaching few felt success might finally come their way.

Political unrest from nationalist movements meant the national side was seeded in Valencia, which was supposed to be a safe ground. Football historian Alberto López Frau recalls how shambolic the preparation for the finals was. 'To take players away from the media frenzy, the Federation sent the squad to train in the Pyrenees, where the temperature was around 14º, nothing like they would find in Valencia, where it was double that, alongside the terrible humidity. Players failed to adapt and never looked fit.'

There was something else that had everyone on their nerves. 'The previous year Quini, Spain's star striker, had been kidnapped and there was a failed coup attempt on Congress, so everybody was extremely nervous something could happen during the World Cup,' the historian remarks. 'Players, especially from Real Sociedad and Athletic Bilbao, had bodyguards 24/7. The squad was terrified of the threats from the Basque terrorist movement ETA and they couldn't cope emotionally.' The side was supposed to have enjoyed a lucky draw. Instead, they were matched by Honduras, had a controversial late penalty in their favour at the last moment against Yugoslavia and proceeded to lose against Northern Ireland. Miraculously they still qualified for the second group stage, moving to Madrid, but proved unable to beat England and West Germany. Supporters were in dismay and many players were never called up again. The 1982 World Cup is a tournament that brings back good memories to many football supporters but not in Spain. Only Naranjito, the tournament mascot and one of the great symbols of the decade, steals back a smile. The same could be said of Manuel Cáceres, a Valencian supporter who became a local celebrity by playing the bass drum during the group stage in Mestalla. Manolo 'del Bombo' became one of the most recognisable football supporters in the world and spent the next 30 years following the national side wherever they went. A time when Spain became famed for the following 20 years as being one of the unluckiest sides in international football.

In 1983 a much-changed side qualified for the Euros finals but only just. Needing to beat Malta in Seville by 11 clear goals to go through at the expense of the Netherlands, they won 12-1 with a very much-needed late goal. José Angel de la Casa, the beloved RTVE commentator, brought the country to tears with his famous cry, 'Gol de Señor,' that served as an appetiser for what was to come. During the finals Spain were never able to play beautiful football, still too much constrained by the *Furia* mentality, but scraped through the group stage and ousted the crowd-pleasing Denmark in a penalty shoot-out. Luis Arconada, hero of the semi-final, floundered at a poor Michel Platini free kick and France came out victors in the final played in Paris.

Two years later, after again thrashing the Danish Dynamite in the last 16 of the Mexico World Cup, Spain were sent home by losing a penalty shoot-out against Belgium. By then the young *Quinta del Buitre* generation was starting to attract attention but, unlike at Real Madrid, they never fully unlocked their potential with the national side. Author Sergio Vilariño believes their lack of international success had everything to do with poor management. 'The 1986 side was the best of that period and Spain seemed unlucky, but that generation suffered the tactical limitations of both national managers. In 1988 Miguel Muñoz should have done the same as Lobanovsky by playing a starting XI of Real Madrid players but, instead, tried to please everyone and it didn't work out.' Soviet Union coach Valeriy Lobanovsky had filled his team with players from his former club side, Dinamo Kyiv, and reached the final, losing to the Netherlands. 'Luis Suárez, who then took the helm, decided to play with a *libero* that disrupted the attacking movement too much. Despite the battles with the press, the truth is that those players always seemed to lack something. Spain wasn't a winning nation then and at the very first sight of trouble everything fell apart like a house of cards.'

In 1992, Javier Clemente, who had led Bilbao to back-to-back league titles, was appointed national coach. It was the last hurrah of the Fury and, once again, they proved unlucky. A Tassoti elbow inside the box left Luis Enrique's nose broken during a tense quarter-final against Italy in the 1994 World Cup. Spain screamed for a penalty and red card that were never forthcoming. They also left the Euros 96 with complaints against the refereeing during the last eight against England. Despite Johan Cruyff's influence in Spanish football, already clear by then, Clemente remained faithful to the old-school playbook of *La Furia* until a very depressing end at the 1998 World Cup.

José António Camacho, who had been a no-nonsense defender in his playing days, believed in many of Fury's values but had in his hands such a talented squad that he began to take things differently. It still wasn't enough. Whether it was Raúl's missed penalty against France during Euro 2000 or several scandalous refereeing decisions in the last eight of the 2002 World Cup against the hosts South Korea, everything seemed to go wrong. For López Frau that 2002 squad was the side that could have gone all the way. 'It was a strange World Cup and Spain was a much better side than Germany, who would then play the Koreans in the semis. There were already a lot of quality players and the team was performing well but sadly it wasn't to be.'

By the turn of the millennium Spain was a much different country than it had been in 1982 but there were still issues unresolved. Terrorism was still a menace, the economic boom was based on the growth of low-cost tourism, there was already a housing bubble fueled by powerful corruption networks that would be exposed years in the future and an ever-present political tension between the central state and the different regional nations. Nationalism became the elephant in the room, more so when the regional federations started to play friendly matches against other countries to raise awareness for their political agenda. *La Roja* became seen as another political weapon, despised by those who pressed for more autonomy or full independence and defended by those who wanted to establish a more powerful central state. So many blunders had Spanish supporters believing they just weren't good enough. It took a group of young players with everything to prove and a hardened veteran ready for a showdown to demonstrate how wonderful Spain could be as a nation if everyone set aside their differences for a long-standing common desire: winning.

* * *

While former national coach José António Camacho screamed his lungs out on live TV, the man who changed Spain's perception of itself as a winning nation was celebrating, shirt off, arms wide out. 'Iniesta de mi vida!' remains today the most iconic moment in Spanish television history. Still, the protagonist wasn't aware of anything other than showing the world what he had painted, with the help of his team-mates, on a white T-shirt: 'Dani Jarque always with us'. Spain was minutes away from winning their first World Cup and all Andrés Iniesta was thinking about was how his best friend should have been there. Only, he wasn't. Since they both started playing in Spain's youth ranks, Jarque – later Espanyol's team captain – became a long-time friend. He had passed away less than a year before, a victim of heart failure after a training session. His death, alongside an injury that tormented him for the entire season, led Iniesta to an emotional breakdown. Few knew about it. His facial expression, a child-like kind of joy, told another story. He had come to represent how Spain seemed to make everybody happy. You didn't have to be Spanish, only to love the game. Jarque's deserved homage was also a throwback to the main reason why Spain were World Champions. Many believed they started to change their football history when they won the 2008 Euros. Yet, it all began a decade before when a generation of formidable players bonded at youth-team tournaments and started to collect silverware at every opportunity.

Iker Casillas was the one who lifted the treble of trophies won during that cycle. Alongside Xavi Hernández, he was also one of the first youth internationals to experience winning consecutive tournaments for his country. In 1997 Spain won the under-16 Euros. Two years later that same generation was under-20 World Champions. It was the first World Cup triumph at any level for Spanish football. They already had minor wins in younger categories, but that moment sounded the alarm inside the Football Federation about the potential of that generation. Over the following years, trophies kept on coming at an astonishing pace, both at club and international level. Since Deportivo Alavés' defeat against Liverpool in the 2001 UEFA Cup Final no Spanish club or national side who reached a final lost: 29 matches played, 29 won. The Spanish Federation understood they had established the right path, by tracking the best under-15 talents around the country, calling them up regularly for get-togethers and bonding players to a common moral code of conduct later embodied by that all-winning side. Rivals on the pitch, many of those players became close friends. Yet, while many believed Spain were on their way to doing something big, something was still missing at the senior level. After failing spectacularly in 2004, there were high hopes for what would happen in the following World Cup. A promising group stage ended when Zinedine Zidane sealed their fate. Worst still, the qualifying stages for the following Euros were not going according to plan. Something had to be done and national coach Luis Aragonés knew exactly what to do and the price it would take.

No man was ever as vilified and attacked by the Spanish sporting press as Aragonés. Almost until the very last second of his stint as national manager, he was the victim of a coordinated hate campaign that showed how few in the press cared about the national side. Known as the Wise Man of Hortaleza, a nickname he detested, Aragonés was the perfect representation of what Spanish managers were all about until the turn of the millennium. Madrid-born, he was a talented footballer, captaining his beloved Atlético de Madrid to their first European Cup Final. When Vicente Calderón decided to sack their Argentine manager Juan Carlos Lorenzo the following season, he proposed to the then-skipper that he should lead the way.

Uncertain, Aragonés accepted the task and famously forced his former team-mates from then on to address him by the formal '*usted*' instead of the common '*tu*'. He was never an inventive tactical manager but he also wasn't just a great motivator. He knew all the tricks in the book, telling his players to call referees by their first name to gain familiarity or to know which rival player was more likely to get himself out of the game if harassed properly. Like most Spanish managers of his days, Aragonés had a great ability to adapt, playing on the counter during some periods of his career, and trying to have more of the ball when he saw he had the players to do so. He was also extremely emotional and raucous. Twice on the brink of retirement after suffering emotional breakdowns, he became the first manager to speak publicly about the importance of psychological assistance. His hardcore working-class values were imprinted all over his man management but in more than 30 years he had also won just one league title in 1977 and three cups. When appointed national manager, in 2004, few believed he would be the man guiding Spain to glory. Thankfully, he was one of the few. 'If I don't win anything with these players I'm a fool,' he claimed. Time would prove him to be nothing short of a genius.

In September of 2006, after losing away against Northern Ireland and Sweden, Aragonés decided Raúl González's time with the national side was up. The hero of Real Madrid, Spain's famed number 7, had been an undisputed figure for almost a decade, besides serving as team captain. The manager believed Raúl's leadership and the group of players that faithfully surrounded him undermined the affirmation of that promising generation he was trying to call up. Some managers in the past had suffered attacks from the press whenever they decided to exclude Real Madrid idols but none so violently as he did. For more than a year and a half, every week, newspapers, TV and radio shows called for Raúl to return and Aragonés to be sacked. For a while, his decision seemed to backfire as Spain played poorly. Then, *La Roja* visited Denmark in a European Championship qualifier and put on a memorable display that ended up in an undisputable 3-1 victory. After that, the side never looked back even if they felt betrayed. At every home match, supporters verbally abused both the manager and the players. Not even a joint press conference alongside the Real Madrid club captain was enough to calm things down.

When Spain left for Austria in June, many in the squad felt everyone expected them to fail. Instead of undermining morale, it only served to boost it. Aragonés had not only excluded Raúl but also many players who had underperformed, paving the way for a complete revamp in attitude. Out were the last gasps of the *La Furia* mentality, in came the love for the ball and the passing culture, even before Guardiola made it world-famous at Barcelona. Xabi Alonso, David Silva, Cesc Fàbregas, Andrés Iniesta, Xavi Hernàndez and Marcos Senna provided quality and tactical awareness. David Villa and Fernando Torres combined perfectly in attack and there were a lot of young talented low-profile options on the bench, like Santi Cazorla or Ruben de la Red.

Aragonés preferred a 4-4-2 with attacking midfielders playing wide, creating multiple passing associations that drove rivals mad. Spain routed their group-stage opponents, beating Russia, Sweden and Greece, showing quality and character alike. Then came world champions Italy. *La Roja* had never won an official match against the Italian side at senior level, a track that went back to the 1934 World Cup right up until that Luis Enrique bloody nose in Boston. But in 2001 a team led by Fernando Torres and Andrés Iniesta defeated the Italian under-16s in a penalty shoot-out during the last eight of that year's Euros, which they won. As it became clear the match in Vienna would be also decided by spot kicks, players from both sides were aware of the fact. Not so at home, where many lived terrified of the famous last-eight curse, a term coined by the press referring to the number of times the Spanish were out at that stage. As the showdown began, both Iker Casillas and Gianluigi Buffon – the world's two greatest goalkeepers – had already saved a shot each when Antonio Di Natale's strike was stopped by Spain's captain. Fàbregas, who like Cazorla before him had never taken a penalty, coolly sent the ball easily past Buffon and unleashed Spain from all its traumas.

The semi-final, a repeat of the match against Russia, became the most memorable display of that period. Not even the early injury to David Villa, the side's most prolific scorer, tainted a masterful night, the 3-0 win planting the seed of what Spanish football would be all about. The final, played at the Praterstadion, pitted *La Roja* against Germany, who showed more composure in the early stages of the match. With 15 minutes on the clock, Spain were already dictating the tempo. Aragonés, who knew already that he was leaving, reminded the players he had promised to take them to the final. Now it was up to them. '*Ganar, ganar y ganar*' had been forever his motto and it became the players', a collective battle cry before each match. Win, win and win. When, in the 33rd minute, Xavi Hernández spotted Fernando Torres moving behind Philiph Lahm, everyone knew what was about to happen. The ball left the boot of the midfield maestro and was picked up by 'El Niño' just as goalkeeper Jens Lehmann moved forward, granting him enough space to put it in the net. It was enough. Spain had finally won. History was about to change drastically.

Celebrations upon their return showed a side of Spain nobody knew. The same people who abused the squad took to the streets to party. In Madrid, more than a million people followed the bus parade. Suddenly, optimism was in the air. José Luis Rodriguez Zapatero's socialist party had just won a second term, pressing for a time of important social advances and political stability. ETA's killing days were over and Spain was living the last breaths of an economic boom that would soon collapse when the housing bubble financial crisis hit the country.

During those years the nation enjoyed one of its most open-minded periods. Not just because of the expansion of tourism, but also in media, culture and through packages of progressive legislation, that granted the LGTB+ movement their first rights, allowed women finally to abort and upgraded labour rights. People felt proud of who they were.

Pedro Almodóvar, Penélope Cruz and Javier Bardem's wins at the Oscars brought worldwide acclaim to the arts, and sports enjoyed a golden age, with the exploits of Rafael Nadal in tennis, Fernando Alonso in Formula One and the national basketball team, crowned world champions. The national football side's success was the only thing missing. Over the following four years, while the country plunged into a housing and financial crisis that brought back the conservatives to government, and with it more tension with nationalist movements and trade unions, the exploits of *La Roja* seemed to be all that was left of those golden years.

Vicente del Bosque had by then been named Aragonés' successor. If anyone could follow in the footsteps of a visionary it was him. He kept the legacy of his predecessor while making some minor but influential changes to the side by bringing in the likes of Gerard Piqué, Victor Valdés, Sergio Busquets, Pedro Rodriguez and Jesús Navas to an already star-packed side. He also moved to a more conventional 4-2-3-1 with Xavi playing in front of a midfield duo of Busquets and Alonso but the identity remained the same. Rivals by that time had become aware of how talented Spain were with the ball and many preferred to sit deep and wait for the counter. The debut at the South Africa 2010 World Cup was the perfect example. Spain dominated and had the most chances, but Switzerland scored with their only shot on target.

Back home, the press once again tried to dictate the manager's choices but found out that, much like Aragonés, Del Bosque was not to be messed around with. Proud son of a left-wing believer, Del Bosque grew up to be a working-class hero, a man with a range of human values second to none. He was part of the first trade union for footballers while Franco was still alive, and after being unfairly sacked from Real Madrid, waited for his opportunity to come. Spain's streak of back-to-back trophies owed much to his ability to sail storms unscathed. Wins over the next two group-stage games and versus Portugal in the last 16 anticipated a showdown against Paraguay. It was a make-or-break moment when Casillas saved an Oscar Cardozo penalty kick before Spain scored the winner. They might not have been playing as fluently as they did under Aragonés but they remained faithful to his philosophy. In the semis, the Germans were once again the opponents, and Carles Puyol, who sustained an injury that almost prevented him from playing, scored the winner with a thunderous header. The Catalan was not the most renowned player in the squad but represented the squad ethos like no other. A natural leader, for him it was all about hard work, providing a much-needed safety net in a defence that included the talented but often easily distracted Sergio Ramos and Gerard Piqué.

In the final, the hero of the hour was Iker Casillas. In a match poorly refereed by Howard Webb, who allowed a borderline violent approach from the Netherlands, the goalkeeper twice met Arjen Robben eye to eye and twice saved Spain from defeat. Then, at the end of extra time, all three substitutes Navas, Fàbregas and Torres, combined to outplay the Dutch and the ball ended at Iniesta's feet before crossing the line. It was the most important goal in the country's history. An avalanche of emotions quickly flourished. Casillas famously kissed his girlfriend, TV reporter, Sara Carbonero during his flash interview, much to the royal family's amusement, while Piqué went to celebrate with his future partner, Colombian superstar singer Shakira, whom he had met weeks before in Barcelona while recording the video clip for the tournament's official anthem, 'Waka-Waka'.

Spain would go on to win the Euros in 2012 as well. Success might have felt inevitable, as the side was playing its best football, sometimes reaching almost 80 per cent of possession of the ball. As Vicente del Bosque explains, 'We didn't want to make mistakes and for that you need the ball, but we also played sides who just sat deep, and we had no choice but to keep playing until we found our moment. For supporters, it might have looked less enthusiastic because we didn't take many shots on goal, but it was just a mix of the type of players we had and the challenges posed.' Yet, things might have turned out quite differently as they were on the brink of losing what had taken them there in the first place: team spirit.

During the 2011 *El Clásico* rumble, the tension built by José Mourinho affected the squad, and many players, friends for years, stopped talking to one another. Mourinho's all-out war attitude almost broke that collective spirit but, finally, both Casillas and Xavi found a way to make peace for the common good. It cost the goalkeeper his place in Real Madrid's goal but helped Spain to win the Euros. After beating France and surviving a tense goalless semi-final against Portugal, the Spanish national side signed off with the biggest-ever win in a final, a 4-0 routing of old foes Italy in Kyiv. Villa's injury and Torres's physical condition allowed Del Bosque to perfect Guardiola's concept of a false nine, deploying six midfielders with Fàbregas rooming freely in attack. 'Titles define our place in history, but from my days as national manager, the most important thing is the values we stood for,' said Del Bosque, one of the most decorated managers in the game. 'In 114 matches we only once had a player sent off and during those difficult months that followed the Madrid-Barça clashes, players found a way to get back together and team spirit prevailed. Nothing made me prouder.'

During that time, Spain became one of the most dominant national sides ever. Perhaps only the 1970 Brazil side has probably been as admired. Not only did they win a treble, but they also popularised a style of play that defined a generation. When Aragonés first took the side to glory the country was living the last breaths of a golden era. By the time Casillas lifted that same trophy in Ukraine, they were in an economic and social nightmare. Yet, all those triumphs had changed the national mentality. Inspired by them, thousands took to the streets to protest, ending up setting up new political parties who became decisive in the forthcoming elections. Within years, under Pedro Sánchez's leadership, the country climbed back from the economic and social pit once again, resurrecting an old-forgotten feeling of self-pleasure. More than just football memories, those glorious summer nights tattooed forever in the Spanish society mindset the old Aragonés battle cry: win, win and win again.

EVEN MORE WHEN WE LOSE

FOOTBALL IS about more than winning or losing; some clubs represent that spirit better than others. In a country as complex as Spain, some herald the flag of a nation or a region, others have learned to survive within a biased society, while some have learned the hard way that the game is more about belonging than results. Time and time again football has proven to be a mirror for the world that surrounds us, whether in the middle of the Atlantic, under the dying heat of Andalusia, in a forgotten corner of Barcelona or a valley up in the north. These clubs may not be the most celebrated worldwide when you first think about football in Spain, but they are certainly those who better represent how it is to be faithful to their roots and beliefs. For they have taken to heart Bill Shankly's iconic stance, that football is much more important than life or death. It has come to be what defines them.

* * *

If you ever had to sum up the passionate spirit of Spanish football, there is only one possible answer: Real Betis Balompié.

There is nothing quite like Betis. There probably never will be. Here is a football club that won the league once, almost a century ago, and three cup trophies, one for a generation since the late 1970s. It's a side that shares a city with a club that recently became a multiple continental cup winner. And yet, despite all of that, it commands love, undying devotion and a sense of belonging few could aspire to in European football. Betis is more than just the biggest club in Andalusia. They are likely Spain's fourth-best supported side, with more members than clubs who have won more titles or played in more continental finals. Winning is not the point. Defeat is. There is only one club in the world who takes pride in it. 'Viva el Betis manque pierda' became the club's motto during the worst time in their history when, once league champions, they were forced to wander in the third tier for almost a decade. 'Long live Betis, even more when we lose' became not only a crowd anthem. It came to define them much in the same way that 'You'll Never Walk Alone' has done for Liverpool. A club that accepts suffering and defeat is part of the game. By embracing it, by making it a part of their DNA, they removed the pain and stuck with what mattered the most: belonging.

Seville is known as the 'frying pan of Spain' with good reason. It hardly ever rains, and it's rarely cold even in wintertime. Heat defines everything. People's relaxed sense of humour and their love for street life contrast deeply with their love-or-hate identity. For Andalusians, there is hardly ever a middle ground. It's like that with religion, politics, art and, of course, football. When they fall in love, they do it like no one else. That alone doesn't explain why Real Betis is such a special club, but it helps. Walk around Triana, Seville's most well-known working-class neighbourhood, and you'll understand how much the club means. Streets are crowded in green and white. Bars, shops and even cars are usually decorated with Betis scarves or flags. Some supporters will even try to explain to you that the city of Seville has one football club – their rivals – and one religion: the *Verdiblancos*.

Betis colours are the same as Andalusia's flag. With time the club became the most popular in the region. Truth is they were the first in Spain ever to wear green and white, because of Celtic. 'It was a trip to Glasgow that kick-started the whole thing,' says Manolo Rodriguez, author and journalist, who is also patron of the Betis Foundation and the person who best knows the club's history. 'During its early days, when the club was still known as Sevilla Balompié, Manuel Ramos Asensio, their first club captain, travelled to Glasgow and got together with some of his former acquaintances from his student days at St Joséph's College, run by Brother Wilfred, who was also the founder of Celtic. Back then the club played in vertical green and white stripes, so Asensio decided to bring back to Seville some of those shirts that were first used in a match in 1910.' At first, it was merely an alternative kit, but when Blas Infante, the left-wing politician who defined the concept of Andalusian political identity during the Ronda Assembly of 1918, decided that the region's flag should bear the green and white colours, the club opted to wear it as their primary kit; 1918 was also the year Ramos Asensio last played for the club. His legacy stayed on and set them apart. 'When we played against Celtic in 2021, the club invited Asensio's son, then 92 years old, to receive a standing ovation from the supporters. Ironically, neither side played in green and white that night,' remembers Rodriguez.

If their rivals Sevilla FC were initially a club connected with the well-to-do families of the city, Betis's beginnings couldn't have been humbler. The club was a fusion between Sevilla Balompié and Betis Football Club, set up by former Sevilla members discontented with the course the club was taking by barring members from the working class. Since their origins, Betis – the Roman name for the Guadalquivir river – had already established their specialness. They would embrace supporters from every social background while becoming key in unveiling the Spanish word for football. Sevilla Balompié's founders had written to some of Spain's most illustrious scholars to ask for the correct translation of the commonly used British term foot-ball, as they wanted the club name to have a national imprint. Balompié – ball in the foot – was Mariano de Cavia's answer, later registered by the Royal Spanish Academy as the only accepted form, despite the popularisation of the anglicised *fútbol*. It was adopted in the club's name when both sides agreed to a fusion under the patronage of King Alfonso XIII, thus becoming Real Betis Balompié.

By then already a well-known side, they were forced to live under the shadow of their better-funded neighbours until the early 1930s. The first seasons of the newly created football league had been played without any side south of Madrid. In 1932, Betis – who had also been the first Andalusian club to play the cup final the previous season – became the first southern side to get promoted. While supporters partied for days, club chairman José Ignacio Mantecón had his eyes on a bigger prize, replacing crowd favourite Emilio Sempere with Patrick O'Connell. With that bold move Mantecón – who would later help thousands to leave Spain at the end of the Civil War before being forced to exile in Mexico where he died – forever changed the club's history.

Born in Dublin, O'Connell enjoyed an illustrious career in English football as a player, signing in 1914 for Manchester United. He famously took part in the infamous match-fixing scandal between the Red Devils and Liverpool. After the war, O'Connell moved to Santander, to replace Fred Pentland who was on his way to Bilbao. An icon for Racing supporters over the following decade, he arrived in Seville amid great expectations. O'Connell immediately fell in love with the city, stating it was a place where people lived like they were about to die the next day. His Irish personality connected with the locals, and he famously was seen joining supporters in dinners and night-long poker matches. During the day the Irishman revamped training methods, brought a new tactical approach and, against all odds, guided Betis to their sole league title in 1934/35. The *Verdiblancos* fought neck and neck with Madrid CF – during the years of the II Republic, all clubs dropped Real from their names – and reached the final day of the season in need of a win against O'Connell's former club. Some Madrid journalists claimed he was seen visiting Racing players the night before the match, but Betis never seemed in need of special help. Five goals without reply proved enough to clinch the title before the side embarked on a long bus journey home. The crowd, in the middle of the famed Feria de Abril celebrations, was eager to party alongside Don Patricio, the name O'Connell went by, without knowing he was on his way to coach Barcelona. Betis became only the fourth different club to win the league and, although they have never won it again since, there's no denying that year's historical triumph turned them into Spanish football royalty. What came next might not have looked so glorious in retrospect but made them the well-loved club they are today.

'The "*Manque pierda*" tag goes beyond football, it's a sense of belonging that can be felt in any aspect of life. I will love you even more when you lose,' Manolo Rodriguez adds proudly. 'It was first mentioned in a song by the *peña* Puerta de Carne – *peñas* are the organised supporter groups in Spain – during the harsh years the club spent in the third division. Those were the days that defined the club identity.' The league title came with a heavy financial cost, and the destruction of the recently acquired ground of the Seville Exhibit at Heliopolis during the Civil War condemned Betis to an unexpected relegation in 1940.

Things were so bad that the club fell into the third tier and for almost a decade they couldn't get themselves promoted despite the massive public show of support of their fans who moved around Spain by the thousands on away days, popularly known as the Green Marches. 'Many wrongly stated the expression means Betis supporters have learned to accept defeat as normal. It's the other way around. It's a cry for hope, a rebellious spirit that knows better days will come and until then our love for the club will remain untouched,' says Rodriguez.

That spirit made Betis what they are today. There are clubs defined by the trophies they win or the support they gather. Real Betis have both won silverware and boast a huge fanbase. But the most important thing they have is their hardcore sense of belonging. It's not just a philosophical stance as they have shown it time and time again. During the years Betis were suffering in the lower leagues, the terrible economic reality of Franco's policies drove almost two million Andalusians away from their homes to other parts of Spain and Europe. Most settled in the Basque Country and Catalonia. They had few possessions to take but the love for their club colours went with them. Many were working-class Betis supporters, turning them into a nationwide institution. As Manolo Rodriguez says, 'If there is something that unites Andalusians wherever they are it is their devotion to the Virgin of Rocío. After that, their love for Betis. When I travel around Spain it never ceases to surprise me the number of supporters who show up. Many are the grandsons and great-grandsons of those forced to leave. Many years have gone by, but they remained faithful to their ancestors' club. It is their way of keeping the family spirit alive.'

Few represent that connection better than Héctor Bellerín. The former Arsenal right-back was born in Barcelona from an Andalusian family who had moved there a generation before in search of a better life. His father is a diehard Betis supporter and, although Bellerín became a Barcelona fan and a La Masía graduate himself before moving to London, he ended up asking the Gunners for a transfer to Seville, so he could play for the club his family had supported for generations. That is the emotional power Real Betis commands, something they are proud of. Over the years the Benito Villamarín stadium – one of the most beautiful football grounds in European football, named after the club's most influential and beloved chairman – has been home to many celebrity supporters, capable of doing the craziest things to show their love for the side. You can always expect the unexpected. It came to a point where they ended up adopting a chant that goes 'They say we are dead crazy'. They are, in a good way.

It's late September, which means Seville is still enjoying its summer weather. It's almost 29º Celsius and people start to flock around the stadium to enjoy the last hours in the sun with a beer in hand, dressed up for the occasion. As with every home match, the Villamariin is packed and exhilarating with a light of its own. It is a stadium that takes you back in time, old concrete stands mixed with the ever-present green and white all around. If they were a club more known around the world it would surely become a place of pilgrimage as happens with other iconic grounds all over Europe. As the club anthem starts to sound, 50,000 people stand up and echo through Seville's night sky what their undying love is all about. Once the ball is kicked, thousands start to clap, but not in the way you would expect. Their hand movement throws you back to the old flamenco bars rather than to other football grounds. Here artistry comes first, always. The match is against Mallorca and, despite an early goal by former Tottenham man Giovanni Lo Celso, the Balearic side comes out winners with a late drama effort. Anywhere else disappointment would be massive but here supporters first find in their hearts the need to applaud the team's effort. They have their priorities clear in their minds. And despite the club having reached the best version of themselves for years, they know it will never be a bed of roses. After all, Andalusians are used to suffering. They are one of the poorest regions in the European Union and, despite its remarkable history and overwhelming cultural legacy, sometimes all they have left is their sense of humour. The *guasa*, or banter, provides entertainment and helps to forget the day-to-day hardships.

Author Colin Millar, who has written about the club in his book *The Frying Pan of Spain*, sums up the importance of the local culture in the club's identity: 'Betis embody Andalusia, certainly in the minds of their fans. They have that self-expression, joy, life, the '*guasa*' always winding others up in a joking way. It's very, very Betis as is that sense of "otherness". Of being different.' Football is one of the best ways to express that sense of humour and Betis supporters have lived that over the years, whether through the traditional local hat used by Nigerian star George Finidi in each goal celebration or the flamboyant step-overs of Brazilian legend Denilson, who became the most expensive football player in the world when he signed for the club. They both arrived in the late 1990s, a time when Real Betis once again felt great.

Under the guidance of Lorenzo Serra Ferrer, the side became regulars in the top half of the first division and were on the brink of reaching a Cup Winners' Cup Final, only to be beaten by Chelsea in the 1998 edition. Then, the ambition of their swashbuckling chairman Manuel Ruiz de Lopera almost took them back to the bottom of the pit once again, although they quickly rose from the ashes. During that short stint, the fans' never-fading love was rewarded with the arrival of the man who became their greatest-ever footballer. Because if Real Betis is a club of passion, banter and belonging there's only one person who represents that identity to the core.

Joaquín Sánchez is a living legend and not just to Betis supporters. One of the greatest wingers ever to grace the

Spanish game, Joaquín played professional football for more than two decades, becoming one of the few world-class players who rejected a move to the Premier League just to enjoy life in his native country. His footballing qualities alone would have sufficed to make him one of the most influential players in Spanish football, but Joaquín is more than that. A practical joker known for his constant banter, he also came to represent the Andalusian way of life like no other sportsman. He's the incarnation of the *guasa* spirit and the most passionate player ever to wear the Betis shirt. When he was promoted to the first team, Betis were playing in the second division and in need of an inspirational figure. Five years on Joaquín was guiding them to Champions League football and their first Copa del Rey win in decades. He also rose to the ranks of the national side, for whom he earned more than 50 caps, giving an assist for forward Fernando Morientes to net a wrongly disallowed goal that prevented Spain from progressing to the semi-finals of the 2002 World Cup.

By the time Luis Aragonés decided to pave the way for a fresher set of players, he was one of those left out but, by all accounts, he should have been there for the Euro 2008 glory run. By then, the El Puerto de Santa Maria-born winger had moved first to Valencia, and then to Málaga and Fiorentina. In 2015, Joaquín returned home for a second stint, which turned out to be a fairy tale. Against all odds, he won the cup again before retiring. 'I could never express what those two nights mean to me,' Joaquín says. 'To win the cup in 2005, my first-ever professional triumph with this club, was something I dreamt of since I was a kid. That night at the Vicente Calderón was just unforgettable. The setting, the sensational team spirit we forged, and everything that happened on the pitch. And then, out of the blue, 17 years later, to be able to end my career with another trophy, in Seville, knowing the end was near, it was special.'

Joaquín is part of the club's history, the only one who won two of the club's four trophies. He embodies it like no other. 'It is hard to explain to people what Betis is about. For me, above all else, it's a privilege and pride to have been able to wear the club's shirt and become a club legend alongside so many great players that Betis had during its history. It made me feel special.' Now a club ambassador and shareholder, the former winger knows the real importance of Betis in Spanish football. 'I think people love Betis because of what we represent. We are usually the second club for most supporters in Spain, and that probably is because we are perceived as a joyful and passionate side. Wherever I go it seems I always bump into Betis supporters, and for a club that has won so little, who have suffered so much, it's incredible how much love we still get from everyone.'

Nono Espinar is one of those supporters who, despite being born in Jaén, a province in northern Andalusia, and living in Madrid, is as passionate for the club as if he spent his days in Triana. 'I was born in a family of *Béticos* and that passion has been with me since I was a kid. For Andalusians, whether you are from Seville or not, Betis represents the best we have to offer to the world and, even when you are away and not able to go to the ground every week, that sense of belonging and love is inside you every day of your life.' When Betis won the 2022 Copa del Rey final that feeling was well felt in Spain, with spontaneous celebrations all around when Joaquín lifted the trophy to the Seville skies.

The league triumph of Patrick O'Connell's side might be a distant memory and hard to replicate but over the past decades, the *Verdiblancos* found in the cup a particular solace. The first time they won the trophy in 1977 was also, for Manolo Rodriguez, the most important moment in the club's modern history. For those who endured the hardships of the previous decades, it was a well-deserved albeit unexpected joy.

It was the first edition after Franco's death, and Betis faced favourites Athletic Bilbao in Madrid. The side coached by Basque manager Rafael Iriondo had in its ranks players who still today are worshipped by Betis supporters and deservedly so. Players like José Esnaola, Francisco Bizcocho, António Biosca, Júlio Cardeñosa and Rafael Gordillo – one of the greatest Spanish players ever and now chairman of the club Foundation – embodied the supporter's enduring spirit in a tense match decided on penalties. 'I would love to see Betis win the Champions League,' says Rodriguez, 'but no triumph will be as important as the 1977 win. I was 18 and felt the joy around me of those who had endured the hard times. People who felt everything had been worthwhile and as we were entering a new democratic period in Spain, it felt appropriate that an underdog like Betis came out victors in the end.'

In 2005, more than 20,000 Betis supporters took again the road to the Vicente Calderón stadium to see their side beat Osasuna with an effort late in extra time by academy graduate Dani. It took the club almost two decades to play another cup final, and when Betis faced Valencia in Seville's La Cartuja, it seemed impossible to believe they would not run out winners. Yet, Betis is a club all about suffering and despite playing almost at home, Borja Iglesias's early goal was soon cancelled out, and the match ended in a draw and, a penalty shoot-out. Memories of 1977 came back to those who had lived that long night in Madrid. Hundreds couldn't cope with the pressure and left the stands to wander in the inside corridors of the ground. Joaquín, of course, scored one of the penalties. With only Valencia's Yannis Musah missing his chance, responsibility came to Juan Miranda, an academy graduate defender who had been in the stands alongside his father for the 2005 final. Making true the dream of every kid in town, he knocked the ball into the net and drove the crowd to ecstasy.

Many knew then and there that they would probably have to wait a decade or two to lift another trophy. Or perhaps not. Real Betis might have a long-standing history of suffering and resistance, but the club is evolving under the presidency of Ángel Haro. After more than a decade of unrest due to former chairman Ruiz de Lopera's unlawful manoeuvres, club members have now recovered majority control and fully support the work done by the board. The club's values and memories are well preserved, and the future lies in the hands of former legends such as Gordillo or Joaquín, who many expect will become chairman one day.

Manuel Pellegrini's managerial stint has been one of sporting success and institutional calm, something the club missed desperately. They were able to sign world-class players such as Nabil Fekir, Giovanni Lo Celso and Isco Alarcón, who brought a greater artistic drive to their footballing sides. The Benito Villamarín is also set to be renewed, the club has expanded their training facilities and the work done by its Foundation has made them even more important within Andalusian society. With more than 50,000 season tickets sold – with 30,000 club members on a waiting list – supporters' devotion is at an all-time high.

Many believe that Real Betis have all it takes to become one of the strongest clubs in Spanish football and yet, ask any diehard fans and they will tell you it doesn't matter. They care only if they live for the club to see another day. There is no other football club with a soul as big as theirs in European football and if you doubt it, take the next flight to Seville and see for yourself. As midnight approaches in the undying Andalusian heat, with supporters heading home, one last look back to that mystical ground captures the last artificial lights being turned off in an already empty Villamarín. It represents to perfection the sense that, even in their darkest hour, Bétis have always found redemption. Spanish football is a place full of great histories but the endless passion of the *Verdiblancos* comes second to none. Win or lose.

* * *

What is left when your neighbour is one of the biggest giants in the history of the game? Go even more local. As FC Barcelona became an international juggernaut, their city rivals RCD Espanyol came to represent, against what many may think, the broader definition of what it means to be Catalan. Despite the regional media blackout and lack of international recognition, they found in their local roots their meaning for existence.

RCD Espanyol was once called Real Español, which helps to understand the nature of their singularity in Barcelona. They not only identified with Spain as a nation – for many in Catalonia an abomination – but also embraced the royal family patronage. Espanyol was the first Spanish football club with an all-exclusive national identity when English, Scots and other European foreigners were still seen as key figures in any sporting project. The name was not an opposition to Catalonia, as Barcelona supporters tend to tell you, but pride in sticking with local players when others, like Barça, were founded by foreigners. In time they would also become the club that better represented the complex Catalan society. Historically they boast more local players on their ranks, have one of the most important youth set-ups in the land and yet, despite that, are still seen as aliens to those who have embraced the narrative of their local rival as the sole representatives of what it means to be from Catalonia. Traditionally at Espanyol's ground you can see sitting side by side supporters with the Spanish flag alongside others with the *Estelada*, the symbol of an independent Catalan state. They are the most inclusive football institution in the region, so much so that even the high-profile speaker in Congress for the left-wing pro-independence party Esquerra Republicana, Gabriel Rufián, is a well-known Espanyol supporter. Rufián is one of many who believe that supporting Catalonia is not exclusive to Barcelona fans. A member of a group that had accepted their fate, to be a proud minority. A symbol of social, political and emotional resistance to the all-absorbing Barça universe.

That has been an ever-present spirit since the club's inception. Born in the well-to-do Sarriá district of Barcelona, the club happened to be because of the enthusiasm of local students for the game. It was also a stand in favour of local Catalan footballers. They turned out to be quite good, taking part in the first-ever edition of the Spanish Cup in 1903. Yet, the lack of available players when many moved abroad to follow up their studies meant Espanyol suffered a silent period that lasted until the 1920s, when their first cup win was followed by the inauguration of the Sarriá stadium and the arrival of Ricardo Zamora, Spain's greatest-ever goalkeeper, nicknamed 'The Divine One'. Zamora was one of history's best and one of its first icons. He starred in movies and advertising ads, was a key figure for the national side and inspired poets and musicians. His fame alone allowed him to be spared a tragic end when he was arrested at the beginning of the Civil War by Republican loyalists. His popularity not only prevented his execution but also allowed him to escape to France. He later returned as a figure acclaimed by Franco's regime and guided Atlético de Madrid to back-to-back league titles.

When Zamora first moved from Espanyol to Real Madrid, in the late 1920s, Barcelona had already established itself as the city's greatest institution, embracing its connection with Catalonia's cry for autonomy, while Espanyol kept a more conservative approach, refusing to mix politics with sports. Participants in the first-ever league tournament, the club was briefly forced to embrace a more local identity during the Republic years, changing its name to the Catalanised Club Esportiu Espanyol. They also suffered deeply during the Civil War, losing more players and club members on the battlefront than any other Spanish club. In 1940, back with the old Español designation, and against all odds, they won the first edition of the Generalissimo Cup, the new name given by the regime to the previously known Copa del Rey.

Many believed them to be a club affectionate to the new regime, but they were not. They did become the meeting point for those in Barcelona who believed Catalonia was as much part of Spain as Andalusia, but that never prevented many fierce nationalists from embracing their colours. Their officially neutral stance cost them dearly and even during the dictatorship years Espanyol was already a minority club within the city and region. On the pitch they were never as successful as Barça but maintained a high profile, playing in more La Liga editions than any other apart from Real Madrid, FC Barcelona, Athletic Bilbao and Valencia. Ladislao Kubala and Alfredo di Stéfano's playing days ended in Sarriá, something that, if it had happened today, would have meant seeing Lionel Messi and Cristiano Ronaldo both playing their trade in *Blanquiazul*. The club also boasted some brilliant local Catalan players and world-class internationals like Thomas Nkono, John Lauridsen and Mauricio Pochettino.

Yet, none were as beloved as their two most celebrated goalscorers. In the 1970s Rafael Marañon, born up north in Navarre, became famed for his prowess in front of goal, netting a record 111 times, one that stood for decades and earned him a move to Real Madrid. He was only rivalled when academy graduate Raúl Tamudo came along to become the club's modern poster-boy, a street-smart footballer, capable of scoring fantastic and unexpected goals. In the 2000 cup final, against Atlético Madrid, Tamudo craftily stole the ball from the hands of his former team-mate, goalkeeper Toni, while he was preparing to toss it forward, before opening the scoring. He became even more beloved by Espanyol and Real Madrid supporters alike when, seven years on, he netted a brace in a derby against Barcelona, allowing Real Madrid to complete an unexpected comeback to claim the league.

Espanyol never got as high as third, won four cup editions – losing other five finals – and even played in two UEFA Cup finals, both lost on penalties, against Bayer Leverkusen in 1988 and Sevilla in 2007. They are not the luckiest of clubs but are notorious survivors. Carlos Marañon, a well-known supporter and writer who is also the son of their greatest-ever forward, stresses how the club would have probably become more popular if only their resistance culture against their neighbours was praised as highly as Sankt Pauli's or Rayo Vallecano's. 'The way we live our identity is not considered politically correct if you compare it with other clubs that are more openly left-wing. We feel double-discriminated against because we are not accepted as part of the concept of a resistance club. It seems many have chosen legend over reality. Truthfully, we are as Catalan as you can be, so perhaps the best thing is not even to try to compete against what others have decided to think we are and go on with our lives, proving ourselves on the pitch.'

As Marañon points out, local media rarely pay much attention to the club. The same can be said of public institutions who have chosen Barcelona as their sole banner. The political *Procés* at the turn of the 2010s highlighted how alone Espanyol was. Not even changing back their name to Catalan made any difference. 'People understood the club's silence during those years as taking a stand against independence when it was just a coherent stance for an all-inclusive club,' Marañon adds. By then the *Pericos* had already moved from the old Sarriá – the same ground where the iconic match between Brazil and Italy was played in the

1982 World Cup – first to the Olympic stadium and then on to the outskirts of Cornella, just outside of Barcelona. With passion for the Catalan cause at an all-time high, the ground change didn't help either, forcing them to keep a low profile to surf the waves that took almost a decade to calm down. When they did, the investment of the City Group up north in Girona, the capital of a province that borders the French Pyrenees, provided a new challenge.

Football in Catalonia has always been a dance of two. Clubs like Gimnastic Tarragona, Lleida, Sabadell or Europa had been the sole representatives of the region apart from Barcelona and Espanyol yet together have played only 24 seasons of first-division football combined. Girona presents a different challenge. The club is on its way to its fifth season in La Liga and yet is already playing Champions League football, something Espanyol was never able to do. They count on important financial backers and a sound sporting structure while sitting in a provincial capital with a hardcore Catalan identity. Espanyol on the other hand have just been promoted from the second division – they went down the season before, never having stayed more than one year outside of La Liga – and are in the hands of foreign ownership who never quite figured out how to create a competitive side. Club supporters are among the most faithful in Spanish football – even if many share a special connection with Real Madrid, as they are the only ones who can topple their noisy neighbours – partly because they have no choice. Even they know the club is living in limbo.

On the one hand, they undoubtedly remain a historic force in Spanish football, yet the absence of regular European football or silverware has forced them to search for a new way to stay relevant, more than clinging to the concept of being different. Espanyol's identity has always been defined by where they are settled and not just by who they want to be.

Perhaps that is what is slowing them down. At some point, RCD Espanyol will have to decide if they are content with being just a resistance club or if they aspire to more. Girona's menace might open their eyes. Even if Barcelona will forever remain the giant of Catalonia, it is possible, with the right leadership, to create a competitive footballing project in their backyard. It is more of a question of when and how than if. Until then, *Pericos* will remain proud of their heritage and uniqueness if nothing else. They might have fewer things to celebrate than their city rivals, but you can't deny they also have found some joy by being themselves.

* * *

Spain is a country of passionate people wherever you look. But when it comes to passion there's no place like the Canary Islands. Sixty miles away from the West African shore lays an archipelago of seven main islands that mix African heritage and South American culture. Life there is lived differently. Despite being part of Spain for more than six centuries now, their culture and identity have more South American vibes than European. There's good reason for it. Located west of south Morocco, the Canaries were the last port of call for Cristobal Colón before he sailed to set sights on a new continent. Since then, they became the main hub of connection for the Spanish Armada in their travels between Seville and their American empire. That defined it as a place for travellers who happened to pass by, no strings attached. The local accent, the cultural heritage and even the physical aesthetics are a testament to a land that most continental Spanish were unaware of. Even their football clubs suffered, vetoed from taking part in any sort of continental competitions until the 1950s for logistical reasons. And things only changed because of Union Deportiva Las Palmas.

Of the main seven Canary Islands, Gran Canaria is not the largest nor the most populated but represents the ethos of the archipelago like no other. It's like a small continent in the middle of the Atlantic. Different climates and landscapes succeed frenetically through its shores and crossroads. The capital city of Las Palmas remains the most populated in the Canary Islands. For years football was played there between locals and British merchants, developing a style of players more similar in artistry to Brazilians and West Africans. However, the Canaries were too far away to be allowed to take part in continental football. Yet, the fame of their footballers had crossed the Atlantic waters by then and the most powerful clubs in the peninsula started to pick up their best players one by one – reality ill-received by the locals, who were fed up with being treated differently. It became the catalyst for five of Las Palmas' main clubs to sit down together and decide to join forces to press the authorities to grant them access to national competitions.

It was a difficult process since it meant erasing decades of local rivalries for the common good but, in the end, UD Las Palmas was formed in 1949, with the crests of the five clubs who paved the way for change proudly represented in the new badge. The following year the club was accepted in the second division, after beating all the continental third-division regional champions in a play-off. They were soon followed by their rivals from Santa Cruz de Tenerife, proving how strong local football was. History would remember Tenerife for its iconic side from the early 1990s yet, on broader terms, despite being more popular among the British expats who moved to the island to enjoy its weather, the club has never achieved the historical relevance of the side from Las Palmas. Nor did they suffer the heartful tragedies that became intertwined with its history.

With their customary yellow-and-blue Brazil-like kit, UD Las Palmas soon became the first club from the Canaries to play in La Liga. Come the late 1960s they surpringly stormed the top half. Coached by local legend Luis Molowny, a former European Cup winner with Real Madrid, Las Palmas finished third and then second to Real Madrid between 1967 and 1969. The club became synonymous with classy, artistic football, supported by thousands of fanatics who made the Insular stadium a hell for visitors. It seemed they were meant for greatness but instead, tragedy struck hard. Twice. Juan Guedes was one of the most talented players from the archipelago and was touted to become a Spanish legend. His love for the island spoke louder than his ambition and for years the cultured midfielder rejected moves to Real Madrid and Barcelona. What few would guess is that just shy of turning 30, Guedes was diagnosed with cancer. He passed away months later, in January of 1971, a devastating blow to a side that was aspiring to challenge for the league title. Four years later his best friend and international teammate Tonono, also died prematurely. The talented *libero* had suffered a liver infection a few hours after a cup match against Málaga and, despite the doctors telling him he would be fine, passed suddenly just ten days after. Losing two of their best players was a hard blow, yet there was a stint of hope with the signing of several Argentinian internationals at the end of the decade as Las Palmas reached the cup final for the only time in their history. After that, everything went sideways. The club was relegated to the third tier and was on the brink of disappearing altogether. Local businessmen, aware of its importance for the island, stepped in. Las Palmas was saved, even if they remained far from first-division football, bar a short spell at the turn of the millennium.

Without elite football, supporters started to focus more on enjoying the talented youth prospects that broke through the ranks until in 2014 they were rewarded with the arrival of manager Quique Setien. Still playing in the second division, Setien's Las Palmas became one of the most inspiring sides in Spanish football. They mixed the vanguard tactical ideals of their manager with the technical skills and ability to improvise of local players such as the returning skipper Juan Carlos Valerón, the ball-playing midfielder Roque Mesa and promising attacker Jonathan Viera. The team got promoted at the end of the season, leaving behind the trauma of a late-hour drama in the final minutes of the previous play-off final against Córdoba, when the crowd invaded the pitch to celebrate a goal they thought would suffice, only to suffer a late equaliser in the dying seconds.

With an island economically revigorated by the boom provided by tourism, Las Palmas played three consecutive seasons in La Liga, remaining forever faithful to their football identity. The new Gran Canaria stadium was regularly packed to back a side that could meet eye to eye any other. Spanish football was entering a low after almost a decade of enjoying a golden age and for many UD Las Palmas became a sort of last hurrah for the passing game style that had made the country a superpower. The island of David Silva – the greatest Canary Island player ever, who sadly couldn't play for his local club as his family moved to Valencia while he was still a teenager – has also proved time they could nurture talent in abundance. So, even when the club lost many of their most talented players, like a young Pedri, another seemed to spring up immediately.

Despite not achieving remarkable results on the pitch, Las Palmas have fulfilled by far the aspirations of those who embraced the spirit of togetherness so popular within the islands. In moments of hardship, the club has been a beacon of pride to the local supporters, who often feel that, as Spanish citizens, they have been left behind. Sitting in a different time zone to the peninsula, the Canaries have always looked more like an exotic summer destination than part of the nation. Others would have felt diminished by it but in Las Palmas, as well as the remaining islands, it became a symbol of specialness. Embracing their African and Latin American roots, through dance, music, race mixing and social values, the Canarians have become the most multicultural and open-minded of all the Spanish. Joyful, passionate and uncaring as their most remarkable footballers. A refreshing world where tears and smiles embody the love of the yellow-and-blue colours. They may not win the league or achieve continental glory but the club has become a flag for a place like no other. Perhaps that's the greatest win of them all.

* * *

If it makes you special, why change?

Athletic Bilbao have become synonymous with homegrown talent, a strong local identity, and a fierce defender of Basque values for more than a century. While football embraced globalisation, with many sides playing with more foreign players than nationals, they remained firm in their stance. As the world moved in a different direction, they embraced localism and tradition. Their shirt was one of the latest in the world to add a sponsor and they agreed only to partner with local Basque companies. Above all else, they remained faithful to fielding Basque players only.

It's forever the romantic touch for many outsiders who still see in Athletic Club the guardians of days gone by. It makes it more incredible if you think their pool of players is reduced to a region with less than three million inhabitants, smaller than Uruguay. And all that without having ever been relegated, something only Real Madrid and Barcelona can equal. Yet not everyone sees it that way. Their Basque rivals point out that Athletic's economic power has stopped them from prospering because when they come knocking it's hard for any local footballer to say no, unless you are a diehard fan of your local team, as most kids in Euskadi grow up wanting to wear the red-and-white shirt. It serves as a flag of the region to the outside world. Players know it, supporters feel it and rival clubs are limited by it. In other parts of Spain, many see it as an endogamy of sorts, a club that has never looked beyond the horizon and evolved. Some even believe it to be an over-nationalist approach. In truth, they fail to understand the true nature of the Basque. There are few places in Europe where tradition, heartfelt rooting in the soil and the power of family exerts such an influence in the community. They rarely feel something from the outside can bring enough value to their lives to even bother.

Athletic resonates with that feeling in sporting terms. If there's *cantera* – a translation for the mining quarries that stands for youth set-up – there's no need for *cartera*, or wallet. If the earth provides, we will be fine. Of course, the definition of an Athletic player has also evolved with time. It wasn't until 1910 that the restrictive policy kick-started after the club board took offence at a protest presented by their rivals from Donostia for fielding an ineligible British player in a cup match. Since then, the club vowed to only play with Basques, but as time went by the definition was stretched. Officially the club recognises all players born in Euskal Herria – which includes besides the Basque Country, the territory of Navarre and the French Basque Country – but also those who were direct descendants of born Basques and even those who, having no Basque heritage, did most of their youth academy years in Euskadi. That explains why someone like French-born Bixente Lizarazu was signed while Antoine Griezmann, who ended up at Real Sociedad, wasn't. Some players have sparked debate even among supporters but in the end Athletic have been able to sustain a policy through time that gathers full support from their fanbase. Enjoying the journey is more important than winning. But that doesn't mean that Athletic is a club that lacks silverware.

Bilbao is a place that echoes different eras in perfect harmony. Crossing the iconic San Antón bridge, you get glimpses of what it was like to live there during the Middle Ages, a time when the city was already a key commercial site. On both sides of the Nervión river, any visitor can jump from bar to bar and never get tired of trying the local *pintxos* and gastronomy musts. Despite being inland, in a small valley, the river stretches to the Bay of Biscay a few miles north, making Bilbao a place for cuttlefish or cod lovers. Land and sea have defined Bilbao's identity for centuries. While the connection with the land can be seen everywhere, it was the sea that paved the way for the Industrial Revolution, changing Bilbao's landscape completely. The richness of its soil made it the perfect place for British companies to settle in at the end of the 19th century. It was the first main industrial site in Spain and soon Bilbao grew to become more like Birmingham and Manchester, its green valleys replaced by the smoke and dust coming from the quarries and factories. Part of its beauty was lost, replaced by the unshakable nature of the modern world. Not all was bad, though, as with it also came football.

Matches were played regularly between locals and British workers so, eventually, when some Basque youths returned home after spending some years studying in the United Kingdom, the idea of forming a local football club grew stronger. 'It was the British dockers that first played football in Bilbao on the Campa de los Ingleses (Englishmen's Field), where the Guggenheim Museum now stands,' explains Christopher Lee, the author of the book *Origins*. From those matches rose in 1898 a club that was not shy to embrace its early British connection. In fact, it made it thrive. 'Many British players took part in Athletic's earlier matches and the club became defined by some of the island's managers who imprinted a direct and physical style of play rooted in the English way,' adds Lee. From those commercial routes with England also came the famous club colours. At first, as mentioned earlier, they used a blue-and-white shirt inspired by Blackburn Rovers, where many workmen came from. When a board member later travelled to the United Kingdom to get more shirts, only to find they had sold out, he decided to pick up new ones. Thus, a legend was born: the famous *Zurrigorri* kit.

'Officially, Athletic Club say this was inspired by Southampton, though there have been some recent rumblings that it could also be to do with Sunderland,' stresses Christopher Evans, the author of *Los Leones*, and one of the biggest experts on the club's history outside the Basque Country. 'Nobody knows where the red and white striped shirt comes from and nobody really cares,' he adds. What is undoubtedly true is that it became a symbol of the club. For the following 50 years, Athletic became the strongest side in the land. San Mamés was the most admired football stadium in the country, known as The Cathedral – echoing its British inspiration – and its football philosophy had evolved with the arrival of Fred Pentland, the man who changed forever how football managers were perceived in Spain to a point they are still called 'Mister'.

Pentland arrived at Santander after a stint in Paris by the recommendation of Steve Bloomer, the great England international who had been his cellmate in a prisoner-of-war camp in Germany during World War I. He then moved to Bilbao, where his knowledge of the game and man-management skills elevated the club further. Pentland famously allowed his players to jump over his bowler hat after each win and took Athletic to national glory, becoming the first-ever Spanish side to win the double in back-to-back seasons. The accolades of those years, alongside the star quality of many of its players, from Rafael Moreno 'Pichichi', José Belauste and Guillermo Gorostiza up to Agustín Gainza or Telmo Zarra, made them a popular club well beyond the frontiers of Euskadi. They remain one of the best-supported sides nationwide, even though their glory days have since long ended. Only the arrival of Ladislao Kubala and Alfredo di Stéfano changed the scales of power. By then Athletic had won five league titles and 18 cups, but since the mid-1950s, they managed only to claim 11 trophies.

Three of those came in the first half of the 1980s, their last golden age. Coached by Javier Clemente, a well-known anglophile, who regularly visited Sir Bobby Robson at Ipswich, Athletic won back-to-back league titles between 1982 and 1984, also clinching the cup for their last-ever double in 1984. It was a successful period for Basque football, as they succeeded their rivals from Donostia as league champions. It was also a period when British football was at an all-time high, making Clemente's route-one football modern. That side counted on the likes of Manu Sarabia and Andoni Goikotxea, and had in Andoni Zubizarreta a powerful figure in goal, who had succeeded probably the club's greatest-ever footballer, José Angel Iribar. The man who defined goalkeeping in Spain for generations – while becoming the best in the world – was a powerful symbol of the Basque identity. Even today he remains probably one of the most admired figures in Euskadi.

After each competition won, it became customary for players and staff to climb to an old metal scrap boat known as the *gabarra*, and then stream from the coastline up the river into Bilbao, followed by supporters in smaller fishing boats as crowds partied on each side of the Nérvion. Many believed it would become a recurrent celebration in the years to come but happiness was short-lived. During those years ETA killings and the economic depression took a toll on the city, and after Clemente and the club parted ways, many tried to recover the old San Mamés spirit to no avail. Managers like Howard Kendall, Jupp Heynckes and Luis Fernàndez had their shots, yet trophies remained a distant memory.

In 1998 the club finished a distant second behind Barcelona with a side comprised of local legends such as Julen Guerrero, Joséba Etxeberria and Ismael Urzaiz, qualifying to play in the Champions League for the first time. Guerrero particularly became one of the first sex symbols in Spanish football, drawing crowds of teenagers and young women to the stadiums at a time when supporters were still almost exclusively male. His cultural impact preceded that of David Beckham in England, but a set of injuries never allowed him to fulfil all his potential. He, like his generation, ended his career trophyless and supporters had to wait a decade to experience some sort of sporting success.

The arrival of Argentine manager Marcelo Bielsa, after a couple of seasons with the club on the brink of relegation, provided a glimpse of hope. Bielsa proposed a fast-forward attacking football mindset supported by a young generation of local graduates such as Ander Herrera, Óscar de Marcos, Javi Martinez, Iker Muniain and Fernando Llorente. In 2012 they lost both the cup final to Barcelona and the Europa League Final to Atlético Madrid but, after routing Manchester United at Old Trafford on their way to the final, the world got to know again who the mighty Lions from Bilbao were. One key player from those days was Mikel San José. He initially graduated from Lezama Academy but then moved to Liverpool only to return after a few years at Anfield. San José became a club legend by scoring the first Athletic goal at the new San Mamés, a memory that lingers.

'It was just the equaliser, so my first instinct was to get the ball to go for the winner but then you realise the importance of that moment,' he said. 'Eventually, we won, and it became a special day for everyone. I was lucky enough to play in the old San Mamés and the new and the good thing is that the club was able to keep its essence. You can still feel that British identity we always had, the supporters close to you and the acoustics of 50,000 people chanting create an incredible atmosphere.' San José played more than 400 matches for Athletic and was club captain for several seasons. Being a local academy graduate he understands better than most the importance of the club being rooted in the community. 'To play for Athletic is a dream for anyone growing up in Euskal Herria. I played cup and European finals and won a Supercup, and there's no better feeling. If you walk the streets in Euskadi, you always see children wearing the club's shirt and that makes us proud,' he adds.

Many don't realise it but Athletic Club is much more than just a football club. Most likely they are the most important social and cultural institution in Euskadi. Events like the Thinking Football Film Festival and the One Club Award are but examples of the extensive work developed by the club's Foundation. Galder Reguera, one of Spain's most talented writers, works for the Foundation and understands well the nature of their social relevance. 'Athletic supporters are like philosophers,' he explains. 'More than discussing match results, we are constantly debating who we are. Our work at the Foundation goes beyond what happens on the pitch. For us it's important to establish a connection with the cultural world and to drive social projects to make life better for people, especially in Vizcaya.'

Few imagine the Basque country without immediately having Athletic come to mind. Over the past years, the city of Bilbao has changed deeply. The old scars of the Industrial Revolution have been replaced with a much more attractive city, full of green areas, modern housing buildings and iconic sites such as the Guggenheim Museum. At the top of a small hill, the new San Mamés exemplifies that futuristic approach. And, as Reguera explains, Athletic is also an institution known for its ability to unite. 'During the worst years of Basque terrorism, when it was difficult to tend bridges in political institutions and the community, the old San Mamés served as a place of union,' he says. 'Nobody cared what side you were on. We were there for Athletic and that was enough. A Basque saw the club standing for Euskadi and a Spanish nationalist could see a side that represented Spain because we only played with national players, so everyone felt represented.'

Modernity also meant the club embraced the new multiculturalism that is reshaping Spanish society. Due to their exclusive policy, Athletic was the last professional football club in Spain to field a black footballer, an important issue in a country that still needs to tackle the ever-presence of racism in society. Jonas Ramalho became the first son of an African immigrant to play with the first team, debuting against Seville in November of 2011. He paved the way for a new era that couldn't have been better represented than by the Williams brothers. 'I believe Iñaki Williams to be the most charismatic figure in the history of Athletic over the past 40 years', says *The Guardian* correspondent Sid Lowe. 'He's the symbol of a new multicultural world flourishing in Euskadi, someone who is both proud of his African roots and being Basque.'

The forward's parents came from Ghana, crossing the Sahara Desert on foot with his mother pregnant, before entering Spain illegally, like so many who cross the fence at the border in Melilla. They were saved, first by declaring themselves political refugees from Liberia, and then welcomed to Bilbao by a Catholic priest who became so important in their lives that they chose his name when they baptised their firstborn. Iñaki owed his Basque godfather the love for the club and debuted with the first team in December of 2014, aged just 20. For over a decade, the forward became one of the side's key figures, appearing in a total of 251 consecutive matches without getting injured or suspended even if for most of the time he was playing with a two-centimetre-long shard of glass in his foot.

'What Iñaki has won, the day he took a flight from the Africa Cup of Nations to play a decisive cup match against Barcelona, scoring the winner, tells everything you need to know on sporting terms,' says Lowe. 'But he is also much more than that, because, thanks to him and his guidance, we have been able to enjoy the explosion of his younger brother Nico, for whom he has been a father figure.' Nico Williams became known worldwide during Euro 2024, scoring the opening goal in the final against England. An electric winger, he was touted by his brother to become the greatest player ever to come out of Lezama. Together they brought a glimpse of the future to such a traditional club. More importantly, they combined forces to give supporters what they most desired.

Forty years had passed since Athletic enjoyed a trophy celebration, and after losing a cup final against their rivals Real Sociedad in 2021, many started to despair. But things took a turn for the best and in 2024 the side coached by Ernesto Valverde reached the final once again. Thousands of supporters marched south to see the side face Mallorca in Seville, for what seemed like the last opportunity for a generation and the perfect moment for the Williams brothers to leave their mark. The match turned out a tense affair with Mallorca opening the scoring and Oihan Sancet grabbing an equaliser in the second half. The night ended with the sides forced to a penalty shoot-out. Two Mallorca misses meant Alex Berenguer's shot ended the largest drought period in the club's history.

After partying all night long in the Andalusian capital, players and supporters returned north where, once again, the old *gabarra* was put to use. More than a million supporters from all parts of Spain joined in to celebrate, proving that, even after so many years of disappointments, their love never faded. And that's what Athletic is all about. Despite having been the most important side in Spanish football history for long, they've learned that nothing is worth more than their identity. A club like no other, supported by millions who don't care if they win or lose as long as they remain true to their roots. There is no side as romantic as the *Leones* – a club deeply connected to their past but one that has learned to embrace the future without having to abandon their principles. If anything, they are special, and their roar will forever echo into eternity.

THOSE LONELY BULLS

CROSS SPAIN by road and they are impossible to miss. Giant black billboards of a defiant bull dominate the horizon representing a very Spanish trait: the bravery of its people, courage in the face of danger. For a while, the iconic giant silhouettes created by the graphic designer Manolo Prieto for the Osborne drinks company were on the brink of extinction. The fact that their announced disappearance was even discussed in Congress explains its relevance. Ultimately, any reference to the company was removed but the proud animal remained. Their cultural significance was such that they were even used as the backdrop to one of the most iconic love scenes in Spanish cinematography. *Jamón, Jamón* not only presented to the world the rising talents of future Oscar-winning couple Penélope Cruz and Javier Bardem but also exploited the visual power of those billboards as a symbol of the meaning of being part of Spain.

Yet they also reflect a country that is fading away. Small pueblos from the interior are disappearing while provincial capitals are emptying, with so many forced to move to the coast or the capital in search of jobs. Those vast areas, once proud hubs of people, ideas and traditions, are getting lonelier. Inevitably football has suffered as a consequence. Each year the number of professional clubs from the interior decreases and many historic sides have been on the brink of disappearing altogether. Cities and clubs with many stories to tell. Like those giant black card bulls who saw millions pass by contemplating the horizon, probably looking ahead to their bitter end.

* * *

Few goals are so enjoyable. David Seaman, lying down, contemplating the meaning of life. Nayim, hands in the air, in a state of complete disbelief. The thousands of Real Zaragoza supporters rolling their eyes. It had all been so sudden. One moment the former Spurs player was controlling the ball with his chest, almost near the halfway line. Instants later it was slowly descending right into Arsenal's net. The impossible goal, culminating in what for many seemed an impossible win. That 1995 Cup Winners' Cup Final came to represent not only the triumph of the underdog, it was also Real Zaragoza's most unforgettable night. A giant of a club, one that, if British, would surely have been the subject of books and documentaries, has since been largely forgotten. Even in Spain.

In a way, Zaragoza represent the disaffection between the nation and its oldest soul, the vast interior, where the Spanish identity was forged during the centuries of Reconquista, the reoccupation of the lands occupied by Muslim armies. Real Zaragoza is probably the biggest club in Spain never to win the league and, despite all that, it remains one of its most decorated sides. Six Copa del Rey, an Inter-Cities Fairs Cup and that iconic trophy won in Paris against the Gunners. But more than accolades, the club, like the city, has been in the vanguard of Spanish football on many occasions – something that the recent seasons spent in the second tier seem to have erased from collective memory.

'We are the Ohio of Spain,' says a smiling Aitor Lagunas. 'The party that wins the election in Aragon also wins nationwide. In a sense, we are a small Spain inside of Spain.

A city that has things typical of an interior city but also things you only get to see in places like Madrid and Barcelona, a social and cultural hybrid landscape.' Indeed, Zaragoza has a special place within the national geography. It sits midway between the two largest cities, and it's the historical capital of Aragon, once a proud medieval kingdom that ruled southern Italy, Sicily, Sardinia and parts of the south of France.

Home of Francisco de Goya, who ranks alongside Picasso and Velasquez as one of Spain's greatest-ever painters, it has twice boasted the nation's most popular rock bands. Héroes del Silencio, for some the Spanish equivalent to Guns N' Roses in the early 90s, was led by the creative force of Enrique Bunbury and attracted crowds like few other acts achieved before them. Then the talented duo Amaral did the same in the first decade of the new millennium, powered by Eva Amaral's breathtaking voice that revolutionised Spain's indie rock scene. When you arrive in Zaragoza, the majestic cathedral known as the *Pilarica* dominates the landscape alongside the bridges crossing the mighty Ebro. Everything screams modernity. Except for La Romareda.

Real Zaragoza's stadium is pretty much the same as when that all-conquering side from the mid-90s was making the club a fan favourite all around Europe. After visiting so many modern stadiums, entering its gates serves as a refreshing experience, a journey back to a time when concrete ruled supreme and the sounds and smells of a football ground were different. But even that too will change soon, as the city is expected to host matches for the upcoming 2030 World Cup, as they did for the 1982 edition, and the ground will enjoy a revamp.

Back then Zaragoza was also reshaping its football identity. Behind it were the successful days of the *Zaraguayos* – a nickname associated with the number of Uruguayan and Paraguayan players in the side – and, above all, the

Magníficos. During the 90s, Zaragoza was home to one of the most exciting sides in European football. The club had been a late bloomer, only taking part in the first division after the Civil War ended, but two decades later everything changed. With a deadly forward line including Canàrio, Santos, Villa, Marcelino and Lapetra, the club became a national powerhouse, playing in four consecutive cup finals between 1963 and 1966, winning two. In 1964 they also won an Inter-Cities Fairs Cup, a trophy UEFA still don't recognise as the predecessor of the UEFA Cup, in an all-Spanish final against Valencia. They were defeated by Bobby Moore's West Ham in the semi-finals of the Cup Winners' Cup the following season and, in 1966, reached another Inter-Cities final, only to be beaten by Barcelona. Those years marked the first time a club from the interior, apart from Madrid, took centre stage at the national level. The best was yet to come.

In 1991 Real Zaragoza were on the brink of relegation. Supporters were getting nervous, and when the board appointed the reserve-team coach, at only 31, as the new manager, many assumed the battle was lost. They were in for a surprise. Víctor Fernàndez had no CV, but he nurtured a clear idea of how Zaragoza should play. The season was tough, and they were eventually forced to a play-off against Real Murcia to keep their place in La Liga. But the return leg ended with a thunderous win that, in hindsight, became one of the most important in the club's history. Fernàndez was given time to start over and grabbed the opportunity with both hands.

Today it still surprises many when a manager emerges in a first-division side so young, so you can imagine what it was like back in 1991. Yet some men are born to do the extraordinary and Fernàndez was one of them. Two years on, his side was playing the Copa del Rey final against Real Madrid. They didn't win but by then it was clear Zaragoza were on the brink of something special. In 1994 once again they reached the final. This time *Los Maños* came out victors. A year later they were beating Arsenal in the Cup Winners' Cup Final. And all while playing some of the most attractive football Spain had ever seen.

Even a young Guardiola pointed to Fernàndez's side as one of the most exciting teams to watch. It was probably because the manager also believed in a free-flowing attacking football similar to what Cruyff was then doing in Barcelona. During the 1993/94 season, when Barça came to town, Zaragoza displayed all their artistry and inflicted one of the most humiliating defeats suffered by the Dream Team, a 6-3 thrashing on a chilly winter night few could ever forget. The runs of Francisco Higuera, the quality passing of Gustavo Poyet and Miguel Pardeza and the clinical finishes of Juan Esnáider proved too much for the *Blaugrana*.

'Víctor was a young manager the same way Spain was still a young democracy in the early 90s, and it is easy to see the similarities between those realities,' explains Aitor Lagunas. 'To have a provincial side, playing positional attacking football, winning trophies and admirers everywhere, was out of the ordinary. But that side played the same sort of football Spain would later be famous for. The passing game of Fernàndez's is similar to Aragonés' Spain's, albeit with lesser players. By that time perhaps only the Real Madrid of *La Quinta*, Cruyff's Dream Team and perhaps Valdano's Tenerife played so beautifully.' Ironically Fernàndez was supposed to have believed he would be appointed national coach in 2004, only to lose the vacancy to Aragonés, who then won the Euros in 2008.

Also, if you talk about that Zaragoza side you have to mention that duel against Chelsea at La Romareda, in the 1995 semi-finals of the Cup Winners' Cup, a night when one of Spanish football's greatest urban myths came to life.

Fernàndez's team was brilliant, thrashing the Blues 3-0. Near the end, a group of hooligans charged the local police, almost forcing the match to a halt. Watching in dismay, local fans started to shout *'pisarlo, pisarlo'*, 'kick him, kick him'. It was a common chant in Spanish grounds ever since Argentine manager Carlos Bilardo made a similar remark to his medical staff when they attended to an injured opponent. It was a cry of support for the police force but that was understood by the hooligans as 'peace and love', which would have sounded very similar. Suddenly the confrontations stopped but, despite what was said later, there was never any mention in the press, neither British nor Spanish, that anyone really took the word *'pisarlo'* for 'peace and love' that night. Yet as John Ford so brilliantly put it in *The Man Who Shot Liberty Valance*, sometimes if the truth doesn't suit you, print the legend.

Peace and love or not, Zaragoza won and Esnaider's brilliant goal, outshone by Nayim's iconic shot, opened the way for their most memorable night a few weeks later in Paris. Players celebrated afterwards around Montmartre alongside their supporters and the following day more than 150,000 fans gathered on the main plaza to hail the newly crowned champions.

Those memories seem now a world away. Fernàndez was sacked two years later, eventually taking the helm of Celta Vigo, which then became one of Spain's most attractive sides. The club lost some of its best players but remained a competitive side, adding a couple of Copa del Rey trophies over the following seasons. The first came against Fernàndez's Celta and then versus the last recognisable version of the Real Madrid *Galácticos* in 2004. But things were getting more out of control each year. Signing quality players like David Villa, Sávio and brothers Gabriel and Diego Milito, players they couldn't afford, cried disaster. In 2007 Agapito Iglesias bought the club and took that risky policy a step too far.

While he got Víctor Fernàndez back, he also added to the squad the likes of Gerard Piqué, Andrés D'Alessandro and Pablo Aimar to fight for a place in the Champions League. Two years later Zaragoza were relegated. All the warning signs were there but no one bothered to notice. As they went up once again, the same mistakes kept being made and in 2013 Zaragoza fell to the pit, this time for good. It was the 58th and last appearance in the first division until now. What happened since is a rumble of failed projects, bad investments and inability to adapt, according to Lagunas.

'Zaragoza is a big club that has failed to understand that, after so many years, we are no longer a first-division side competing in the second division. We have become a second-division side, and to get out we need to adapt.' It has been a hurtful situation for a club from Spain's fifth-largest city. 'Sadly, we are one of the great anomalies in European football, alongside Hamburg in 2. Bundesliga, or all those years Leeds spent in the Championship,' says Lagunas. 'We have exiled ourselves from our history as we are not up to what we should stand for as a football club, as a city and as a region.' While the city has grown, becoming an ever-important hub between Madrid and Barcelona, with people enjoying the visual riches left by the unique Mudejar culture or the rich gastronomy found in the ever-crowded El Tubo quarter, football has become a thorn in the side for locals.

During these past seasons, Zaragoza suffered a fate similar to other great Spanish clubs like Málaga, Racing Santander or Deportivo La Coruña. The second division is, in the words of Lagunas, like being in 'a foreign league'. There are no television revenues, no visibility and no income. At the same time, the fair play restraints imposed by the Spanish league have made it even more difficult for clubs to turn their situation around. Until the 2010s it was usual for sides as big as Zaragoza to count on the help of public institutions or local companies who would pour money into the club regularly. Now the degree to which the league controls every cent invested has made that extremely hard to replicate. Much smaller sides with a sound management team at the helm are beating big badly managed clubs.

The lack of first-division football is also hurting the community. For a club once a proud symbol of localism in a very centralised country, it's hard to see how young kids are turning their backs on the local team. 'If you exclude the clubs relegated from La Liga and those promoted sides from the 1RFEF, at the start of every season you have around 15 clubs with similar budgets,' explains the *Panenka* director. 'You need to be very precise and lucky to survive in this jungle.'

During the 2023/24 season, up until the last two fixtures, no team had been either relegated or promoted. Only 15 points separated sixth place, the last play-off spot, and the drop zone. Not even the return of Víctor Fernàndez for a fourth time proved enough, yet the tears of the man, during his first press conference, spoke volumes of the club's importance in the community. Real Zaragoza is not just a sleeping giant but one that lives inside a never-ending nightmare like Goya's paintings, waiting to awake to better, sunnier days.

* * *

Spain is one of Europe's biggest countries in area and demographics. If you exclude nations with a vast territory in Asia, it ranks third in area, just behind Ukraine and France. It is also fifth in population, after Germany, France, the United Kingdom and Italy. It includes Europe's only desert, some of its highest mountains, never-ending yellowish plains, and valleys painted in green. Yet, most of that territory is not inhabited. When you look at a satellite view during the night, there's a highway of lights that stretches from the west coast of Galicia all around the Atlantic north and follows along the coastline of the Mediterranean. Right in the middle, a nebula of radiant white covers the area where Madrid sits. Almost everything around is black. A silent void.

Historically Spain has built its identity as a nation of nations through the Reconquista, a period when the Christian kingdoms in the north marched against Muslim territories in the south until, seven centuries later, they reconquered it all. During that time, as a policy of self-defence, large chunks of land were left empty, to discourage raids from both sides. As time went by those areas were kept wild, a reason why Spain still has so many protected forests, wildlife reserves and national parks compared with others. The political map of the reunited kingdom was then reorganised into territorial provinces first, and then, in the 1980s, into autonomous communities. For each, particularly inland, the capital province became almost the only relevant urban centre, a lighthouse of sorts. As time went by though, Madrid's economic and political relevance started to suck all life around it. Many who didn't relocate to the capital were left to contemplate a future with no prospects and eventually moved elsewhere.

As with every important shift in economics and demography, football was deeply affected by it and, in the 21st century, finding professional football clubs from those provincial sides competing in La Liga has become a challenge. The budgets needed to compete made all the traditional local investment from impoverished areas irrelevant and rarely have any outside backers showed a willingness to put their money in clubs with few chances of flourishing. Clubs and supporters became stuck in a world where they couldn't get promoted but remain too important to simply disappear. Like the cities around them, some of which rank amongst the most beautiful and historically important in Spanish history, they languish slowly.

Take the regions of Castilla y Leon and Castilla la Mancha, the two cornerstones of what was once the kingdom of Castile, the backbone of Spanish identity. It's a deserted albeit beautiful world where nature remains important in everyday life, with its national parks, the vast fields of crops, or the hills where bulls wander in peace. In almost a hundred years of the football league, only seven local sides have played first-division football. Of those, only Real Valladolid have spent more than 12 seasons at the top. UD Salamanca, ranking second in that particular list, no longer exist. Albacete, Burgos, Numancia and Cultural Leonesa add up to just 21 seasons between them. They all come from vibrant, important provincial capitals but in the reality of Spanish football they are minnows.

Those two vast central regions also boast provinces that have not once had a side playing professionally in La Liga, from Ponferrada, Palencia, Zamora, Ávila and Segovia in the west to Toledo, Ciudad Real, Cuenca and Guadalajara to the east. Yet, all those cities have strong local identities, and despite the growing lack of economic muscle and demographic influence, they are still important tourist sites and guardians of pride in being Castilian. Ernesto Rosado, who comes from Cebreros, a small pueblo in Ávila, knows well the regional reality and believes the problem resides in a culture that lacks ambition. 'There's no investment in provincial football and that is not only visible in the more important sides of the region but in the youth set-ups as well,' he says. 'For instance, there has only been one player born in Ávila who has played in La Liga for the past 25 years, and that's too depressing even for our small reality. If you don't start from the base, creating the necessary conditions for kids to grow, they become Real Madrid or

Barcelona supporters and lose interest in playing the game altogether.'

The interior of Spain is full of places where landscapes can steal your heart. It is also a land of dreamers who had to seek fortune elsewhere. It is no coincidence that Don Quixote, Cervantes's iconic character, is from around there. The way he and his faithful companion Sancho travel around Castile, fighting imagined demons disguised as windmills, inspired generations. Pedro Almodóvar was one of those dreamers. The most celebrated Spanish filmmaker, winner of several Oscars among other cinematographic accolades, comes from a village in Ciudad Real, a province where football supporters have pledged their hearts to Real Madrid. It wasn't until he moved to the capital, where he became one of the leading figures of the popular *Movida* movement, that he was able to express all the creativity that burned inside him.

Almodóvar is one of Spain's most iconic celebrities worldwide. But even he loses in affection and celebrity status to another son of La Mancha. Andrés Iniesta was born in Fuentealbilla, a pueblo in the province of Albacete. While growing up, the club from the provincial capital was rocking La Liga, baptised by the Spanish press as the 'Clockwork Cheese', a funny cross-over between their version of total football and the economic relevance of cheese production in the region. In 1989 a young coach named Benito Floro took Albacete from the third tier to La Liga in back-to-back seasons. To prove it was no fluke, in their first-division debut season Albacete finished seventh, almost reaching a UEFA Cup spot.

The side played spirited attacking football, inspired by the love Floro had for the iconic Cruyff's Netherlands team. In Zalazar, Geli, Urzaiz, Conejo and Soler they boasted some of their most memorable players. Real Madrid briefly signed Floro but that didn't work out and he was soon back at the Carlos Belmonte ground, guiding the club to their first-ever cup semi-final in 1995. The following year Albacete were relegated, beaten in a play-off by Extremadura UD, the passing of the torch between the only club from Castilla-La-Mancha ever to play in La Liga to one of the most iconic sides from the western neighbouring region of Extremadura, who have long since disappeared from professional football as well.

That same summer, Iniesta took part in the Brunete tournament, a get-together for under-12s first-division sides, and caught the eye of scouts from Barcelona and Real Madrid. If Albacete had not been playing in the first division, perhaps they would never have noticed him, but that week changed the history of Spanish football. Iniesta's family, after much thought, accepted Barça's offer and Andrés and his father drove by car for six hours until they reached La Masia. The youngster would live there for the following years. It was emotionally hard for him but, in a sense, it was also something people from Albacete had been used to by then.

Poverty and lack of job opportunities meant many had to move to the outskirts of big cities like Barcelona, where they were often treated as second-rate citizens by right-wing Catalans. The same happened to Manolo García, Spain's greatest musical poet. His family was forced to take the road in similar circumstances during the 60s and he grew up in the working-class streets of Poblenou, alongside many who, like him, were not from around there. He later became the frontman of Ultimo de la Fila, one the most beloved pop-rock bands in the 1980s, before having an extremely successful solo career. His music, full of poetry, often recalls places lost to the collective memory in the middle of nowhere, a homage to his family roots.

Iniesta and García are not just two of Spain's greatest cultural icons of our time. They share something else. Football, like music, brings joy to people. And if there was ever a footballer who excelled in making others happy that was Iniesta. It was not just his brilliance as a player, nor the ability to control the ball like few have been able to. Nor how he could create late-minute dramas like the effort at Stamford Bridge that allowed the legend of Guardiola's Barcelona to come to life. Or the one that finally gave Spain their much-deserved World Cup title in 2010. It was because of who he was and what he stood for; a man loved by all. That goal in Johannesburg made him a star but his best performance with *La Roja* came two years later during Euro 2012, a tournament where he was famously pictured, like in a *Captain Tsubasa* Japanese anime, surrounded by Italian rivals as if he was a titan. He should have won the Balón d'Or that season, making him only the second Spanish footballer to do so. His partnership with his fellow team-mate Xavi Hernández has since become the stuff of legends. It is hard to say between Xavi and Iniesta who was the better player but there's no doubt who's the most beloved. Despite all those years in Catalonia, Iniesta remained proud of his origins, an all-around Spanish icon, not just a Barcelona legend.

Football is always a reflection of the world we live in, and Spain has yet to come to terms with its deserted interior. Long gone are the days when the magical realism of filmmakers such as José Luis Cuerda, author of *Amanece Que no es Poco*, were able to depict a faithful, albeit metaphoric, portrait of the nation through its rural historical identity. Small pueblos all around the country have become simply summer residences for those families who were forced to move out and now only come back to their parents' empty homes on weekends or vacations as Almodóvar so well depicts in the Oscar-nominated movie *Volver*. Tourism and local businesses have been the only solace for breathtaking places such as Cuenca and its Casas Colgadas, Toledo and its streets full of history, Ávila's perfect medieval walls or

Segovia and its Roman aqueduct. Football as a business is nowhere to be seen.

Few expect things to change, making these lands the perfect place for giants like Madrid or Barcelona to spread their already huge influence. The absence of localism and investment has forever determined the sporting fate of this immense region that covers almost half of the country. The future doesn't look bright but, as they always have, Castilians will find a way to prevail. If they can't compete at club level, at least expect them to keep producing world-class talent. Probably the next Iniesta is already playing somewhere there. Quixote's dream remains well alive in those parts.

* * *

If ever there was a place that has fought against the tide and tried to establish itself as a beacon of hope, it's Valladolid. Of all the cities in the region of the old Castilian kingdom, they are the ones that remain politically and economically relevant. Crossed by the rivers Duero and Pisuerga, Valladolid has retained part of the industrial identity that opened the doors for important multinational companies to settle, like Michelin and Renault. The high-speed train that connects it to Madrid in one hour has helped to keep the city close enough to the capital and, at the same time, to retain its provincial identity. It was its industry and strong-minded mentality that allowed Valladolid to prosper and with it its football club.

Real Club Valladolid have spent more than 40 seasons in the first division, the only club, besides Real Zaragoza, from the interior regions that sit in the top 30 historical ranking sides of La Liga. The *Blanquivioletas* won a League Cup in 1984, lost two Copa del Rey finals and have played European football. Although they don't carry the same prestige and supporter fanbase as Zaragoza, they remain a well-respected side and a fundamental part of the Spanish football identity. Now owned by former Brazilian superstar Ronaldo Nazário, the club has recently been promoted back to La Liga.

Juan Arroita, one of Spain's most popular content creators, is a local supporter and sees the arrival of Ronaldo as an important step for the club's future. 'At first expectations were sky-high, Ronaldo being a much-loved figure, but he made the mistake of telling supporters he was trying to build a project that would fight for a Champions League spot and now here we are, just fresh out of the second division,' he says. 'However, what people don't grasp is what is being done in the background. Ronaldo cleared the club's debt and helped modernise the stadium, the training facilities and the youth set-up. And those are the steps that are going to take us far in the long term.'

For football author Miguel Ruiz, those much-needed steps might not suffice. 'We see what is being done but it's not enough to take the club back to where it belongs, and while supporters don't see those changes at first-team level, it will be hard to mobilise the local core fanbase. Especially when some people hint that the ownership is not as interested in creating a winning sporting side in Valladolid as they are in the economic side of the project.' People are still waiting for a miracle, like the one in 1984 that took them to the final of the League Cup, a short-lived cup tournament in Spanish football, lasting only three years. It was played at the end of the season and the club, who had recently opened their current ground José Zorilla, overcame the opposition of Zaragoza, Betis and Sevilla before playing Atlético Madrid in a two-legged final.

The *Colchoneros* were coached by Luis Aragonés and had Mexican forward Hugo Sánchez as their greatest asset, but Valladolid secured a goalless draw in Madrid before scoring three in the return leg. Today, whenever you walk the streets of Valladolid and happen to enter any local bar, it's likely that you see photos or memorabilia of that team hanging on walls. For a club that aspires to much more, that memory lingers as a signal of hope, but Arroita is extremely sceptical that Valladolid will ever be able to lift silverware soon. 'There were moments the club got into debt because some of the owners hoped to build teams capable of fighting against sides who belong to different economic realities than ours,' he says. 'We must learn from past mistakes and be aware that in Castilla y Leon it's difficult to establish winning projects due to our demographic and economic situation. And when you don't win, particularly in Spain, people easily lose interest, especially if they are faced with the prospect of a late-night match on a snowy Sunday against all the other entertainments now available from the comfort of your home.'

That seems to be the issue with the old Castile and Aragon, two mighty kingdoms trying to find their way into a different and modern Spain, ever more centred on its coastline and its capital city. Places where past and present are forever intertwined. While many defend the importance of keeping alive those old cultural elements that define the DNA of the Spanish idea of a nation, whether it's the famous windmills of La Mancha or the mighty bull who still symbolises bravery, few are prepared to take the necessary political measures to make sure that all this chunk of land remains attractive to live in and to invest in. Football awaits its moment as well, aware of the hard tasks ahead. As songwriting genius Antonio Vega sings in 'Lucha de Gigantes', while the historic and forgotten lands of the interior may feel themselves part of an immense world, they also feel the inevitability of their fragility.

KINGS OF EUROPE

'*COMO NO te voy a querer sí has sido campeón de Europa por décima quinta vez.*' The cloudy London sky opens as Real Madrid supporters sing in ecstasy. Every football club has its anthem for moments of celebration. Some are about connection, others about suffering. Only Real Madrid supporters know how to sing about absolute sporting success. 'How am I not supposed to love you if you have been crowned European Champion for the 15th time,' they shout. In Madrid, love is measured in trophies. One particularly stands out. Real Madrid is the club that won most leagues in the history of Spanish football and that is all very well. But what matters is how they have dominated continental football for the past 70 years. Like Marvel's Thanos, they are inevitable.

For every other football club, even the great ones, glory cycles are limited in time and are usually attached to star players or managers. Not at the Bernabéu. Here, the sole star is the club. Players and managers who have come to understand that are loved forever. Their merits may value the ones who don't but no one regrets seeing them go. Someone else will take their place and be victorious in the end. The club knows it. The fans know it. The anthem that roars in London tells the tale. You can change the number of European Cups won. You won't change how they feel about it. Madrid supporters are absolute winners and nothing else matters. Perhaps that is what made them the undisputable Kings of Europe.

***

Two moments in the 2024 Champions League Final against Borussia Dortmund sum up the essence of Real Madrid. In the 20th minute, a perfect cross pass from Matts Hummels finds Karim Adeyemi running alone, with only Thibaut Courtois in front of him. The German striker would have scored any other day, but he tries to nutmeg the Belgian goalkeeper and squanders the chance. A scene repeated time and time again. Real Madrid, as invincible as they might appear, always give chances away. But, somehow, rivals never seem to take advantage of them. Some may say it's divine protection, others a mental block. After all, seeing those white shirts in a European match has come to be like watching a horde of Vikings ravaging medieval Europe. If you are playing against a predator and only have one shot, you'd better not miss. Because, if you do, you're dead.

Fast forward to the second half, when a Toni Kroos corner gets cleared. Federico Valverde receives the ball and shoots without aiming. The ball should have gone out but then gently touches a Dortmund defender. What could have been a blunder becomes an opportunity. A corner is taken by the genius German midfielder who was playing his last professional club match. Out of nowhere, Dani Carvajal, a six-foot defender, storms in and heads into goal. It is his first European goal in half a decade. For the boy who once stood alongside Alfredo di Stéfano at the inauguration of the Valdebebas training centre in his early teens, it's a dream come true. A youth player, a fanatic supporter, becoming the hero of yet another European triumph.

Despite all the famed star players signed over the years, Carvajal represents a side of Madrid that is often disregarded. The club fosters some of the best talent in Spanish football. They might not get the same credit as Barcelona's La Masia but are equally brilliant. To measure things up, the second goal is scored by Vinicius Junior, the last of a long line of stars who have made the Bernabéu their home. Zidanes and Pavones, a Florentino Pérez dream that bears fruits two decades later. Stars and local youth players paving the way to success.

Toni Kroos may have left by now and Luka Modrić is no longer the key figure he once was. But the club knew how to prepare for the future without conceding to the present. The signing of youth prospects like Eduard Camavinga, Aurelien Tchouameni, Rodrygo, Vinicius and superstars like Jude Bellingham and Kylian Mbappé guarantee Real Madrid will still be one of the strongest sides in European football even after the last living legend of their most decorated generation leaves the pitch. That is sound management.

Everything that explains Real Madrid's dominance in continental football today began 15 years ago when the club was at a low. From 2005 until 2011 Madrid never went as far as the last 16 for five consecutive Champions League editions, their worst record ever. Worse, at the same time, eternal rivals from Barcelona won it twice, boasting what were arguably two of the best teams ever to grace the game. Florentino Pérez, who had left the club's presidency years before, returned in 2009 with a promise to save the day. He eventually did but it took time. Pérez started by splashing millions on the transfer market to bring the two previous Balón d'Or winners, Cristiano Ronaldo and Kaká, and quality players like Karin Benzema and Xabi Alonso. But that wasn't enough so he then hired a star manager.

José Mourinho saved Real Madrid's pride by beating Barça in the Champions League semi-final, thus avoiding a *Blaugrana* triumph at the Bernabéu. The Portuguese vowed he would knock Barcelona off their perch. In three seasons he eventually won a Copa del Rey – in one of the best football matches ever – and a league trophy, clinched precisely at the

Camp Nou with an iconic goal and celebration by Cristiano Ronaldo. But he failed to deliver what was most precious for the *Madridistas*, the European Cup. However, what he did was return the club to the continental elite. Madrid reached the 2010/11 Champions League semi-final and would do so again in the following two seasons with him in charge. But that was as high as it got. In 2011 Real were beaten by Barcelona, during a three-week period in which the two sides played four times against each other. The following year, while celebrating their first league trophy in four years, *Los Blancos* dramatically lost against Bayern Munich in a penalty shoot-out. Then it was Jürgen Klopp's Borussia Dortmund, who prevailed in 2013. Mourinho's project was over, but the Portuguese manager had spent the previous seasons creating the template of what would become Madrid's golden age.

Mourinho transformed former right-back Sergio Ramos into a commanding force as centre-back, pairing him with Pepe, a formidable and ruthless combination, while signing youth prospect Raphael Varane who would become key in the future. Xabi Alonso was given the keys to control the midfield, while Luka Modrić was bought to be the creative force. Benzema by that time had developed into a cultured forward and Ronaldo was at his peak as a goalscorer, helped by the fact that Angel Di Maria was providing balance on the other flank. Mourinho's personality proved to be his doom, but his quality work was undeniable and his successor, Carlo Ancelotti, greatly benefited from it.

The Italian had already proven in Milan he was a talented tactician and great at man-management, commanding the last triumphal period of Berlusconi's AC Milan. Pérez wanted a low-profile man able to drive that talented side on to end the 12 years without European glory and he got it. Of course, signing Gareth Bale helped. The Welsh winger proved decisive as he offered more firepower in front and allowed Ancelotti to move Di Maria alongside Alonso and Modrić in midfield. For the first time in a decade, Madrid reached the Champions League Final, after beating a much-favoured Bayern Munich team in the semi-finals. It was the first time Guardiola would experience the sour taste of defeat in a European clash against his historic rival. It wouldn't be the last. Bayern were far superior in the first leg in Spain but were overcome by a single goal and then, as they went full force against Iker Casillas's goal in Munich, ended up thrashed by a spectacular counter-attacking performance from the visitors. Four goals without reply and a ticket to a final, in Lisbon, against their city rivals and recently crowned league champions Atlético Madrid. A team they had beaten regularly over the years to a point that one day a group of supporters took on a card to the Bernabéu that said: 'Worthy opponent needed'. What could possibly go wrong?

Well, at first, everything. Simeone's Atlético were no team to toy against. Contrary to what Madrid were used to, they took the first chance they got. Atlético dominated the game, frustrating their rivals and even when Ancelotti went into full attack mode, they held on. Except, with two minutes of added time, Atlético conceded a corner, something they rarely did. It proved to be fatal. Luka Modrić crossed beautifully and Sergio Ramos attacked the box to score one of the most important goals in the club's history. Atlético were left for dead and Real stormed extra-time with Bale, Marcelo and Ronaldo scoring one each to take the trophy home. Twelve years had passed and, most importantly, this was the tenth time Real Madrid were crowned European champions, a landmark moment many believed would be impossible to achieve in their lifetime. For years the club supporters had suffered the mockery of their rivals from Barcelona, who claimed that their four trophies had been won in an era when television was technicolour, while Madrid celebrated six of their titles in the black-and-white days. Well, they were in for a surprise.

The Italian lasted only one more season. The reason was the semi-final knockout against Juventus, who prevented the world from witnessing the first *El Clásico* Champions League Final. Of course, Barcelona winning the trophy didn't help either. After a short period when Rafa Benítez took the helm, only to be sacked amid distrust from players and fans alike, in came Zinedine Zidane. The Frenchman had been a crowd favourite during his playing days and worked alongside Ancelotti as an assistant. He knew the players and they knew him. Better still, they worshipped him. Even Cristiano Ronaldo was in awe of his figure.

The Barcelona press mocked Zidane at his arrival but a few months on nobody was laughing. Madrid reached yet another final, against their city rivals once again, at the San Siro. Ramos scored a dubious goal that probably wouldn't have stood today and Griezmann equalised from the spot. There was no last-minute drama this time, and the game went to penalties. From the first nine spot-kickers, only Juanfran failed his attempt so when Ronaldo walked to take his everyone knew it was over. Many would have believed Madrid had won two trophies in three editions out of pure luck but the following year they would once again prove everybody wrong, fielding what was probably one of the best teams in history. By then Isco Alarcón had become a central figure in a midfield diamond that included Brazilian holding midfielder Casemiro, Modrić and Toni Kroos, who had arrived to replace Xabi Alonso. The attacking trio of Ronaldo, Benzema and Bale was no more, with the Welshman often deployed as supersub, while Varane had taken Pepe's place alongside Ramos in a defence that included Marcelo and Carvajal on the wings and Keylor Navas in goal. Spanish football was living its most glorious period, a trend set with the Euros

2008 win followed by Barcelona's Pep Team and Del Bosque's national side the following seasons. That era ended with this Real Madrid side and in 2017 they reached their zenith.

By May they had already won the league on course to another Champions League Final, against Juventus, after thrashing Napoli, Bayern Munich and old foe Atlético in the knockout stages. The final match was to be played in Cardiff but, unfortunately for local supporters, Bale was benched as Madrid put on one of their most remarkable displays. Ronaldo opened the scoring and, although Mandžukić brilliantly tied the match for Juve, there was no stopping the *Merengues*. A Casemiro long-range effort, followed by a second Cristiano goal and a late-minute effort by Marcos Asensio made it 4-1 for the reigning champions. It was not only the third time in the club's history that they had managed to clinch a double league-European Cup win, but also the first time a side had won back-to-back Champions League trophies since the new format kicked off in 1992. The following season they made it three in a row, beating Liverpool in the final with a fantastic display by Gareth Bale, who scored two brilliant goals in the second half.

But it was a triumph tarnished by a sense of farewell. Zidane made it clear he would step down as manager, after a disappointing third place in La Liga, and the final also saw Cristiano Ronaldo announce he would depart the club. Ronaldo had been as pivotal for this generation as Alfredo di Stéfano was in the 50s. The winning mentality, the sheer number of impossible goals and the superhuman ability to make a difference when it mattered made him the star figure of the side. The overhead kick goal against Juventus not only meant he would end up signing for the *Bianconeri* but was also a visual testament to the greatness of that Madrid side. Many believed without him Madrid would go back to being just another big European name, but not the feared competitor it had become. They were wrong. Time has proven no player ranks higher than the club, not even one of the all-time greats. Bale also entered semi-retirement but Madrid didn't take long to resurface, particularly thanks to the old guard who had served as backups and were finally ready to take centre stage. Modrić, Kroos and Benzema led the way for a new Madrid full of youth prospects signed cautiously by Pérez to guarantee they remained competitive over the years.

After a quick spell with Zidane back in charge that coincided with the COVID-19 years, the chairman turned again to Ancelotti. The Italian came to finish the job he had started almost a decade before. In his first season back, 2021/22, he won the double. It was known in Spain as the season of miracles. With a side that depended heavily on the goalkeeping skills of Thibaut Courtois, Vinicius's speed and how Kroos, Modrić and Benzema controlled the game, Madrid entered the Champions League knockout stages a world away from being the favourites. A PSG side with the attacking prowess of Kylian Mbappé, Neymar and Lionel Messi was higher ranked and proved it by beating Madrid at home. Yet a goal was a narrow advantage to take to a stadium that usually comes alive for return legs.

The Bernabéu proved once again to be the much-needed 12th player that evening, echoing the legends of the famous *Remontadas*, the come-backs, of the mid-80s. PSG were never comfortable from the start and Madrid smelled fear and acted accordingly, with Benzema scoring a decisive hat-trick. During the last-eight first leg, against Chelsea at Stamford Bridge, another three goals from the French striker and an incredible amount of luck in decisive moments made the difference. Come the return match, and once again magic happened. The reigning continental champions scored three goals without reply and were on their way to the semis when a late perfect pass by Modrić found Rodrygo in the box. The

Brazilian netted the goal that took the match to extra time where Benzema headed the second, guaranteeing Madrid would then face the heavily favoured Manchester City. The first duel at the Etihad was a rollercoaster that ended with a 4-3 victory for the locals, but Pep Guardiola knew it wasn't enough. Few believed Madrid would be third-time lucky but that is not to understand who they become during those European nights: predatory killers. City scored first, and as seen before, a series of impossible saves by Courtois kept Madrid alive. Then substitute Rodrygo came on and scored twice in just three minutes to take yet again the match to extra time. Everyone knew then how that would end. Benzema, from the spot, put City out of their misery and booked a place in the final for the *Merengues*.

After Chelsea and City, it was Liverpool's turn. Madrid had pending issues with the Reds in Paris, as their last European Cup Final defeat had been precisely there, against Bob Paisley's men, back in 1981. Once more, Liverpool had the better chances, but Courtois proved impossible to beat and Vinicius turned hero by scoring the only goal. For many this win was a vindication of what they are all about. By proving they could win without Ronaldo's influence, overcoming the mighty power of the Premier League three times in a row, this became for supporters one of the most celebrated triumphs ever. But it was not going to be the last.

Fast forward two years and with Benzema on his way to Saudi Arabia, and Kroos preparing to say his goodbyes, Real bounced back to clinch their 15th title. Jude Bellingham's leadership and the affirmation of Vinicius as a world-class player made all the difference during the knockout stages and into the final against Dortmund. The footballing world had by then become accustomed to the idea that Madrid was always the prime contender, independent of who came in, who went out or who their rivals were. That's the biggest lesson of the past 15 years, their modern golden age. Madrid's emotional connection with the Champions League has no match in the history of the game. There may have been arguably better sides during those winning seasons but none as capable of believing in themselves as *Los Blancos*, a feeling that stretches from the dressing room to the stands of the Bernabéu. Real Madrid now have nine Champion League wins since the competition was revamped in 1993, more than any other club in the history of the tournament. They are not just remembered for what they achieved in the days of the European Cup, 70 years ago. Even if that helps to understand what the club is all about.

* * *

Real Madrid are in love with the European Cup partly because they invented it. Well, at least they helped. Back in 1954, when Stan Cullis's Wolverhampton Wanderers beat Honvéd on a rainy night at Molineux, the English press was eager to claim Wolves as European champions. The memory of the infamous defeat against the Hungarians at Wembley still lingered and there was a sense of pride restored but the claim was badly received overseas. Gabriel Hanot, editor of the French newspaper *L'Équipe*, was quick to dismiss the idea and proposed a continental competition between the best sides in Europe to find out who would come out on top.

Hanot's project was similar to the modern Superleague, a round-robin tournament between teams invited by the newspaper, not necessarily national league champions, and had much to do with the work of the forgotten figure of Julius Ukrainczyk, a Polish facilitator and football agent. His role has been forgotten over the years but was recently restored to light thanks to Spanish podcast *Brazalete Negro*. He was a key figure, connecting a list of famous football clubs with the *L'Équipe* staff to prepare the blueprint for the competition.

The original idea was soon discarded for its impracticality, transformed into a knockout competition with home and return legs and a final to be played at a neutral venue.

Invitations were sent all around Europe. Chelsea were warned by the Football League not to take part and went along with it. They weren't the only ones. *L'Équipe* and Ukrainczyk tried to get Barcelona on board, the *Blaugrana* being the most renowned side in Western Europe at the time, but the club declined. They had invested their future in a project that had the blessing of UEFA, the Inter-Cities Fairs Cup, a fatal error of judgement. In Madrid, Santiago Bernabéu saw the enormous potential behind the Hanot project and was quick to join in. His club would not only take their rivals' place in the competition but also lend a hand to the organisation.

Back then Real Madrid was not the prestigious club we now know but as the celebrated author of *The Undisputed Kings of Europe* Steven Scragg points out, 'The Real Madrid of the early era of the European Cup found themselves to be in exactly the right place at the right time. Their 1953/54 La Liga title success was their first domestic league win for 21 years, and only their third in total at that point. Barcelona, Atlético Madrid, and Valencia had all stolen a march on them since the end of the Spanish Civil War, but Real's rise really couldn't have been better timed.'

Real was founded in 1902 and, despite becoming one of the capital's early football forces, they were no giants. Also, despite all the allegations over the years, they were far from being a club favoured by Franco's political regime. Their best years came during the II Republic when they won their first league titles as Madrid CF with a board full of renowned left-wingers, including chairman Rafael Sánchez-Guerra. It was he who did everything in his power to save the Chamartín ground from destruction when the rebellious army surrounded

Madrid in the early stages of the Civil War. After the conflict ended, Sánchez-Guerra was forced into exile, but he was on the lucky side. Many of the club's players either died or were arrested. Antonio Ortega, a Republican soldier who was also briefly club chairman, was shot in a death camp by the victors.

A couple of years after, Santiago Bernabéu, a former player and manager of conservative ideals who enlisted voluntarily to fight in Franco's army, was named chairman. He had hoped to stay for a few years to sort things out but ended up dying in office, becoming the sport's greatest-ever chairman. A visionary, Bernabéu invested everything in transforming Chamartin – the stadium that bears his name – into one of Europe's finest. It was located then on the outskirts of Madrid, but he foresaw that the city would expand north and was right. The area alongside the famed Paseo de la Castellana became a new central hub, especially around Nuevos Ministerios and AZCA, where new governmental headquarters were built. The Chamartin stadium was at the centre of it all but all that took time to take shape, and during his first years in charge, Real Madrid never won the league and were even occasionally close to relegation.

Everything changed when they finally signed Alfredo di Stéfano in 1954, a much-discussed affair between them and Barcelona. Few remember how they had once tried to do the same with Ladislao Kubala, only to be warned by the fascist government that the player was bound for Catalonia as part of a public relations coup. The signing of the Argentine genius and the complete revamp of Chamartin transformed the club's history. Yet, it was the birth of the European Cup that made them immortal.

Guillermo Gonzalez, journalist and author, explains the historical relevance of that moment. 'Real Madrid was always a club trying to get ahead of things,' he says. 'Santiago Bernabéu was key to moulding the European Cup because he was aware of the relevance a competition like that would have and he wasn't wrong. He wanted the world to know all about Madrid. It's also because of that connection that the European Cup is part of the club's DNA and today, for a club supporter, a season is good or not, primarily if Madrid wins the Champions League.'

With his right-hand man Raimundo Saporta on the organising committee and Di Stéfano shining on the pitch, Real Madrid entered the first edition of the new competition as one of the top contenders. There were only seven league champions present. Initially, the Spanish champions travelled to Switzerland, where they faced Servette. Bernabéu took the opportunity to take the team to pay their respects to the exiled son of former king Alfonso XIII, infuriating Franco. Madrid won the tie but were soon close to being knocked out by Partizan, during the return league of the last eight, played in Belgrade. They had a four-goal cushion but, on a snowy pitch and against a talented side, lost 3-0 and were saved in the dying minutes by a ball that smashed against the post and went out, a moment that would repeat itself time and time again in the years to come.

Beating AC Milan was trickier, but they eventually reached the final. The match, unsurprisingly, was to be played in Paris, home of *L'Équipe*, and against a French side, Stade Reims. The locals scored two early goals, and when Di Stéfano and Héctor Rial tied the match, the French went one up again. However, Real Madrid were already showing their predatorial skills. Sensing the rival was physically exhausted, the Spanish propelled Francisco Gento, a young Cantabrian winger, to disrupt their defence over and over again with Marquitos and Rial once more turning the game in their favour. Fewer than 40.000 witnessed what would become the first-ever European continental cup final. What was more important, it was Madrid's first win.

That team was still years away from the famous forward line-up they would be known for. Raymond Kopa, the star of the Reims side, was signed that summer. He was deployed as a right-winger and was key to leading Madrid to back-to-back finals, now to be played in front of 124,000 home fanatics at the Chamartin. It would become a trend. Bernabéu would sign one of the best players in the world, they would deliver immediately, and Madrid retained the trophy. A record five consecutive wins while adding players like Didi and Ferenc Puskás to the side came as a result of Bernabéu's policy. They consecutively beat Fiorentina, AC Milan, Reims and finally Eintracht Frankfurt at Hampden Park in what became known as the 'Final of all Finals'.

The match was at risk of not being played until Puskás publicly apologised to the German federation for stating to the press that their international side had taken forbidden substances during the 1954 World Cup Final against Hungary. Thankfully it went ahead, and Madrid won 7-3. Puskás scored four goals, Di Stéfano netted three times. Alex Ferguson watched in awe from the stands. No other side had played so brilliantly in a European Cup final. It was mesmerising.

Puskás, of course, had been one of the great players in his day but when he arrived at Madrid, after two years without competitive football, was overweight and no longer capable of playing as a mobile false nine. He was still deadly though, and the Chamartin was quick to nickname him 'Cañoncito Pum', literally 'little cannon, boom', a reference to his plumpness as well as his scoring skills.

That side was probably one of the best of all time. But were they superior to the one that has dominated European football for the past decade? Phil Kitromilides is a journalist and TV host for La Liga broadcasts and of the awarded *The Spanish Football Podcast*. In his view, the historical relevance of the 1950s side cannot be understated. 'I think it is very difficult to compare sides from different periods and different contexts,' he says. 'The contexts of Real Madrid, football and the world were extremely different in the 1950s to what they are now. The Di Stéfano team is revered and always will be because they sowed the seeds of Madrid's historical link with the European Cup. Without those five in a row to start with I don't think Real Madrid would view themselves as the Kings of Europe, even with their latter-day success.'

For Spanish author Sergio Vilariño, the two teams stand side by side in historical terms. 'Without Di Stéfano, there wouldn't be a Real Madrid. Without Cristiano, there wouldn't be a modern Real Madrid. They changed absolutely everything, each during their time at the club. They are equally decisive and both generations are fundamental to understanding the club culture and DNA.'

Glorious as they were, they were also passing their peak. Barcelona, who by then had won back-to-back league titles, became the first side to beat the perennial reigning champions in the inaugural round of the 1960/61 edition. The following season Madrid reached the final once again, only it was Eusébio's Benfica who came out victors after a thunderous 5-3 display, with Puskás scoring yet another hat-trick. They would lose another final in 1964 against Inter. Di Stéfano was gone, after a row with Miguel Muñoz, the captain in their first winning seasons who, by then, had been promoted to manager. The man who had helped the club to become a European giant went out by the back door. He and Bernabéu never spoke for years.

Only Paco Gento remained from the golden days, and it was he, alongside a young generation of promising footballers like Amancio Amaro, Manuel Sanchis, Ignacio Zoco, Manuel Velásquez, Ramon Grosso and Pirri, who surprised everyone by winning the competition a sixth time in 1966. They beat Partizan in a tight match, once again coming from behind as they often did. It was also the first and only time a team from Spain would win the European Cup with a line-up exclusively of Spanish players. That generation became known as the Yé-Yés, because of the long hairs reminding of the Beatlemania, but they would also be famous for something else. After that night, Madrid spent 32 years without winning 'their' competition. And for a club whose affection is measured in honours, it was a hard blow to take. Generations of great players passed through without touching the sky. In 1981 they reached the final – the only time in three decades – and faced mighty Liverpool.

Vicente del Bosque was by then a leading figure in the squad. He recalls it with a mixture of sadness and pride. 'People usually forget how difficult it was back then for teams from Southern Europe to reach the final,' the future European Cup-winning manager remembers. 'Those were the years of dominance of Dutch, German and English football. The game was played differently, and it was hard for us more technical sides. But even if we were not the most brilliant team ever to play for Madrid, we were a good side and put up a fight against Liverpool.'

During those years Madrid became undisputed champions of Spanish football, winning more accolades than all their rivals combined. But they kept on failing to reclaim their place among the continental elite. That is partly why many of those sides are less talked about today, although there is one that despite all those years of hurt, is still fondly remembered.

* * *

'Valdano said one day that the *Quinta* was the sporting arm of the *Transición*. And he was right.' Alberto López Frau is a sports analyst and a Real Madrid supporter. The *Quinta del Buitre*, as for so many who grew up in the 1980s, remains his Madrid favourite side. A team that won five consecutive leagues yet never reached a European Cup Final. Yet, they remained fondly in *Madridistas*' hearts, an anomaly in the history of a club that measured success based on continental glory. The reasons behind it are both sporting and social. That 1980s generation played football like few have done. A free-flowing attacking side, playing high-tempo, sometimes even recklessly, with an approach that resonated with an era of liquid football as expressed by the likes of the *Le Carré Magique* of France, Tele Santana's Brazil or the Danish Dynamite. They mixed talented attacking players like Michel, Martin Vásquez and Emilio Butragueño, hard-tackling defenders in the shape of José Antonio Camacho and Manuel Sanchis, classy midfielders such as Rafael Gordillo or Bernd Schuster and clinical finishers in the style of Carlos Santillana, Jorge Valdano or Hugo Sánchez. A team based on the club's youth academy represented a positive approach to the game after years of dominance by the Basque sides, who preferred a more direct and physical approach. They also came from a city living a decisive period in its history.

'Madrid was an optimist place in the mid-1980s,' says Frau. 'It was a moment of great social changes, a time to transgress, to do the unthinkable, and I think the football expressed by that generation also represented that.' It was the *Movida* years, a period after the political transition that began with Franco's death followed by the smashing victory of the Socialist Party in the national elections of 1982. Known as a contracultural artistic movement their protagonists were young, hedonistic, and rebellious and set up the template of what Spanish culture would become in the following years, getting equally critical and public acclaim. Football would have its representatives of *La Movida* as well.

In 1984, while Di Stéfano was coaching Madrid's first team, a young journalist by the name of Julio César Iglesias visited the Castilla reserves team, managed by another club legend, Amancio, who was on course to win the second division championship. Iglesias was enwrapped by their talent and took particular notice of five young promising players. The following days he penned a story on the newspaper *El País*, claiming Madrid's future would be on their shoulders. By that time whenever Castilla were allowed to play at the Bernabéu the crowd would be even bigger than the first team's matches. The journalist particularly fancied a young forward called Emilio Butragueño, nicknamed 'El Buitre', The Vulture, so he christened that generation as 'La Quinta del Buitre', Quinta being the local word for class. So, the Vulture Squad was born.

Butragueño was the role model of a generation. Quiet, handsome, well-behaved, the perfect son-in-law, he was also ruthless on the ball and a great goalscorer. Michel was the most flamboyant of them all, a talented winger who passed the ball like few could. Rafael Martín Vázquez was, perhaps, the lowest in profile of the bunch but he knew how to read a game, and Manuel Sanchís, the son of the European champion player of the Yé-yé generation of the same name, was already seen as a fantastic centre-back. Miguel Pardeza was included in the group, although he would not last long in Madrid.

The five names quoted by Iglesias in his famous piece played fewer than 20 matches together but the nickname stuck. Between 1985 and 1986, they all had a role to play in Real's triumphant UEFA Cup campaigns, famed because of the countless matches won at the Bernabéu after losing away in the first leg. During those two seasons, the *Merengues* managed to overcome deficits of two goals or more in eight different knockout rounds, eliminating opponents such as Anderlecht, Rijeka, Inter (twice), Borussia Mönchengladbach and AEK Athens. The era of comebacks, known as

Remontadas, became famed for Juanito's rant after a defeat in Milan when he stated in poor Italian: '90 minutes in the Bernabéu is too long.' Valdano coined the expression 'stage fright' to sum up those years. The atmosphere was electric, the stadium was packed and believed diehard in the team, while the players were up to it. Before every match club captains Santillana and Camacho instructed the younger members that they had to commit the first foul, take the first shot on goal and score early to intimidate opponents. They always obliged.

The *Quinta* was forged during those years but reached its peak afterwards, winning La Liga for a record five times, something no team had ever done before or would do again. They beat all the points and goalscoring records and made the Bernabéu the Bolshoi of European football. Yet something was missing and that became the Holy Grail. The Vulture Squad played in three consecutive European Cup semi-finals and, like Mourinho's side, always ended up on the losing side. Arrigo Sacchi's AC Milan twice beat them but the one that stuck in the memory happened before, in the 1987/88 edition.

Steven Scragg, who wrote about that iconic generation in his seminal work *Where the Cool Kids Hang Out*, states: 'I think the *Quinta del Buitre* version of Real is the best Real side not to have lifted a European Cup. Those five successive La Liga titles between 1985/86 and 1989/90 can't be dismissed as insignificant, and their UEFA Cup wins of 1985 and 1986 played a huge part in that revival. It was a wonderfully balanced side, which seemed cursed in the European Cup. The one that truly got away was in 1987/88 when they were beaten by a pragmatic PSV Eindhoven, with a place in the final in the palm of their hand. That Real side was talented, fluid, skilful, and exciting to watch, yet ever so slightly flawed. This last element is one we don't naturally associate with the club. It made them hypnotic, yet human.'

Beaten by Bayern Munich in the 1987 semi-final, they had it all in their favour the following season. They left behind Maradona's Napoli in the first round and beat reigning champions FC Porto before meeting PSV in the semis. Unfortunately, after managing only a 1-1 draw at home, Real were unable to score in the return leg. The Dutch side went on to win the trophy on a penalty shoot-out having drawn every single one of their last five matches.

That defeat emotionally broke the side. They kept on winning at home but were soundly beaten twice by Milan and then put out of their misery at their last attempt by Spartak Moscow. The trophy eluded them, but their memory lives on. Juanito is still remembered by the fans, who chant his name in the seventh minute of every home game. He was the one who made the number iconic at the club, a tradition followed by Butragueño, Raúl and Cristiano Ronaldo. However, despite all those missed opportunities, people still remember them more fondly than the side that in 1998 finally ended the long drought of titles.

Sanchís was the sole remaining member of the Vulture Squad on that team, where Fernando Redondo, Clarence Seedorf, Davor Šuker, Pedrag Mijatović and a young Raúl were now the star players. The unexpected victory over Juventus sent a clear message. The king was back. Two years later they were at it again. Vicente del Bosque had just been appointed head coach in mid-season and, while the team was languishing in La Liga, things turned out rather differently in Europe. A particular night stood out in time when the Spanish side visited reigning champions Manchester United at Old Trafford. The backheel self-pass by Redondo followed by a clinical Raúl finish clinched a place in the semis, a round decided by a solo effort of Nicolas Anelka against Bayern.

In the final *Los Blancos* met Valencia in what became the first Champions League Final with two sides from the same nation. Valencia were heavily favoured, but Madrid turned out to be clear winners. Fernando Morientes, Steve McManaman and the inevitable Raúl scored the goals. Two-time European champions in just three seasons, after 30 years of hurt, seemed enough for chairman Lorenzo Sanz to call a vote. It turned out that it wasn't. Sanz was ousted by the promise of the signing of their rival's captain. The *Galácticos* era had just begun.

* * *

Florentino Pérez had already lost twice in the presidential ballot when he decided to do things differently. Weeks before the 2000 elections he announced an agreement with Portuguese star Luís Figo, club captain of FC Barcelona. If he won the vote, he would pay Figo's release clause and the player would sign for Madrid. If that didn't happen, he promised to pay for the season tickets for an entire season for all club members. What nobody knew then was that it was Figo, who had signed a secret agreement through his agent, that would have had to put up the money to pay for those. Figo never expected Pérez to win and went along just to try and get a better contract deal with Barcelona's newly appointed chairman, Joan Gaspart. When Pérez duly won, the Portuguese winger had no option but to go through with it.

A few months later he was awarded the Balón D'Or, more for what he had done during the Euro 2000 finals and as a Barcelona player than for his achievements with the Real Madrid shirt. But that transfer helped to raise his popularity as he became the most loved and hated figure alike in club football. And that was also the story behind the *Galácticos*. They were equally revered and loathed. A mix of superheroes from the Marvel universe, years before it became fashionable, assembled at the Bernabéu, representing the greatest form of football entertainment. They were also seen as opening the door for a more commercial view of the game, one that would eventually triumph in time.

The end of the romantics and the beginning of the star system, they also made Madrid European champions once again. Figo was the first to be signed but in his debut season the Del Bosque side only won the league, losing against Bayern in the Champions League semi-finals. The following year though, Pérez again broke the transfer record and brought in Zinedine Zidane. The French playmaker became the symbol of the *Galácticos* era. His sheer quality, mixed with Figo's verticality, Raúl's sense of opportunity, Roberto Carlos's runs and the work ethic of Claude Makélélé, Steve McManaman and Fernando Hierro, brought balance to the side. Madrid went on to the Champions League Final of that year, won after an iconic finish by the Frenchman.

All seemed to be going according to plan when Ronaldo Nazário was added after an outrageous performance during the Japan and Korea World Cup. With the Brazilian striker, the team played as they had never done before and won the league again. An unforgettable Ronaldo hat-trick at Old Trafford showed the world just how good they were. However, a penalty miss by Figo in the dying minutes of the return leg of the semis against Juventus meant they missed out on the final. For Pérez, it was too much. The chairman decided to sack Del Bosque and release Hierro, then club captain. By doing so he dismembered everything that brought equilibrium to his project, the quiet leadership of two men who understood the club better than anyone.

Twenty years on Del Bosque recalls that time fondly: 'I think numbers sum up perfectly well what we achieved in those years. We won the European Cup twice and were only out of the tournament in the semis on two different occasions, after many years when Madrid hardly competed against the top sides. We helped the club to be respected once again and I am very proud of that.' It was a team for the ages, remembered both for its blissful football quality and all the corporate marketing strategy behind it. 'There was a perfect mix of players from the youth system, Spanish internationals who understood the club well, and people who came from other countries that integrated well like Redondo, Makélélé, McManaman, Figo, Zidane and Ronaldo,' says Del Bosque. 'Of course, if I have to point out someone, it would be unfair to forget how much Sanchís and Hierro meant in the dressing room but Raúl was something else, both as a footballer and as a leader of men.'

Raúl was the man who survived Pérez's purges the following seasons when players like Fernando Morientes or Makélélé were also sold to pave the way for the arrival of David Beckham and then Michael Owen in his attempt to make Madrid more popular in Asia and in the United States. Great players as they were – and Beckham was particularly popular among supporters – they disrupted any sort of balance and, despite the first promising months of Carlos Queiroz's stint as head coach, in the end the *Galácticos* ended up imploding. That 2003/04 season marked the beginning of the end. Madrid were fantastic until February but then all collapsed, and they lost the league to Valencia, the cup final to Zaragoza and went out of the Champions League in the last eight against Monaco.

Over the five following seasons, they would never reach as high as the last 16 in Europe. Coaches came and went, and even Pérez finally left, like all the star players he signed. Real may have been more popular than ever but they were never as successful as they hoped. That remains a lesson for the future. Kylian Mbappé might have been added to the roster, but he arrives at a different club, especially compared with those days.

Florentino Pérez seems to have learned his lesson. Although recently he has become a much-demonised figure for his role in the Super League project, threatening to kill the very competition that gave meaning to the club, he managed to create the perfect environment for the club to thrive. His obsession with this new competition model comes, according to football historian Sergio Vilariño, as much as a defence mechanism against the economic muscle of the Premier League and the state-funded clubs as a way to emulate his teen idol, Bernabéu. 'I believe Florentino is obsessed with surpassing the legend of Bernabéu and the only thing missing now is to be the godfather of the most important club competition in the world,' he says. 'The club is indeed afraid of the Premier League's economic muscle but there's something of an ego issue also around his project.'

Until that happens, if it eventually ever comes to pass, Real Madrid have put themselves in a position where they have everything to remain a dominant force. The club found space to sign superstars like the Frenchman and, at the same time, guarantee that the football structure remains balanced. On learning from past mistakes they became even more powerful. They are the undisputed Kings of Europe. It seems to be their destiny. The cries of *Hala Madrid* will echo throughout many European grounds for years to come. A mixture of fear and awe. What Real Madrid is all about.

ACKNOWLEDGEMENTS

IT IS extremely difficult to put down in words the amount of work and joy this project has given me over the past months. I have never spent so many hours talking to so many different and wonderful people or travelling around, watching as many live matches at iconic grounds, while grasping the true sense of the soul of an entire country. It has been a rewarding experience at every level and one I'm grateful to share with so many. Football has been part of my life for as long as I remember but, as years went by, I gradually came to understand the reason I love the game the most: it is because it opens an uncountable number of windows to understand the world around us. Or, in this case, a country. I'm Portuguese by birth, but Spanish at heart. It was the country that taught me everything I know about life. I always felt I owed something back and this book is a testament to that, a love letter that I hope, if only by a fraction, captures the magical essence of what Spain is through the lenses of its football identity. Because of all that, this book means something special to me. It's one of adventures on the field, trips down memory lane and tales few talk about or, at least, not enough. Most of all, it's a book about people, past and present. And it could not have been brought to life without the help of so many.

First and foremost, I thank Paul and Jane for once again trusting in my writing and ideas. Also to Nick Szczepanik and Duncan Olner for their brilliant work. It is a privilege to

ACKNOWLEDGEMENTS

be part of the Pitch family. Also, a special thank you to a living legend, Don Vicente del Bosque, a man who has won everything yet still managed to sit down and chat about his life and career with his usual ease. And to Joaquín Sánchez, one of the most beloved and brilliant footballers Spain ever produced. It was also a wonderful experience to talk with icons such as Carlos Cuellar, Mikel San José, and Alberto Cifuentes. I also thank the welcome from the people inside football clubs such as Real Bétis, Athletic Club Bilbao, Cádiz CF, Unionistas Salamanca, SD Logroñés and Independiente de Vallecas, who opened their hearts and shared their stories for this book.

Spain is a complex sum of realities, and I was lucky enough to have been able to talk with many experts, many of whom I count as friends, who come from different backgrounds and geographical points and who have a close connection to the game's roots and identity. People like Adrián Blanco, Aitor Lagunas, Alberto López Frau, Alejandro Arroyo, Alex Vendrell, Angel Iturriaga, António Espinar, Borja Pardo, Bruno Alemany, Carlos Castellanos, Carlos Marañon, Ernesto Rosado, Fermín Suárez, Fran Guillen, Francisco Iborra, Galder Reguera, Guillermo Gonzalez, Ignacio Pato, Javier Olivares, Javier Roldán, José Luis Ouro, José Maria Nolé, Juan Esteban Rodriguez, Juan José Montero, Juanma Romero, Juan Arroita, Manolo Rodriguez, Martí Perarnau, Mercedes Torrecillas, Miguel Gutierrez, Miguel Quintana, Miguel Ruiz, Nacho Sanchez, Nahuel Miranda, Oscar Abou-Kassem, Pablo Bueno, Paco Caro, Paulo Silva, Rafa Escrig, Raúl Rota, Roger Xuriach, Sergio Vilariño and Toni Padilla. It was also pivotal to get an external perspective on some issues and for that I was lucky enough to count on the help of friends such as Sid Lowe, Simon Kuper, Michael Cox, Colin Millar, Chris Lee, Andy Brassell, Steven Scragg, Christopher Evans, Phil Kitromilides, Mark Harrison and

Euan McTear, journalists and authors who have been covering Spanish football for years now and understand the country and its multiple identities all too well.

Spain was also the place I called home for almost two decades and for that this book is also dedicated to all the people I crossed paths with over the years. Friends, neighbours, co-workers, and even people I walked by on the street. Everyone contributed to my love of the land and to understanding the essence of what Spain is all about. Without them, I would never be able to grasp it and live it to the fullest. And of course, this book is for Sharma, who was born on the same plains that Don Quixote rode along. And to Cris, who taught me how to say *I love you* in Spanish.

BIBLIOGRAPHY

Azparren, N., *El Mitico Oviedo* (Oviedo, Hoja de Lata, 2023)

Balague, G., *Pep Guardiola: Another Way of Winning* (London, Seven Dials, 2018)

Ball, P., *Morbo* (London, WSC Books Limited, 2010)

Ball, P., *White Storm* (London, Mainstream, 2003)

Ballester, E., *Infrafútbol* (Madrid, Libros del KO, 2014)

Ballester, E., *Otro Libro de Fútbol* (Madrid, Libros del KO, 2020)

Burns, J., *Barça: A People's Passion* (London, Bloomsbury, 1999)

Burns, J., *La Roja* (London, Simon and Schuster, 2012)

Carlin, J., *White Angels* (London, Bloomsbury, 2004)

Carretero, N. *Nos Parece Mejor* (Madrid, Libros del KO, 2018)

Castelló, I. *Salvaje* (Madrid, Contra, 2017)

Castellón, A., *Rayo Vallecano: Un Equipo de Barrio* (Valencia, Fuera de Ruta, 2024)

Cox, M., *The Mixer* (London, HarperCollins, 2024)

Cox, M., *Zonal Marking* (London, HarperCollins, 2020)

Cosin, A., *Delanteras Miticas* (Buenos Aires, LibroFutbol, 2020)

Cruyff, J. *My Turn* (London, MacMillan, 2017)

Del Riego, M., *La Biblia Blanca* (Madrid, Corner, 2018)

Di Stéfano, A. *Gracias Vieja* (Madrid, Aguilar, 2000)

Dunne, R., *Working Class Heroes: The Story of Rayo Vallecano* (London, Pitch, 2017)

Evans, C., *Los Leones: The Unique Story of Athletic Bilbao* (London, Pitch, 2024)

Gendre, M., *Branquiazul* (Barcelona, Contra, 2019)

Goldblatt, D., *The Ball is Round* (London, Penguin, 2007)
Gonzalez, E., *Una Cuestión de Fe* (Madrid, Libros del KO, 2021)
Gonzalez, G., *Las 100 historias de leyendas del Real Madrid* (Madrid, Anaya, 2024)
Gutierrez, M., Pacheco, A., *Saber y Empatar* (Madrid, Corner, 2020)
Hunter, G., *Spain: The Inside Story of La Roja's Historic Treble* (London, BackPage, 2013)
Hunter, G., *Barça: The Making of the Greatest Team in the World* (London, BackPage, 2012)
Iborra, F., *Getafe: Sueños de Primera* (Madrid, MCS Sports, 2017)
Jabois, M., *Grupo Salvaje* (Madrid, Libros del KO, 2013)
Kuper, S. *Barça: The Rise and Fall of the Club that Built Modern Football* (London, Shortbooks, 2022)
Lee, C., *The Defiant* (London, Pitch, 2022)
Lee, C., *Origin Stories* (London, Pitch, 2021)
López Frau, A., *11 Equipos, 11 Huellas* (Buenos Aires, Librosfutbol, 2021)
Lourenço Pereira, M. *Cruyff: Anatomia de um Génio* (Rio de Janeiro, Corner, 2022)
Lourenço Pereira, M., *Noites Europeias* (Porto, Amor à Camisola, 2013)
Lourenço Pereira, M., *Sueños de la Euro* (Barcelona, Panenka, 2021)
Lourenço Pereira, M., *Bring Me That Horizon* (London, Pitch, 2024)
Lowe, S., *Fear and Loathing in La Liga* (London, Yellow Jersey Press, 2013)
McTear, E., *Eibar the Brave* (London, Pitch, 2015)
McTear, E., *Hijacking La Liga* (London, Pitch, 2017)
Millar, C. *The Frying Pan of Spain* (London, Pitch, 2019)
O'Brien, J., *Euro Summits* (London, Pitch, 2021)
Padilla, T., *El Historiador en el Estadio* (Barcelona, Principal, 2021)
Pato, I., *Grada Popular* (Madrid, Panenka, 2022)
Pato, I., *No Es Fiera para Domar* (Madrid, Altamarea, 2024)

Perarnau, M., *La Evolución Táctica del Futbol* (Barcelona, Corner, 2021)

Perarnau, M., *Pep Confidential* (London, Arena, 2013)

Perarnau, M., *Pep Guardiola: The Evolution* (London, Arena, 2016)

Perarnau, M., *The Pep Revolution* (London, Ebury, 2024)

Relaño, A., *Memorias en Blanco y Negro* (Madrid, Córner, 2022)

Reguera, G., *Hijos del Fútbol* (Bilbao, Seix Barral, 2022)

Roldán, F. J., *Rinus Michels* (Buenos Aires, LibrosFutbol, 2020)

Rodriguez, J. E., *Recuerdos del Doblete* (Madrid, Al Poste, 2016)

Rodriguez, M. *Historias del Betis* (Sevilla, Bétis Libros, 2021)

Scragg, S. *The Undisputed Champions of Europe* (London, Pitch, 2021)

Scragg, S. *Tournament Frozen in Time* (London, Pitch, 2019)

Scragg, S. *Where the Cool Kids Hang Out* (London, Pitch, 2020)

Simón, J. A., *España 82: La Historia de Nuestro Mundial* (Madrid, TB Editores, 2012)

Smith, R. *Mister* (London, Simon and Schuster, 2016)

Taboada, L., *Como Siempre lo de Siempre* (Madrid, Libros del KO, 2019)

Torres, A., *11 Ciudades* (Barcelona, Contra, 2017)

Triana, J., *Goool en Las Gaunas* (Madrid, Libros del KO, 2014)

Valor, A., *1994: El Mundial en la Frontera* (Valencia, Fuera de Ruta, 2024)

Vázquez Montalbán, M. *Fútbol: Una religión en busca de Dios* (Barcelona, Debolsillo, 2006)

Vignoli, L., *In the Shadow of Giants* (London, Pitch, 2021)

Villalobos, C., *Fúbtol y Fascismo* (Madrid, Altamarea, 2020)

Williams, A., *Euro 1984* (London, Pitch, 2024)

Wilson, J., *Inverting the Pyramid* (London, Orion, 2014)

Wilson, J., *The Barcelona Legacy* (London, King's Road, 2019)

Newspapers and Magazines
Panenka
Líbero
Don Balón
Marca
As
Mundo Deportivo
Sport
Super Deporte
El País
El Mundo
When Saturday Comes
These Football Times
World Soccer
Four Four Two
The Blizzard
Jot Down
Cuadernos de Fútbol